POSSIBILITIES OF
LYRIC

Cultural Inquiry

EDITED BY CHRISTOPH F. E. HOLZHEY
AND MANUELE GRAGNOLATI

The series 'Cultural Inquiry' is dedicated to exploring how diverse cultures can be brought into fruitful rather than pernicious confrontation. Taking culture in a deliberately broad sense that also includes different discourses and disciplines, it aims to open up spaces of inquiry, experimentation, and intervention. Its emphasis lies in critical reflection and in identifying and highlighting contemporary issues and concerns, even in publications with a historical orientation. Following a decidedly cross-disciplinary approach, it seeks to enact and provoke transfers among the humanities, the natural and social sciences, and the arts. The series includes a plurality of methodologies and approaches, binding them through the tension of mutual confrontation and negotiation rather than through homogenization or exclusion.

Christoph F. E. Holzhey is the Founding Director of the ICI Berlin Institute for Cultural Inquiry. Manuele Gragnolati is Professor of Italian Literature at the Sorbonne Université in Paris and Associate Director of the ICI Berlin.

POSSIBILITIES OF LYRIC
Reading Petrarch in Dialogue

MANUELE GRAGNOLATI
FRANCESCA SOUTHERDEN

ISBN (Paperback): 978-3-96558-014-5
ISBN (Hardcover): 978-3-96558-015-2
ISBN (PDF): 978-3-96558-016-9
ISBN (EPUB): 978-3-96558-017-6

Cultural Inquiry, 18
ISSN (Print): 2627-728X
ISSN (Online): 2627-731X

Bibliographical Information of the German National Library
The German National Library lists this publication in the Deutsche
Nationalbibliografie (German National Bibliography); detailed
bibliographic information is available online at http://dnb.d-nb.de.

Cover design: Studio Bens with an image by Claudia Peppel, collage detail,
2013

In Europe, the volume is printed by Lightning Source UK Ltd., Milton
Keynes, UK. See the final page for further details.

The digital edition can be downloaded freely at:
https://doi.org/10.37050/ci-18.

ICI Berlin Press is an imprint of
ICI gemeinnütziges Institut für Cultural Inquiry Berlin GmbH
Christinenstr. 18/19, Haus 8
D-10119 Berlin
publishing@ici-berlin.org
www.ici-berlin.org

Contents

A 'Miscellaneous Enterprise'

> From cocoon forth a butterfly
> As lady from her door
> Emerged — a summer afternoon —
> Repairing everywhere,
>
> Without design, that I could trace,
> Except to stray abroad
> On miscellaneous enterprise
> The clovers understood.
>
> Emily Dickinson,
> 'The Butterfly's Day'

TEXTUAL ENCOUNTERS

Opening to passion as an unsettling, transformative force; extending desire to the text, expanding the self, and dissolving its boundaries; imagining pleasures outside the norm and intensifying them; overcoming loss and reaching beyond death; being loyal to oneself and defying productivity, resolution, and cohesion while embracing paradox,

non-linearity, incompletion. These are some of the possibilities of lyric that this book explores by reading poems in
dialogue with one another.

Most of the poems belong to Italian authors from the
late thirteenth and fourteenth centuries who have contributed to shaping the Western lyric tradition: Guido Cavalcanti (c. 1255–1300), Dante Alighieri (1265–1321), and
Francesco Petrarca (1304–74). They stem from 'courtly'
poetry of *fin'amors*, which originated in Provence in the late
eleventh century and which in Italy developed beginning
from the early thirteenth century, first in Sicily and then
in the central and northern parts of the peninsula.[1] These
poets were in dialogue with one another, both directly
through poetic exchanges and debates and less excipli-
citly through various forms of intertextuality. For instance,
the relationship between Guido Cavalcanti and Dante has
been one of the most fascinating and explored parts of
Dante Studies, alongside the equally discussed issue of
Petrarch's position with respect to Dante. Our analysis
sometimes begins with the dialogue that these poets' texts
explicitly establish among themselves, but the form of
comparison that we employ also opens up other less apparent dialogues. These are all forms of 'textual encounter',
and by proposing this term we aim to convey the dynamics
that a dialogue between texts produces beyond a linear
sense of influence, source, or genealogy.

In this endeavour, we have been inspired by Donna
Haraway's and Anne Carson's ways of reading texts with

---

1   For an overview of the relationship between early Italian lyric and
        courtly poetry, see the chapter 'Dante and the Lyric Past' in Teodolinda
        Barolini, *Dante and the Origins of Italian Literary Culture* (New York:
        Fordham University Press), pp. 23–46. On the development of me-
        dieval love lyric, see also Peter Dronke, *The Medieval Lyric* (London:
        Hutchinson, 1968), pp. 109–66.

one another. With the notion of 'diffraction', Haraway has proposed a shift of optical metaphors for a new critical mode of thought and practice. Taking as its point of reference the optical phenomenon of diffraction, according to which lightwaves striking an object do not reproduce its exact form but give way to interference patterns that depend equally on the object and the lightwaves themselves, Haraway argues that diffraction produces a different critical consciousness. Unlike reflection, a diffractive reading has texts interact beyond the hierarchy of original and copy and studies them one through the other, with the aim of offering a different perspective and producing something new.[2]

Carson's scholarship provides a beautiful example of creating conversations between authors and texts that are not based on pre-existing connections between them but nonetheless use one to better understand the other. As she has written about her reading of Simonides of Keos with Paul Celan in *Economy of the Unlost*, 'With and against, aligned and adverse, each is placed like a surface on which the other may come into focus.'[3] This rich and creative mode of comparison also informs her reading of Sappho,

---

2   Donna J. Haraway, *Modest_Witness@Second_Millennium.FemaleMan_ Meets_OncoMouse^{TM}: Feminism and Technoscience* (New York: Routledge, 1997), p. 273. See also Donna J. Haraway, 'The Promises of Monsters: A Regenerative Politics for Inappropriate/d Others', in *Cultural Studies*, ed. by Lawrence Grossberg, Cary Nelson, and Paula A. Treichler (New York, Routledge, 1992), pp. 295–337; and Birgit Mara Kaiser and Kathrin Thiele, 'Diffraction: Onto-Epistemology, Quantum Physics and the Critical Humanities', *Parallax*, 20.3 (2014), pp. 165–67. On the difference between reflection and diffraction, see Astrid Deuber-Mankowsky, 'Diffraktion statt Reflexion. Zu Donna Haraways Konzept des Situierten Wissens', *Zeitschrift für Medienwissenschaft*, 1 (2011), pp. 83–92.

3   Anne Carson, *Economy of the Unlost: Reading Simonides of Keos with Paul Celan* (Princeton, NJ: Princeton University Press, 1999), p. viii.

Marguerite Porete, and Simone Weil in *Decreation*. Taking her cue from a lyric by Sappho that implicitly poses the question: '*What is it that love dares the self to do?*', Carson has explored striking affinities in the three writers' experience and expression of ecstasis, of 'standing outside oneself'. Not only love, but also writing, emerges as a state of 'absolute daring' that involves having the self 'disappear' from its own narrative in a paradoxical endeavour of 'telling'. Carson has replicated the mysterious non-consequentiality of this undertaking in a three-part essay that has four parts rather than three.[4]

The textual encounters that we propose in this book do not erase the differences or specificity of the individual poems, nor do they overlook their histories or context, but they always try to open new avenues of interpretation. When poems are part of a larger collection, we consider their position within it, but our approach has been to read them one through the other. Often this approach allows for fresh insight on the poems, even when they are some of the most famous or explored of the Italian tradition, and what drives our endeavour is a conceptual interest in understanding how these poems articulate a particular dimension of lyric textuality. Thus the first two chapters may focus on Petrarch, and he may be the author most frequently mentioned throughout, but he is always read as part of a larger interest in the lyric that doesn't necessarily begin or end with him. In Chapter 3, for example, a sonnet by Shakespeare is read together with sonnets by Dante and Petrarch, not on the basis of a possible poetic genealogy (in this case mediated by Petrarch) but as a means

---

4   Anne Carson, 'Decreation: How Women Like Sappho, Marguerite Porete and Simone Weil Tell God', in her *Decreation: Poetry, Essays, Opera* (New York: Knopf, 2005), pp. 155–83.

to understand different ways in which lyric textuality can convey the irresistible force of passion and how different degrees of control and abandon articulate different pleasures. Furthermore, in the final chapter we propose a textual encounter that shows such a force reappearing in two later works by Dante and Petrarch that have supposedly left the lyric behind.

Careful close reading has been our main tool for investigating lyric textuality. This includes in-depth consideration of rhetorical, linguistic, and syntactic features, as well as analysis of conceptual and philosophical complexity in relation to cultural context. At the same time, an important interlocutor has been some late twentieth-century theory that has shown how textuality is imbued with desire and gives shape to subjectivity. In particular, we engage with Leo Bersani's theory of 'aesthetics', according to which textuality does not transcend desire but enacts its movement.[5] This engagement with theory — which also includes a more recent interest in affect, queer temporality, and the post-human —offers some concepts and perspectives for looking at medieval and early modern poems and developing from them new readings. It is a creative operation that, in turn, enables us to produce some new concepts that both illuminate the poems analysed and offer possibilities for thinking further about poetry and its possibilities for the present.

This book affirms the transformative potential of passion by focusing on lyric as a space for affect, wherein a receptive subject is unsettled, moved, and shaped by desire. While in the wake of Augustine, many medieval authors,

---

5   Leo Bersani, *The Freudian Body: Psychoanalysis and Art* (New York: Columbia University Press, 1986). See in particular Chapter 1 of the present study.

including Dante and Petrarch, reflected at length on the risks of letting reason and will be overcome by desire, in the texts we read, the 'I''s susceptibility to love coincides with a heightened capacity for feeling, expansion, and abandon. Passion breaks the hardness and strictures of control, allowing the lyric subject to imagine new possibilities and stray into the pleasures of paradox, instability, and non-linearity.

In his interpretation of Spinoza's *Ethics*, Gilles Deleuze famously highlighted that 'we do not even know of what a body is capable' and that 'we do not even know of what affections we are capable, nor the extent of our power'.[6] Deleuze insisted that such knowledge can be attained, not through reasoning, but only if we 'concretely try to become active' through a series of trials leading to the full experience of our bodies' potential. In this book we suggest that, likewise, we don't know what lyric can do until we experience it, and that lyric is a privileged realm to explore our power of being affected.

While maintaining a profound respect for the texts, we have given ourselves the freedom to roam with and among them, finding pleasure in a 'miscellaneous enterprise' that tries to capture and convey not a theory or

---

6   Gilles Deleuze, *Expressionism in Philosophy: Spinoza*, trans. by Martin Joughin (New York: Zone Books, 1992), p. 226. On passion see in particular, Erich Auerbach, '*Passio* as Passion', in *Time, History, and Literature: Selected Essays of Erich Auerbach*, ed. by James I. Porter, trans. by Jane O. Newman (Princeton, NJ: Princeton University Press, 2013), pp. 165–87. On affect see Brian Massumi, *Parables for the Virtual: Movement, Affect, Sensation* (Durham, NC: Duke University Press, 2002), Simo Knuutila, *Emotions in Ancient and Medieval Philosophy* (Oxford: Oxford University Press, 2004), and *The Affect Theory Reader*, ed. by Melissa Gregg and Gregory J. Seigworth (Durham, NC: Duke University Press, 2010). For a comparative study of affect in Petrarch and Dante, see Francesca Southerden, 'The Intensity of Affect', in *Dante and Petrarch in the Garden of Language* (in progress), with additional bibliography on these authors.

comprehensive definition of lyric as a genre but some moments of 'lyric in action'.[7] Each chapter is dedicated to one of these moments, and if in gathering and arranging them we have suggested some possible connections, each chapter also interacts with all the others in a transversal way through recurring concepts and resonances. It is a movement that hopefully retains some trace of the lyric potential for non-linearity and resistance to closure, which many of these poems powerfully convey. We also like to think that Dickinson's butterfly that moves freely and 'repair[s] everywhere' is a suggestive image for a less systematic and more open, 'lyric' way of reading and thinking, which we have tried to follow and which we hope the reader may also find inspiring — and even take pleasure in.

LYRIC IN ACTION

The book opens with a diptych that explores different articulations of desire in the lyric Petrarch. Chapter 1 reads together two *canzoni* belonging to Petrarch's lyric sequence, the *Rerum vulgarium fragmenta* (*Fragments in the Vernacular*). This first textual encounter was suggested by Petrarch himself and inscribed in the textuality of the so-called 'canzone of citations' (*Rvf* 70, 'Lasso me, ch'io non so in qual parte pieghi'). This *canzone* cites texts by earlier poets at the end of the first four stanzas (the pseudo-Arnaut Daniel, Cavalcanti, Dante, and Cino da Pistoia) and concludes the

---

7   For a recent theorization of lyric, see Jonathan Culler, *Theory of the Lyric* (Cambridge, MA: Harvard University Press, 2015). See also *The Lyric Theory Reader: A Critical Anthology*, ed. by Virginia Jackson and Yopie Prins (Baltimore, MD: Johns Hopkins University Press, 2014), and Virginia Jackson, 'Lyric', in *The Princeton Encyclopedia of Poetry and Poetics*, ed. by Roland Greene and others, 4th edn (Princeton, NJ: Princeton University Press, 2012), pp. 826–34.

fifth and final stanza by citing Petrarch's own '*canzone* of metamorphoses' (*Rvf* 23, 'Nel dolce tempo de la prima etade'). In the past, the *canzone* of citations has often been read as a palinode through which the poet renounces the erroneous desire of the past and formulates a new, correct way of loving and writing. By reading the two *canzoni* together, we question this teleological narrative of conversion and show that the only significant change takes place in the earlier *canzone* and is the metamorphosis into a love poet. In our reading, rather than a recantation, the later *canzone* indicates a return to the previous one, and the impulse towards 'conversion' and change coexists with an irresistible attachment to the past and to passion's torments. We also develop the idea that Petrarch's paradoxical form of pleasure is replicated by textuality and can be visualized in terms of a Möbius strip, in which forward movement is in reality a movement backwards that returns to the beginning endlessly, with no way out of the loop. This same shape, we suggest, can be found in other crucial moments of Petrarch's lyric sequence.

In Chapter 2, it is our own analysis that returns to *canzone* 23 and engages it in a different textual encounter, this time with the sonnet 'Amor co la man dextra il lato manco' (*Rvf* 228). This encounter has been suggested to us by an unusual reversal in these texts. Usually the *Rerum vulgarium fragmenta* stage the transformation of the beloved Laura into a laurel tree, and in analogy with the Ovidian myth of Apollo and Daphne, this motif emphasizes desire for possession and ensuing frustration. Instead, in the poems we are putting in dialogue, it is the poetic subject who is transformed into, or implanted with, the laurel. By engaging these poems with recent philosophical works that consider the nature of plant existence as a form of interconnectedness and porosity to the outside, our analysis explores the possibilities for subjectivity and desire that are imagined in the relationship to the laurel. Most importantly, we show that rather than emphasizing the traditional dynamics of desire in Petrarch's lyric, these poems bring into play a radical passivity that opens up the subject and expresses a sense of desire not as lack but as intensity.

Passivity is also at the core of Chapter 3, which proposes more surprising textual encounters between sonnets by Dante, Petrarch, and Shakespeare that all explore the relationship between will, reason, and passion: Dante's 'Io sono stato con Amore insieme'; Petrarch's *Rvf* 132, 'S'amor non è, che dunque è quel ch'io sento?' and Shakespeare's sonnet 129, 'Th'expense of spirit in a waste of shame'. This chapter shows that while these sonnets share a concern with desire as compulsion, an irresistible and ineluctable force which paralyzes reason and makes the will impotent to act, they also articulate it with differing degrees of abandon, which are visible in their different lyric textualities. While Dante maintains a certain scientific lucidity that holds together the subject and the poem, and Shakespeare embraces a devastatingly masochistic impulse that annihilates the subject and radically unbalances the poem beyond any sense of measure or control, Petrarch cultivates an 'art of imbalance' that finds pleasure in a state of contrariness and conveys a radical instability without dissolving the subject into the Shakespearian abject.

While retaining an interest for passivity, Chapters 4 and 5 form another diptych that focuses on the intersubjective and relational dimensions of lyric. Chapter 4 opens a new perspective on three of the most famous sonnets of the Italian lyric tradition: Cavalcanti's 'Chi è questa che vèn

ch'ogn'om la mira', Dante's 'Tanto gentile e tanto onesta
pare', and Petrarch's 'Erano i capei d'oro a l'aura sparsi'
(*Rvf* 90). They are all praise poems and all engage with
the notion of epiphany, understood as an experience of
instantaneity and a manifestation of presence, associated in
each case with the appearance of the beloved and its effects
on the poetic 'I'. In dialogue with recent interest in queer
forms of temporality and its relationship with desire and
embodiment, our analysis focuses on the different declen-
sions of the 'now' in the three poems and shows that they
articulate three different forms of subjectivity and pleasure.
Cavalcanti's poem stages a fulguration that cannot be sustained, and the subject finds himself in a space of negativity
where the 'now' both initiates desire and precludes fulfilment. By contrast, Dante's sonnet is characterized by pure
positivity, and the 'now' of the beloved's epiphany, which
the poem enacts and the reader also experiences in all its
affective intensity, consists in an ecstatic excess of sweetness that is impervious to time. Petrarch's sonnet begins
negatively by displacing the 'now' of epiphany into the past
and so qualifies it from the outset as imperfect. And yet
with a paradoxical twist that is typical of Petrarch, memory
and poetry remake a 'now' in which desire perseveres and
pleasure thrives notwithstanding the violence of time.

An encounter with the beloved is also at the centre
of Chapter 5, which similarly reads three poems by Cavalcanti, Dante, and Petrarch: the *ballata* 'Perch'i' no spero
di tornar giammai' and the sonnets 'Oltra la spera che più
larga gira' and 'Levòmmi il mio pensier in parte ov'era'
(*Rvf* 302). This textual grouping is perhaps more unex-
pected than the previous one insofar as Petrarch's sonnet
is a clear rewriting of Dante's (both staging the possibility of reaching the beloved after death), but Cavalcanti's

ballata is usually read independently. What interests us is that Cavalcanti's poem also conceives of the lyric space as a means of extending desire and imagining a post-mortem possibility to bridge the gap with the beloved. Our analysis explores the different modalities of this encounter and its outcome: a posthumous pleasure that is more imagined than experienced and remains on an horizontal axis; a vertiginous journey through the universe that reaches heaven and realizes desire beyond all limits; and an earthly fantasy of the afterlife that manages to give pleasure in its tenuousness and instability.

The last chapter offers a comparative reading of the significance of the body and the enduring presence of lyric in two later texts by Dante and Petrarch that do not strictly belong to the lyric genre and are meant to depart from eros insofar as it is incompatible with God: Dante's *Paradiso* and Petrarch's *Triumphus Eternitatis*, which is his most 'Dantean' text. By studying the representations of heaven and eternity in both works, we explore how they relate to and differ from the eschatological tenets of the time. In particular, we focus on the doctrine of the resurrection of the body and show the different ways in which, for both poets, a theological concept becomes an opportunity to reaffirm the affective component of lyric. Dante's text reveals a profound anchorage in God and a drive towards fusing with Him in the beatific vision yet also maintains an erotic attachment with the beloved that is contained in the body and the desire for it. It is a paradoxical sense of fullness that culminates with the anticipation of the Resurrection that the final cantos of *Paradiso* not only stage but enact through a powerful, pyrotechnic textuality. Petrarch, instead, reveals a less strong drive towards the Divine and turns the doctrine of bodily return into the possibility for curing Laura's body of its earthly imperfections. Significantly, in the *Triumphus Eternitatis*, the ultimate pleasure consists not in the vision of God but in the eternal contemplation of Laura's perfected beauty. However, even when turning the traditional understanding of heaven upside down, Petrarch's poetry leaves space for desire not to be satiated but to keep its affective power and to be experienced as a paradoxical pleasure. For Petrarch (as also for Dante), once a love poet, always a love poet.

The book concludes with an epilogue by the contemporary poet Antonella Anedda Angioy, who traces other lyric possibilities and extends them into the present. She explores the encounter between Petrarch, Paul Celan, and Osip Mandelstam, in particular Celan's sense that 'Petrarch's | in sight | again' and Mandelstam's translation of four sonnets by Petrarch into Russian. She thereby identifies the creative power that poetry has 'to reread the texts, to bring them closer by further questioning, to annul time so as to make it live again in the space of language'. By offering her own variation on one of Mandelstam's renditions of Petrarch, she beautifully enacts that power. Anedda Angioy's epilogue is presented in the original Italian and is followed by a translation into English by another contemporary poet, Jamie McKendrick, who expands the dialogue between poets even further.

ACKNOWLEDGMENTS

The dialogue between the authors of this project has extended over many years and places, especially Oxford, Berlin, and Paris. We have also been in dialogue with numerous friends and colleagues, and we take this opportunity to thank all of them for enriching our endeavour and making it even more pleasurable. In particular, thanks are due to Gian Maria Annovi, Isabelle Battesti, Igor Candido, Franco Costantini, Pascale Drouet, Anna Pia Filotico, Marco Formisano, Francesco Giusti, Lisa Gourd, Philippe Guérin, Thomas Harrison, Andrew Kahn, Giuliano Milani, Jennifer Rushworth, Laura Scuriatti, Almut Suerbaum, and our colleagues in the Medievalist Research Group at Somerville College, Oxford, Natascia Tonelli, Raffaella Zanni, and Fabio Zinelli. We would also like to thank Caroline Dormor and Lachlan Hughes for their beautiful translations of poems by Cavalcanti, Dante, and Petrarch and for enthusiastically embarking on that enterprise. A special thanks to Antonella Anedda Angioy for generously accepting the invitation to write an epilogue to our book, and to Jamie McKendrick for translating it into English. As always, Christoph F. E. Holzhey and Elena Lombardi have accompanied us as precious interlocutors throughout the project, and we would like to thank them wholeheartedly for their insightful comments and generous support. Without them, this book would not have been possible.

The multifarious encounters and conversations that have contributed to the miscellaneous character of this enterprise are also evident in the rich textual lives of its parts. Other versions of most chapters have been published or are about to be published elsewhere, often in other languages. They have been rewritten for this book, but it is a pleasure to acknowledge the other venues in which they appear, the occasions for which they were originally thought, and the others in which they were discussed. The first version of Chapter 6 was presented at the conference 'The Unity of Knowledge in the Pre-modern World: Petrarch and Boccaccio between the Middle Ages and the Early Renaissance' (Freie Universität Berlin, June 2014), organized by Igor Candido and Bernard Huss. It was published as 'From Paradox to Exclusivity: Dante's and Petrarch's Lyrical Eschatologies', in *The Unity of Knowledge in Premodern World*, ed. by Igor Candido (Berlin: De Gruyter, 2018), pp. 129–52. Chapter 4 began its life as part of a collaborative Oxford project on Medieval Temporalities by the Somerville Medievalist Research Group (SMRG), and the version written for that project, 'From Loss to Capture: Temporality in Cavalcanti, Dante, and Petrarch's Lyrical Epiphanies', is forthcoming in *Medieval Temporalities: The Experience of Time in Medieval Europe*, ed. by Almut Suerbaum and Annie Sutherland (D. S. Brewer). Another version was presented in Italian at the workshop 'Les deux Guidi (Guinizzelli et Cavalcanti): quelques prolongements' (Université Sorbonne Nouvelle, February 2017), organized by Marina Gagliano, Philippe Guérin, and Raffaella Zanni, and was published as 'Dalla perdita al possesso. Forme di temporalità nelle epifanie liriche di Cavalcanti, Dante e Petrarca', *Chroniques italiennes web*, 32 (2017), pp. 137–54. Chapter 1 was originally presented at the conference 'The Shape of Return Progress, Process, and Repetition in Medieval Culture', organized by Francesco Giusti and Daniel Reeve (ICI Berlin, September 2017). Two versions have appeared as 'Poetry Without End: Reiterating Desire in Petrarch's *Rvf* 70 and 23', in *Ends of Poetry*, ed. by Gian Maria Annovi and Thomas Harrison (= *California Italian Studies*, 8.1 (2018)), pp. 1–13 and 'Petrarca e la forma del desiderio: tra metamorfosi e soggettività ibrida in *Rvf* 70 e 23', *Per Leggere*, 18.35 (2018), pp. 27–41. We began thinking of Chapter 3 for the conference 'Dante et Shakespeare: cosmologie, politique, poétique' (Université de Poitiers, April 2019), organized by Isabelle Battesti and Pascale Drouet, and an early version of it was also presented in Paris at the newly created 'DanteLab@Sorbonne Université' in October 2018. It has appeared in French as 'Compulsion, plaisir, regret: volonté et passivité dans trois sonnets de Dante, Pétrarque et Shakespeare', in *Dante et Shakespeare: cosmologie, politique, poétique*, ed. by Isabelle Battesti and Pascale Drouet (Paris: Classiques Garnier, 2020), pp. 105–23. Like Chapter 4, Chapter 2 took shape as part of a SMRG project, this time on the subject of Openness in Medieval Culture. It was presented at the Symposium, 'Openness in Medieval Culture' (ICI Berlin, June 2019), organized by Manuele Gragnolati and Almut Suerbaum, and a version is forthcoming in *Openness in the Middle Ages*, ed. by Manuele Gragnolati and Almut Suerbaum (ICI Berlin Press).

We are also glad to acknowledge the support of our institutions: ICI Berlin, Somerville College, Oxford, and Sorbonne Université.

BERLIN/OXFORD, 30 SEPTEMBER 2020

1. The Shape of Desire
Metamorphosis and Hybridity in *Rvf* 23 and *Rvf* 70

This chapter, like the ones that follow, explores lyric textuality as a privileged space for articulating a particular form of desire and subjectivity. It focuses on two *canzoni* from Petrarch's lyric sequence, 'Nel dolce tempo de la prima etade' (*Rvf* 23) and 'Lasso me, ch'io non so in qual parte pieghi' (*Rvf* 70).[1] By reading them together, we investigate how they blur the distinction between transformation and return and between beginnings and ends, and how, defying conclusion, they give shape to a paradoxical form of pleasure.

Rvf 70, the so-called '*canzone* of citations', opens by staging a state of impasse where the 'I' is overwhelmed by

---

1   We refer to Petrarch's lyric sequence using the authorial Latin title. All quotations are taken from Francesco Petrarca, *Canzoniere*, ed. by Marco Santagata, rev. ed. (Milan: Mondadori, 2010). Unless otherwise stated, English translations of lyric poems by Dante, Petrarch, and Cavalcanti are by Caroline Dormor and Lachlan Hughes. All emphasis is ours.

sensual desire, and contemplates correcting it. It is an intertextual poem (and part-cento) that culminates in an expli-
cit textual return of the poet's own poem 23, the so-called
'*canzone* of metamorphoses', in which the poetic subject
undergoes a series of transformations explicitly modelled
on Ovid. The incipit of *canzone* 23 forms the final line of
canzone 70 and is the last in a series of quotations of the
incipits of earlier poems, each of which closes one of the
stanzas of Petrarch's *canzone* and reconstructs what Franco
Suitner has termed 'il retroterra della lirica romanza' (the
hinterland of romance lyric).[2]

All the incipits closing the five stanzas relate to a
concept of love as essentially tyrannical, obsessive, and
compulsive. The first stanza ends with the incipit of the
Occitan poem now thought to be by Guillem de Saint
Gregori, 'Drez et rayson es qu'ieu ciant e· m demori', which
Petrarch attributed to Arnaut Daniel and which depicts
the state of subjecting oneself to love even to the point
of death, and finding pleasure in it.[3] The other incipits
belong to the Italian lyric tradition. The second stanza ends
with Guido Cavalcanti's 'Donna me prega, per ch'io voglio
dire', the doctrinal *canzone* that explains the nature and
effects of love as a sensual passion that infects the body
and annihilates reason and the faculty of judgment.[4] The
third stanza incorporates the incipit of Dante's 'Così nel

---

2   Franco Suitner, *Petrarca e la tradizione stilnovistica* (Florence: Olschki,
     1977), p. 12.

3   On this misattribution see Sarah Kay, *Parrots and Nightingales:
     Troubadour Quotations and the Development of European Poetry* (Phil-
     adelphia: University of Pennsylvania Press, 2013), pp. 189–95 (espe-
     cially pp. 189–92); and Petrarca, *Canzoniere*, ed. by Santagata, p. 352,
     which both provide a survey of literature on the subject.

4   On Cavalcanti's concept of love as lethal in a moral and physical sense,
     respectively, see Giorgio Inglese, *L'intelletto e l'amore: Studi sulla let-
     teratura italiana del Due e Trecento* (Florence: La Nuova Italia, 2000),
     pp. 3–55, and Natascia Tonelli, *Fisiologia della passione: Poesia d'amore*

mio parlar voglio esser aspro', one of four *rime petrose*, or 'stony rhymes', which also express the lethal and paralyzing effects of sensual love and in which the harshness of the content is matched by the harshness of the style. The fourth stanza ends by citing the incipit of Cino da Pistoia's *canzone* 'La dolce vista e 'l bel guardo soave', an exile poem that laments the anguish and torment of being separated from the lady but in a sweeter style, one of *dolcezza*.[5] Finally, the last stanza ends by returning to Petrarch's own *canzone* 23, whose incipit closes the poem.

The trend has been to read *Rvf* 70 teleologically and as a narrative of conversion,[6] where conversion is not about turning to another faith or confession but rather about moving towards a better moral position and a greater coherence of the self, to which would also correspond a better poetics.[7] In this way the poet is said to renounce the errant desire of his youth, represented by all these incipits, achieving a new mode of loving and speaking. As each voice of the earlier romance tradition is reiterated and surpassed, so the 'I' apparently learns how to control his desire and

---

    e medicina da Cavalcanti a Boccaccio (Tavarnuzze [Florence]: SISMEL · Edizioni del Galluzzo, 2015), pp. 3–70.

5   Cf. Teodolinda Barolini, 'The Making of a Lyric Sequence: Time and Narrative in Petrarch's *Rerum vulgarium fragmenta*', *MLN*, 104.1, Italian issue (Jan. 1989), pp. 1–38 (p. 23), in which she notes that 'Cino's verse [...] is tonally similar to the Petrarchan verse with which the poem ends [...] — the main difference, in fact, is the temporal anxiety that Petrarch fuses into Cino's unalloyed sweetness'. On Cino's prolific use of the adjective 'dolce', see Maria Corti, 'Il linguaggio poetico di Cino da Pistoia', *Cultura mediolatina*, 12.3 (1952), pp. 185–223 (p. 193).

6   See in particular Petrarca, *Canzoniere*, ed. by Santagata, p. 349; Kay, *Parrots and Nightingales*, pp. 194–95; and Martin Eisner, *Boccaccio and the Invention of Italian Literature: Dante, Petrarch, Cavalcanti, and the Authority of the Vernacular* (Cambridge: Cambridge University Press, 2013), pp. 91–92.

7   In this sense, Petrarch's project dovetails with Dante's in the *Vita Nova*, in which the meditation on desire is also a discourse on poetry.

sets out to relinquish the sensually-directed eros that is the hallmark of the courtly lyric, including his own poetry up to this point in the collection, thereby transforming the poet he is — or can be.

Petrarch's decision to end *Rvf* 70 by referring to the beginning of his earlier poem thus inserts his poetry within a specific lyric and romance genealogy that culminates with him.[8] That point of culmination has been read by Marco Santagata and others as conveying a linear and vertical temporality that leads to conversion.[9] The poem is thereby interpreted as a palinodic gesture through which the poet is at once evoking and recanting his poetic past, specifically its bonds with purely sensual desire, which *Rvf* 23 is taken to represent. Sarah Kay, too, has argued that in *Rvf* 70, through the technique of quotation, Petrarch creates a genealogy of texts that are surpassed one by the other. In the new context of 70, the Petrarchan 'I' would 'disengage' from the earlier subject position implied in the romance lyrics he quotes in order to occupy a different place and thereby 'desire differently'.[10] Kay has also supported her forward reading through analysis of another rhetorical feature of the *canzone*, namely the *coblas capfinidas* structure, which consists of connecting the end of one stanza to the beginning of the next through the repetition of the same word. She argues that 'the resulting interplay of quotation and reaction impels the song forward via a process of self-reappraisal, in which the impulse to break with past guilt and progress toward a new future has to

---

8   On poetic genealogy, see Giuseppe Mazzotta, 'Petrarch's Dialogue with Dante', in *Petrarch and Dante: Anti–Dantism, Metaphysics, Tradition*, ed. by Zygmunt G. Barański and Theodore J. Cachey, Jr (Notre Dame, IN: University of Notre Dame Press, 2009), pp. 179–81.

9   See the works cited in n. 6.

10   Kay, *Parrots and Nightingales*, pp. 194–95.

contend with wistfulness, reluctance and inertia' (193) but ultimately prevails over them.

Kay sees *canzone* 70 as a new beginning, and her reading is thereby in line with those critics who consider the *canzone* as a prelude to the following three poems, the so-called 'canzoni degli occhi', which would express a new lyric mode and, in the vein of the most positive poems of the *dolce stil novo*, celebrate the spiritual improvement brought about by the encounter with the beloved, as though Laura had morphed into Dante's Beatrice.[11] The fact that the poem lacks a *congedo* (the leave-taking that usually concludes a *canzone*) — a feature which is unusual within the *Rvf* and occurs in only one other poem (105) — can also be read formally as a sign of this apparent opening up to what follows and as a projection forwards.[12]

Therefore, for Kay and Santagata (but also for many others), the fact that *canzone* 70 ends with a quotation from *Rvf* 23 is the sign of a 'subjective transformation' and a move beyond the domain of the earlier lyric.[13] Instead, our interpretation is in tune with the more ambivalent reading that Rosanna Bettarini and Marco Praloran have given of *Rvf* 70, and proposes that the quotations from the previous poems do not mark a complete departure but function as traces of desire that are reactivated in and by the text.[14]

---

11 See Petrarca, *Canzoniere*, ed. by Santagata, pp. 349–50; and on the 'canzoni degli occhi' sequence, see in particular Barolini, 'The Making of a Lyric Sequence', pp. 21–24; and Corrado Bologna, '"Occhi solo occhi" (*Rvf* 70–75)', in *Canzoniere: Lettura micro e macrotestuale*, ed. by Michelangelo Picone (Ravenna: Longo, 2007), pp. 183–205. For a discussion of Petrarch in relation to the poets of the *dolce stil novo*, see Suitner, *Petrarca e la tradizione stilnovistica*.

12 On the *canzone*'s lack of *congedo*, see for example, Barolini, 'The Making of a Lyric Sequence', p. 23.

13 Kay, *Parrots and Nightingales*, pp. 194–95.

14 See Bettarini's commentary to *Rvf* 70 in Francesco Petrarca, *Canzoniere. Rerum vulgarium fragmenta*, ed. by Rosanna Bettarini, 2 vols

Therefore, the questions we are posing differ from the ones previously considered by critics: what if we take *canzone* 70 not as the end of a phase but as a literal return to *Rvf* 23? How would that change our reading of the poems, especially the relationship between them, including the supposed palinode that one makes of the other? Can our analysis tell us something about the subjectivity shaped by textual return in these two poems and in Petrarch's collection more broadly?

TRANSFORMATION

In order to answer these questions, it is important to consider *canzone* 23, 'Nel dolce tempo de la prima etade', which relates how the lyric 'I' was first struck by love. The *canzone* can be interpreted as a manifesto or blueprint

(Turin: Einaudi, 2005), I, pp. 343–50; and Marco Praloran, *La canzone di Petrarca: Orchestrazione formale e percorsi argomentativi*, ed. by Arnaldo Soldani (Rome-Padua: Antenore, 2013), pp. 52–65. Unlike Santagata and the other scholars mentioned above, and closer to our reading, in her commentary on *Rvf* 70 Bettarini is not interested in the idea that the *canzone* expresses a conversion and a new departure relative to the poetry of the past, but instead proposes that the citation of *Rvf* 23 with which *Rvf* 70 concludes establishes a line of continuity between the two texts and makes the youthful *canzone* appear 'come testo lontano dove il poeta si riconosce e da dove comincia a fluire la memoria poetica di se stesso' (p. 344). Praloran has identified another kind of tension in the Petrarchan *canzone*: on the one hand, he persists with the idea of a new interpretation of desire, according to which through a superior form of sublimation the beloved would no longer be the cause of alienation and anguish, but the means of spiritual elevation. Praloran has also maintained that the different interpretation of amorous desire would result in a new model of the *canzone*-form in which the lyric element perfectly blends with the rational intent (pp. 61–62); on the other hand, Praloran has argued that in spite of the different role of the lady in the process of falling in love, the poet does not manage to diminish the destructive force of desire; on the contrary, he amplifies it because the distance between Laura's 'innocence' and 'the subject's infirmity' is unbridgeable (p. 63).

of Petrarch's early poetry, one centred on the unrequited love of the troubadour and the Ovidian traditions.[15] As mentioned above, it is constructed around the Ovidian paradigm of metamorphosis and entirely focused on the 'I''s transformations through the effects of love — first into a laurel, then into a swan, stone, fountain, flint, voice, and stag, evoking respectively the Ovidian myths of Daphne, Cygnus, Battus, Byblis, Echo, and Actaeon.[16] All these are done to a completely passive and powerless subject who cannot but submit to the power of sensual desire.[17] More significantly, they are all forms of punishment, both for a

---

15   For a detailed reading of *Rvf* 23, see Robert M. Durling, 'Metamorphosis', in his introduction to *Petrarch's Lyric Poems: The Rime Sparse and Other Lyrics*, trans. and ed. by Robert M. Durling (Cambridge, MA: Harvard University Press, 1976), pp. 26–33; Petrarca, *Canzoniere*, ed. by Santagata, 101–02; John Brenkman, 'Writing, Desire, Dialectic in Petrarch's *Rime* 23', *Pacific Coast Philology*, 9 (1974), pp. 12–19; Annalisa Cipollone, '"Né per nova figura il primo alloro…": La chiusa di *Rvf* XXIII, il *Canzoniere* e Dante', *Rassegna europea di letteratura italiana*, 11 (1998), pp. 29–46; Giovanna Rabitti, '"Nel dolce tempo": sintesi o nuovo cominciamento?', in *Petrarca volgare e la sua fortuna sino al Cinquecento*, ed. by Bruno Porcelli (= *Italianistica*, 33.2 (May–August 2004)), pp. 95–108; and Gur Zak, *Petrarch's Humanism and the Care of the Self* (Cambridge: Cambridge University Press, 2010), pp. 121–57, in which the author traces an Ovidian style in the poet's corpus that is linked to the inability or unwillingness to renounce sensual desire, which is in tension both with the Virgilian and Stoic styles, aimed at cultivating virtue and resisting passion, respectively; and with the Augustinian style that necessitates a renunciation of both desire for Laura and for poetic glory.

16   On the paradigm of Ovidian metamorphosis as intrinsic to the *Rerum vulgarium fragmenta*, see Sara Sturm-Maddox, *Petrarch's Metamorphoses: Text and Subtext in the 'Rime Sparse'* (Columbia: University of Missouri Press, 1985); Lynn Enterline, *The Rhetoric of the Body from Ovid to Shakespeare* (Cambridge: Cambridge University Press, 2000), pp. 120–45; and Gregory Heyworth, *Desiring Bodies: Ovidian Romance and the Cult of Form* (Notre Dame, IN: University of Notre Dame Press, 2009), pp. 179–227.

17   See Zak, *Petrarch's Humanism*, p. 148, in which he argues that 'the language of Ovid, of metamorphosis, stands […] for the loss of reason, of self-control, the succumbing to the grip of the passions'.

desire represented as transgressive and for the urge to voice it in spite of the prohibition to do so.

After describing how 'in the sweet season of [his] first youth' the subject lived in freedom ('libertade'), that is, immune from the effects and pains of love, the second part of the second stanza ends by describing how Love, with the help of a 'powerful lady', who is clearly the poet's beloved Laura, transforms him into a laurel:

> prese in sua scorta una possente donna,
> ver' cui poco già mai mi valse o vale
> ingegno, o forza, o dimandar perdono;
> *e i duo mi trasformaro in quel ch'i' sono,*
> *facendomi d'uom vivo un lauro verde,*
> che per fredda stagion foglia non perde.

> ([he] took into his service a powerful lady, | against whom neither cunning, nor force, | nor begging for mercy ever was (or is) much use; | *and these two transformed me into what I am,* | *making of me,* *a living man, a laurel tree,* | which, though winter come, never sheds a leaf.) (*Rvf* 23, 35–40)

Thus, the first transformation into the laurel is a punishment for not yet bending to love. As we shall see in more depth in the following chapter, this transformation is astonishing for anyone familiar with Petrarch's poetry for the reversal of roles it implies — usually it is Laura who is turned into a laurel (*lauro*) with reference to the Ovidian myth of Apollo and Daphne.[18] In other words,

---

18   See for example, *Rvf* 22, *Rvf* 34, and *Rvf* 197. On the myth of Apollo and Daphne, see Sturm-Maddox, *Petrarch's Metamorphoses*, pp. 35–40; Philip Hardie, 'Ovid into Laura: Absent presences in the *Metamorphoses* and Petrarch's *Rime sparse*', in *Ovidian Transformations: Essays on Ovid's 'Metamorphoses' and its Reception*, ed. by Philip R. Hardie, Alessandro Barchiesi, and Stephen Hinds (Cambridge: Cambridge University Press, 1999), pp. 254–70; and Natascia Tonelli, *Per queste orme: Studi sul 'Canzoniere' di Petrarca* (Pisa: Pacini, 2016), pp. 40–41.

the way in which Laura rejects the poet's love is usually presented as analogous to Daphne's refusal to succumb to Apollo's advances and subsequent transformation into a laurel tree. In this case, however, it is the poet who is turned into the laurel. As Santagata and others have explained, this metamorphosis is to be understood in terms of the lover's complete identification with the desired object, the concept that, as Petrarch will later convey in his *Triumphus Cupidinis*, 'the lover turns into the beloved' (l'amante ne l'amato si transforme; III, 162).[19] This transformation of the poetic subject into the laurel confirms the extent to which the poem is about his transformation into a poet dominated by desire: the encounter with Laura is the encounter with poetry.[20] It is also an experience of dispossession of identity and loss of self, and, as the Romantic poet Giacomo Leopardi first suggested, this experience is forever: the image of the evergreen laurel 'signifies the intensity and constancy of the poet's love: first, by saying that he has been turned into the very form of his lady; and second by stating that he, like the laurel, never loses his leaves'.[21]

---

19 The *Triumphi* are quoted from Francesco Petrarca, *Trionfi, Rime estravaganti, Codice degli abbozzi*, ed. by Vinicio Pacca and Laura Paolino (Milan: Mondadori, 1996). Translations are ours. For Santagata's observation, cf. Petrarca, *Canzoniere*, p. 109. On the relationship between the expression in the *Triumphi* and the Christian idea of compassion, see Chapter 2, pp. 54–55.

20 In her reading of *Rvf* 23, Carla Freccero commented on how Petrarch's poem simultaneously marks the poet's falling in love and his becoming a poet. See Carla Freccero, 'Ovidian Subjectivities in Early Modern Lyric: Identification and Desire in Petrarch and Louise Labé', in *Ovid and the Renaissance Body*, ed. by Goran Stanivukovic (Toronto: University of Toronto Press, 2001), pp. 21–37.

21 See Francesco Petrarca, *Canzoniere*, ed. by Ugo Dotti, with notes by Giacomo Leopardi (Milan: Feltrinelli, 1979), p. 68; our translation. For a related observation on these lines of Petrarch's poem, see Leonard

If poem 23 is a manifesto of a certain kind of poetics, as it has so often been read, then the image of the poet it reveals is twofold. It communicates not only that poetry feeds off a painful form of desire-as-loss but also that the poet is controlled by his senses and completely at the mercy of the beloved: he even loses his shape and takes on hers.[22] This concept is already made evident at the end of the first stanza, which identifies:

> un penser che solo angoscia dàlle,
> tal ch' ad ogni altro fa voltar le spalle,
> e mi face oblïar me stesso a forza:
> ché tèn di me quel d'entro, et io la scorza.

> (a single thought which causes only anguish, | and makes me deaf to all other thoughts, | and forces me to forget myself entirely: | for it governs all that is in me, and I only the shell.) (*Rvf* 23, 17–20)

In Robert Durling's words, in the transformation of the lover into the laurel 'the idea is that of the movement of love from potency to actuality in the will's taking on the form of the desired object'.[23]

The first metamorphosis into the laurel is followed by all the others in the subsequent stanzas, but we discover in the *congedo* that all the other metamorphoses have taken

Barkan, *The Gods Made Flesh: Metamorphosis and the Pursuit of Paganism* (New Haven, CT: Yale University Press, 1986), p. 211.

22   On the concept of desire-as-loss, see Elena Lombardi, *The Syntax of Desire: Language and Love in Augustine, the Modistae, Dante* (Toronto: University of Toronto Press, 2007), pp. 12–13 and 163–64. See also Elena Lombardi, '"I Desire Therefore I Am": Petrarch's *Canzoniere* between the Medieval and the Modern Notion of Desire', in *Early Modern Medievalisms: The Interplay between Scholarly Reflection and Artistic Production*, ed. by Alicia C. Montoya, Wim van Anrooij, and Sophie van Romburgh (Leiden: Brill, 2010), pp. 19–41.

23   Robert M. Durling, 'Petrarch's "Giovene donna sotto un verde lauro"', *MLN*, 86.1 (1971), pp. 1–20 (p. 11 n. 14).

place within the laurel and that the 'I' has actually remained fixed in the outcome of the first metamorphosis.

> Canzon, i' non fu' mai quel nuvol d'oro
> che poi discese in pretïosa pioggia,
> sí che 'l foco di Giove in parte spense;
> ma fui ben fiamma ch'un bel guardo accense,
> et fui l'uccel che piú per l'aere poggia,
> alzando lei che ne' miei detti honoro:
> *né per nova figura il primo alloro*
> *seppi lassar*, ché pur la sua dolce ombra
> ogni men bel piacer del cor mi sgombra.

> (Canzone, I never was that cloud of gold | that rained in precious drops | to douse Jove's fire, at least in part; | but, yes, I was a flame lit by a lovely gaze, | and was the bird that soars highest in the sky, | elevating her whom I honour in my verse: | *nor could I ever leave the first laurel behind* | *for a new form*, for its sweet shade | expels all lesser pleasure from my heart.) (*Rvf* 23, 161–69)

Canzone 23 is thus framed around a series of metamorphoses, but it is a strangely circular kind of process that goes back to the first metamorphosis without perhaps ever having left it. Only the first transformation into the laurel can be considered a proper metamorphosis, while all the subsequent ones ultimately seem to be reiterations of the first experience of desire as punishment and self-loss. Thus, the *congedo* clarifies what we have already seen announced at the end of the second stanza, where — by saying that 'i duo mi trasformaro in quel ch'io *sono*', that is, that Love and Laura turned him into what he *is* — the poet already indicates that, having been turned into a laurel, he continues to be one at the time of writing. It is as definitive a type of transformation as the laurel is evergreen: it is

irreversible. In this sense, *Rvf* 23 is a very Ovidian text.[24]
However, what appears as very Petrarchan (and will be
explored further in the following chapter) is the particular kind of pleasure with which the poem ends and which
seems to turn it around. The laurel, which the poet cannot
bring himself to relinquish and which represents the painful experience of self-loss provoked by love, is also a site
of pleasure, albeit a paradoxical one.[25] Significantly, the
adjective *dolce* (168), which is present in the incipit and
refers to the time before desire, returns here unexpectedly
bound to desire, with which it seemed incompatible.

NON-RESOLUTION

At this point, we can consider *canzone* 70. This poem opens
with a sense of frustration and reprises the motif of being
forbidden to give voice to desire, which *Rvf* 23 articulates
through an Ovidian paradigm emphasizing its transgressive aspect (in the sense that the metamorphoses are pun-
ishments not only for desire but also for the urge to voice
it). In *Rvf* 70, the problem of adequately voicing desire
is articulated by tracing the genealogy of courtly poetry.
As noted earlier, the final stanza incorporates a quotation
from a poem that Petrarch thought was by Arnaut Daniel, a
twelfth-century singer of sensual, uncontrollable love. The

---

24   On the Ovidian dimension of Petrarch's poem, particularly the inter-
      relationship between transformation, poetry, and passion, see Barkan,
      The Gods Made Flesh, pp. 206–14.

25   On paradoxical pleasure, see Christoph F. E. Holzhey, 'The Lover of a
      Hybrid: Memory and Fantasy in *Aracoeli*', in *The Power of Disturbance:
      Elsa Morante's 'Aracoeli'*, ed. by Manuele Gragnolati and Sara Fortuna
      (Oxford: Legenda, 2009), pp. 42–58; and Christoph F. E. Holzhey,
      *Paradoxical Pleasures and Aesthetics: Masophobia, Sexual Difference,
      and E. T. A. Hoffmann's Kater Murr*, Ph.D. Thesis (Ann Arbor, MI:
      University of Michigan, 2002).

stanza also reprises the Ovidian motif and locates the intensity of desire in the failure to possess the beloved and the violent, anguished struggle to write about it. The ultimate fantasy here seems to be that of speaking freely, which would reverse the prohibition that was the mark of *Rvf* 23:[26]

> Non gravi al mio signor perch'io il ripreghi
> di dir libero un dì tra l'erba e i fiori:
> *Drez et rayson es qu'ieu ciant e· m demori.*

> (let it not displease my Lord if I ask again | to give me leave to say, one day, among the grass and flowers: | *Drez et rayson es qu'ieu ciant e·m demori.* [It is right and just that I should sing and be happy])
> (*Rvf* 70, 8–10)

The following two stanzas — which quote two poems by Cavalcanti and Dante embodying irrational and painful desire — emphasize and reiterate the trap of sensual attraction, centred on the subject's obsession with the 'phantasm' of the lady and his enslavement to it, so powerfully expressed in Cavalcanti's and Dante's poems.[27] In particular, stanzas 1 and 2 play with the fantasy not only that it might be possible to 'dir libero' — make an open avowal of one's love and receive satisfaction from the beloved — but even, in the Cavalcantian stanza, that she might call on the lover to speak, which reverses Laura's command in *canzone*

---

26 On the frustrated desire for speech in *Rvf* 23, see especially Brenkman, 'Writing, Desire, Dialectic', pp. 15–18.

27 Cf. Dante's *rime petrose* and the so-called 'canzone montanina', 'Amor, da che convien ch'io mi doglia', his last *canzone* of exile which is also 'a testament to deadly, Cavalcantian eros' (Barolini, 'Dante and the Lyric Past', p. 41). On the phantasm in medieval lyric poetry, see Giorgio Agamben, *Stanzas: Word and Phantasm in Western Culture*, trans. by Ronald L. Martinez (Minneapolis: University of Minnesota Press, 1992).

23, 'di ciò non far parola' (make no word of this; 100). In *Rvf* 70, the movement is that of a katabasis into the pain of love, and the nadir is reached at the end of the third stanza, where the *aspro* — harsh — language is meant to match the harshness of suffering:

> Ella non degna di mirar sì basso
> che di nostre parole
> curi, ché 'l ciel non vòle
> al qual pur contrastando i' son già lasso:
> onde, come nel cor m'induro e 'naspro,
> *così nel mio parlar voglio esser aspro.*

> (She does not deign to look down so low | as to take note of our words, against the will of heaven, | so that I'm already weary from the struggle: | and so, as my heart grows hard and harsh, | *così nel mio parlar voglio esser aspro.* [so in my words I want to be harsh]) (*Rvf* 70, 25–30)

Having reached this 'hell-like stasis' of being trapped in sensual love, there is a turning point at the start of stanza 4.[28] Here the poet acknowledges the excessive desire expressed in the poem and in the lyric sequence itself up to this point — what the poem calls 'disïar soverchio' (excessive desire) — just as he begins to reflect on his actual responsibility in letting himself be taken by this excess. If up to this point the poem stresses the ineluctable force of love, which does not leave any room for the will to resist it, here the fault is acknowledged as belonging to the poetic subject alone:

---

28 See Zygmunt G. Barański, 'Petrarch, Dante, Cavalcanti', in *Petrarch and Dante: Anti–Dantism, Metaphysics, Tradition*, ed. by Zygmunt G. Barański and Theodore J. Cachey, Jr (Notre Dame, IN: University of Notre Dame Press, 2009), pp. 50–133 (p. 85). On petrified immobility as the hallmark of *canzone* 23, see Barolini, 'The Making of a Lyric Sequence', p. 30.

Che parlo? o dove sono? e chi m'inganna,
altri ch'io stesso e 'l desïar soverchio?
Già s'i'trascorro il ciel di cerchio in cerchio,
nessun pianeta a pianger mi condanna.
Se mortal velo il mio veder appanna,
che colpa è de le stelle, o de le cose belle?
Meco si sta chi dí et notte m'affanna,
poi che del suo piacer mi fe' gir grave
la dolce vista e 'l bel guardo soave.

(What am I saying? Or where am I? And who is
deceiving me, | other than me and my excessive de-
sire? | If I search the heavens from sphere to sphere,
| no planet condemns me to tears. | If a mortal veil
dims my sight, | what fault is it of the stars, | or of all
that is lovely? | Tormenting me night and day, she
has dwelt in my heart | since the day I was burdened
with pleasure by | *la dolce vista e 'l bel guardo soave.*
[the sweet countenance and the lovely, soft gaze])
(*Rvf* 70, 31–40)

Critics have stressed the change happening in this stanza.
Santagata, for instance, has argued that with these questions 'the overturning of the discourse so far put forward
begins: both the desire for reciprocation expressed in the
first two stanzas and the impossibility of realizing that desire, because of the lady's fault and an adverse destiny, now
appear as a delirium and as guilty self-delusion'.[29] However, we argue that the poet's recognition of the possibility
to control desire (and therefore of his own responsibility in
yielding to it) coexists with the reiteration of his passivity
and the pleasure of meditating obsessively on the lady's
image and ceding all control of himself to it. This paradoxical sweetness was already a feature of Cino's exile *canzone*,
where the absence from the lady was lamented in a *dolce*

---

29 Petrarca, *Canzoniere*, ed. by Santagata, p. 354; our translation.

style.[30] Therefore, rather than seeing the fourth stanza as a pivotal conversion point, we propose reading it in dialogue with Caroline Walker Bynum's distinction between metamorphosis and hybridity.[31]

For Bynum, metamorphosis is a kind of change that relates to a 'labile world of flux and transformation'. Metamorphosis is a 'process', 'encountered through story'. It 'goes from an entity that is one thing to an entity that is another, and the relative weight or presence of the two entities suggests where we are in the story'.[32] Thus, it seems to us that metamorphosis corresponds to an Ovidian paradigm of change or, in a Christian context, to that of conversion as the abrupt and definitive break with the past that is articulated through a linear temporality and that implies, in Foucauldian terms, 'renunciation' or 'dying to oneself', the idea of 'being reborn in a different self'.[33]

Hybridity, by contrast, 'expresses a world of natures or substances' (often diverse or contradictory to each other) and is 'encountered through paradox' — 'in the instant'. So we understand the hybrid as more static, and Bynum

---

30   On Cino's exile poems and his use of the motif of *lontananza* to articulate his obsession with the phantasm of the lady, see Catherine Keen, 'Images of Exile: Distance and Memory in the Poetry of Cino Da Pistoia', *Italian Studies*, 55.1 (2000), pp. 21–36. She notes the Cavalcantian dimension to many of Cino's exile poems, in which the fragmentation of the lady's image corresponds to the lyric subject's own fragmentation. On Petrarch's relationship to Cino more broadly, see Edward L. Boggs III, 'Cino and Petrarch', *MLN*, 94.1, Italian issue (Jan. 1979), pp. 146–52; and Suitner, *Petrarca e la tradizione stilnovistica*, pp. 99–156.

31   See Caroline Walker Bynum, *Metamorphosis and Identity* (New York: Zone Books, 2001).

32   Ibid., p. 30.

33   Michel Foucault, *The Hermeneutics of the Subject: Lectures at the Collège de France, 1981–82*, ed. by Fréderic Gros, trans. by Graham Burchell (New York: Palgrave-Macmillan, 2005), p. 211. As our analysis goes on to show, the primary exemplum of this form of conversion is Augustine's *Confessions*.

underscores that the hybrid is 'not just a frozen metamorphosis' and is 'certainly not the end point or interruption
of metamorphosis'. It is rather 'a double being, an entity
of two parts — or more'. It makes 'twoness and the simultaneity of twoness visible'. As such, it can be a figure of
contradiction rather than change.[34]

On the basis of Bynum's distinction, our reading is
that in stanza 4 of *canzone* 70, there is no conversion, and
if anything changes, it is only Laura: she is no longer the
'possente donna', the powerful lady of *Rvf* 23, who was
blamed for the poet's demise. Instead, in *Rvf* 70 she is
exonerated from any fault:

> Se mortal velo il mio veder appanna,
> che colpa è de le stelle,
> o de le cose belle?
>
> (If a mortal veil dims my sight, | what fault is it of
> the stars, | or of all that is lovely?) (*Rvf* 70, 35–37)

However, although the poet recognizes Laura as the supreme of the 'cose belle' and turns the 'guilt' (colpa)
towards himself, this acknowledgment does not liberate
him from desire. In this sense, rather than progressive
movement or metamorphosis, we see hybridity here as the
paradoxical coexistence of recognizing the possibility of
resisting desire and yet compulsively surrendering to it.

In a similar vein, the last stanza points to the goodness
of creation but ends up confirming the 'I''s continued errancy and powerlessness:

> Tutte le cose, di che 'l mondo è adorno
> uscïr buone de man del mastro eterno;
> ma me, che cosí adentro non discerno,

---

34   Bynum, *Metamorphosis and Identity*, p. 30–31.

abbaglia il bel che mi si mostra intorno;
et s'al vero splendor già mai ritorno,
l'occhio non po' star fermo,
cosí l'à fatto infermo
pur la sua propria colpa, et non quel giorno
ch'i' volsi inver' l'angelica beltade
nel dolce tempo de la prima etade.

(All things with which the world is adorned | came
forth good from the hand of the eternal creator; |
but I, who do not see beneath the veil, | am dazzled
by the beauty in front of me; | and whenever I return
to the true splendour, | my eyes cannot stay focused,
| made so weak by their own fault, | and not by the
day | when I turned towards such angelic beauty
| *nel dolce tempo de la prima etade.* [In the sweet
season of my first youth]) (*Rvf* 70, 41–50)

In this last stanza, though there may be Biblical and even
Augustinian elements, the latter of which stand in Petrarch
for the necessity to turn towards God, the poem reaches
an impasse or a suspension, not a point of conversion or
change. Therefore it seems that *Rvf* 70 ends in a similar
vein to Petrarch's *Secretum* and the supposed 'conversion'
canzone Rvf 264.[35] In all these texts, when compared to the
Augustinian paradigm that comes to the fore in book 8 of
the *Confessions* as the fervour to convert that accompanies
the recognition of the split will, there is no sense in which
Petrarch urgently desires God, nor that he is desperately
trying to throw off the chains binding the self. There is just a

---

35 The *Secretum* is a fictional dialogue in Latin in three books staged
between two characters named 'Franciscus' and 'Augustinus', usually
taken to be alter egoes of the poet. On the close connection between
this work and *Rvf* 264, see Hans Baron, *Petrarch's 'Secretum': Its Making
and its Meaning* (Cambridge, MA: Harvard University Press, 1985),
pp. 47-57 and Klaus W. Hempfer, 'La canzone CCLXIV, il *Secretum* e
il significato del *Canzoniere* di Petrarca', *Studi petrarcheschi*, 14 (1994),
pp. 263-87.

slightly greater self-awareness, without the impulse to then push it a step further. As Christian Moevs has insightfully put it, in Petrarch one can only join with God through a superhuman effort, through a 'macho act of the will', a kind of superego trip that wants to impose a change and never manages it.[36] In this sense, the conclusion of *Rvf* 70 is a non-conclusion similar to that of the *Secretum* and *Rvf* 264, in which, with Michelangelo Picone, we can say that 'the truth that the Petrarchan "I" manages to achieve is related not to his eternal fate but to his earthly destiny; it is not a transcendental revelation but the recognition, rooted in immanence, of his being a sinner and of his living "a brief dream"'.[37]

36   Christian Moevs, 'Subjectivity and Conversion in Dante and Petrarch', in *Petrarch and Dante*, ed. by Barański and Cachey, Jr, pp. 226–59 (p. 246). On this aspect of Petrarch's poetics, see Francesca Souther-den, 'The Art of Rambling: Errant Thoughts and Entangled Passions in Petrarch's "Ascent of Mont Ventoux" (*Fam.* IV, 1) and *Rvf* 129', in *Medieval Thought Experiments: Poetry, Hypothesis and Experience in the European Middle Ages*, ed. by Philip Knox, Jonathan Morton, and Daniel Reeve (Turnhout: Brepols, 2018), pp. 197–221. On Augustine in Petrarch, see Carlo Calcaterra, *Sant'Agostino nelle opere di Dante e del Petrarca* (Milan: Vita e Pensiero, 1931); Nicolae Iliescu, *Il canzoniere petrarchesco e Sant'Agostino* (Rome: Società accademica romena, 1962); Carol E. Quillen, *Rereading the Renaissance: Petrarch, Augustine, and the Language of Humanism* (Ann Arbor: University of Michigan Press, 1998); and Dino Cervigni, 'The Petrarchan Lover's Non-Dialogic and Dialogic Discourse: An Augustinian Semiotic Approach to Petrarch's *Rerum Vulgarium Fragmenta*', *Annali d'Italianistica*, 22 (2004), pp. 105–34.

37   Michelangelo Picone, 'Petrarca e il libro non finito', in *Petrarca volgare*, ed. by Porcelli, pp. 83–94 (p. 88; our translation). For a reading of *Rvf* 264 in relation to the *Secretum*, see Teodolinda Barolini, 'The Self in the Labyrinth of Time: *Rerum vulgarium fragmenta*', in *Petrarch: A Critical Guide to the Complete Works*, ed. by Victoria Kirkham and Armando Maggi (Chicago: Chicago University Press, 2009), pp. 33–62; and Giuseppina Stella Galbiati, 'Sulla canzone "I' vo pensando" (*Rvf* 264): L'ascendente agostiniano ed altre suggestioni culturali', in *Petrarca volgare*, ed. by Porcelli, pp. 109–21.

This is how we read Petrarch's decision to conclude
Rvf 70 by returning to the beginning of *Rvf* 23. With
Bynum, we could say that *Rvf* 70 exhibits the movement
of metamorphosis and the fixity of hybridity together. The
subject feels the onus to shake the trap of sensual desire
in which he is fixed, but there is no change.[38] He is a hybrid: the 'I' neither dismisses self-control nor exercises it,
acknowledging the weakness in itself without correcting
or renouncing it. What interests us here is that by turning incipits into explicits and, in particular, by concluding
canzone 70 with a return to the beginning of *canzone* 23,
Petrarch interrupts forwardness and embraces backward-
ness. In this sense, the same formal features of *Rvf* 70 (the
use of *coblas capfinidas* and the poem's lack of *congedo*)
that, as we indicated earlier, seem to imply progression
and an overcoming of past desire simultaneously embody a
contrapuntal state of immobility and unwillingness to take
leave of the past. Thus, rather than take the quotation with
which the poem ends as a sign of surpassing the previous
tradition and Petrarch's own earlier poetics, we see it as a
literal return to them. As *Rvf* 23 makes clear, the advent of
love is the only and definitive transformation:

> e i duo mi trasformaro in quel ch'i' sono,
> facendomi d'uom vivo un lauro verde,
> che per fredda stagion foglia non perde.

> (and these two transformed me into what I am, |
> making of me, a living man, a laurel tree, | which,
> though winter come, never sheds a leaf.) (*Rvf* 23,
> 38–40)

In other words, a joint reading of *Rvf* 70 and 23 confirms
that the only event in Petrarch's collection is the encounter

---

38   On this point see ibid., p. 110.

with Laura, which is also the making of the poet as a poet of love — the only 'conversion' that takes place in the *Rerum vulgarium fragmenta*. As we shall see in Chapter 2, his state (of being a laurel) will not change; if anything, it will only intensify. Rather than move towards an end point, the poetic subject remains where it is, and the corresponding non-linear and non-teleological temporality operates at both a subjective and a textual level. Textually, 'firstness and lastness collapse into the same point' in *canzone* 70, in the same way that, as Teodolinda Barolini has argued, *Rvf* 23 problematizes the 'nature of all beginnings and endings' within the collection's first poetic micro-sequence (1–23) and in the *Rvf* as a whole.[39] Ultimately, the effect is to dissolve the boundaries between the two poems and to create a kind of hybridity in movement insofar as the poems are distinct within the sequence's macro-structure and yet merge so that the end of one is the beginning of the other, and vice-versa, endlessly.[40]

SHAPE IN MOTION

In order to understand what kind of subjectivity corresponds to this non-linear temporality, we propose engaging with Leo Bersani's concept of aesthetics in his reading of Freud's *Beyond the Pleasure Principle* and *Three Essays on Sexuality*. Bersani has argued that sexuality is fundament-

---

39   Teodolinda Barolini, 'Petrarch as the Metaphysical Poet Who Is Not Dante: Metaphysical Markers at the Beginning of the *Rerum vulgarium fragmenta* (*Rvf* 1–21)', in *Petrarch and Dante*, ed. by Barański and Cachey, Jr, pp. 195–225 (pp. 196–97). See also Rabitti, '*Nel dolce tempo*'.

40   On the openness of the form of the *Rerum vulgarium fragmenta*, see Picone, 'Petrarca e il libro non finito', pp. 91–93, in which he proposes the concept of 'in-finite' work. On the 'canzoni degli occhi' (*Rvf* 71–73) as a particular embodiment of this dynamic, see Barolini, 'The Making of a Lyric Sequence', pp. 21–23.

ally paradoxical insofar as it retains the masochistic character of its infantile stage, notwithstanding later attempts
to domesticate it according to the normative, teleological
model of sexual reproduction. For Bersani, sexuality is
characterized by a simultaneous production of 'a pleasurable unpleasure', which is not about final satisfaction or
release of sexual tension but rather its increase through
repetition and replication. This masochistic repetition produces an 'insistent stasis' and inverts the idea of a movement towards completion: 'the end of the story is already
in the beginning of the story; the teleological movement
goes into reverse at the very moment when it reaches its
goal; and the narrative line of sexuality completes itself as
a circle'.[41]

Bersani has also reformulated Freud's concept of sublimation, seeing 'artistic sublimation' as the possibility for
textuality not to purify or transcend sexual pleasure but,
on the contrary, to extend it to the movement of the text,
replicating its paradoxical character and making the reader
experience it. More specifically, he has argued that the fundamentally masochistic character of sexuality cannot be
articulated through scientific discourse, which inevitably
tends to resolve paradox into a linear logic or narrative
development, but it is conveyed through the aesthetics of
Freudian texts, which engage in self-sabotage and have the
proposed arguments continuously fail instead of progress-
ing linearly and reaching a logical conclusion. In this way,
Bersani considers aesthetics as 'a perpetuation and replic-
ative elaboration of masochistic sexual tensions', which do
not aim for resolution, but rather prolongation and intensification.[42]

---

41   Bersani, *The Freudian Body*, p. 35.
42   Ibid., p. 43. See also Leo Bersani, *Homos* (Cambridge, MA: Harvard
      University Press, 1995) and the volume of collected essays by the same

Bersani's concept of aesthetics can help us better understand the tensions deployed in Petrarch's textuality and link it to an inherently masochistic form of pleasure: by concluding with the return to *Rvf* 23, *Rvf* 70 not only signals the tenacity with which the subject clings to sensual desire and his identity as a love poet, but also embraces the non-linear temporality of non-conversion as continual deferral and intensification of pleasure. In this sense, rather than working as paradigms of desire to be overcome, the lyric citations that Petrarch includes in *Rvf* 70 reactivate the sensuality of desire, which keeps pleasure in the picture and resists the transformation of the poetic subject.

Rvf 70's return to *Rvf* 23 can even be seen as the poet's tenacious attempt to recuperate the masochistic impulse that concluded *Rvf* 23, 'ché pur la sua dolce ombra | ogni men bel piacer del cor mi sgombra' (168–69), where the 'beautiful pleasure' was that of surrendering the self to passion and its torments, represented by remaining in the sweet shade of the laurel. While in *Rvf* 23 the paradoxical pleasure derives from enjoying the pain of self-loss imposed through punishment, in *Rvf* 70 it consists of lingering in the impasse of assuming responsibility for a transgressive desire without ever relinquishing it.

As is by now evident, our interpretation differs from the more common reading of *Rvf* 70 as the end of one phase of desire and poetry and the start of a new one. Instead,

---

author, *Is the Rectum a Grave? And Other Essays* (Chicago: University of Chicago Press, 2005). On Bersani in relation to early modern literature, including Petrarch, see Cynthia Marshall, *The Shattering of the Self: Violence, Subjectivity, and Early Modern Texts* (Baltimore, MD: Johns Hopkins University Press, 2002). On the Bersanian notion of sublimation in relation to Petrarch, see Jennifer Rushworth, *Discourses of Mourning in Dante, Petrarch and Proust* (Oxford: Oxford University Press, 2016), p. 71.

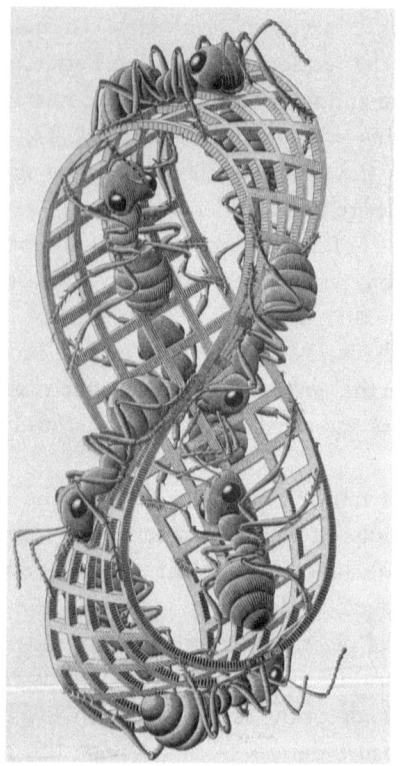

M. C. Escher, *Möbius Strip II*, 1963, woodcut. All M. C.
Escher works © 2018 The M. C. Escher Company – the
Netherlands. All rights reserved. Used by permission
<www.mcescher.com>.

it seems to us that *Rvf* 70's return to *Rvf* 23 signals a non-conversion that keeps the first phase of desire going and even revendicates it, particularly since, in the end, *Rvf* 70 defers to 23.

This conjunction of hybridity and metamorphosis, of movement and return, can be aptly represented as a Möbius strip. Discovered in 1857 independently by the

German mathematicians August Möbius and Johann List-
ing, the Möbius strip is formed by taking a strip of paper
and giving a half twist and joining the ends of the strip to
form a loop. The Möbius strip is a surface with only one
side and only one boundary, and its most significant mathematical property is that 'it is a non-orientable surface'.[43]
As a result of the twist in the strip, 'the inside surface of
the strip becomes the outside surface, and viceversa, endlessly'.[44] There is a beautiful illustration of the strip by M.
C. Escher (Fig. 1), and what we find interesting is that 'if an
ant were to crawl along the length of the strip, it would return to its starting point having traversed the entire length
of the strip (on both sides of the original paper) without
ever crossing an edge'.[45] The Möbius strip can therefore
be thought of as conjuring hybridity, movement, and return and offers a suggestive parallel with Petrarch's poetry:
it looks like it has two sides but actually has only one,
and what looks like difference is ultimately about identity. In its combination of oneness and twoness, the strip
corresponds to the hybrid Petrarchan subject of *canzone*
70, which appears on the verge of change but does not
ultimately change, instead remaining double in its combination of incompatible parts. Moreover, much like the
movement of the Möbius strip, which seemingly exits one

43   Robert Tubbs, *Mathematics in Twentieth-Century Literature and Art:
     Content, Form, Meaning*, (Baltimore, MD: John Hopkins University
     Press, 2014), p. 50.

44   Robert M. Fowler, *Let the Reader Understand: Reader-Response Criti-
     cism and the Gospel of Mark* (Harrisburg: Trinity Press International,
     2001), p. 221. For discussion of the Möbius strip as a figure for reading,
     specifically in relation to medieval textuality, see Alexandre Leupin,
     'The *Roman de la Rose* as a Möbius Strip (On Interpretation)', in *The
     Medieval Author in Medieval French Literature*, ed. by Virginie Greene
     (New York: Palgrave-Macmillan, 2006), pp. 61–75.

45   Stanley Gudder, *A Mathematical Journey* (New York: McGraw-Hill,
     1994), p. 108.

plane for another only to return, Petrarch's poem 70 in its relation to 23 does not lead outside of the loop but always reinserts itself within the same arc and literally returns to the beginning. In this way, the return gives form to a desire that holds together contradictory impulses without resolving them in a linear process but instead inserting them into an infinite process of retroaction, as in a Möbius strip.

***

As a final coda, we could add that this process of retroaction is not limited to the relationship between *Rvf* 70 and *Rvf* 23 but could be considered as the form of movement that shapes the whole *Rerum vulgarium fragmenta*. First, if the poetic subject of the *Rvf* never moves beyond the position it assumes in *canzone* 23, then the paradoxical nature of Petrarch's 'lyric sequence', which Barolini has argued combines fragmentation and sequentiality,[46] is given another dimension and made more ambivalent still. Second, the paradigm of deferral and non-conversion that we have identified in *canzone* 70 can illuminate other moments in the collection that stage an impulse for change and conversion. Remaining in the vicinity of our *canzone* 70, we could consider the three poems that follow, the 'canzoni degli occhi' mentioned above. These poems are meant to prove the change that *canzone* 70 effects in the poetic subject and indeed do express a new lyric mode, one that appears more 'positive'. However, this mode exhausts itself, and the following poems regain the usual Petrarchan tone of the ineluctable submission to Laura and to the forces of eros.[47] Moreover, the old, more 'negative' mode

---

46   See Barolini, 'The Making of a Lyric Sequence', especially pp. 6–7.
47   Cf. Praloran, *La canzone di Petrarca*, pp. 66–109, who underscores how this series of poems highlights the impasse of Petrarchan desire

remains and takes over in the last poem of the sequence, *Rvf* 73 ('Poi che per mio destino'), where reason is 'killed' (la ragione è morta) and abandons itself to sensuality, to the extent that 'dolcezza' (sweetness) becomes 'soverchia' (excessive), the way in which we have seen that 'desir' (desire) was 'soverchio' in *canzone* 70. In this way, even when Petrarch's poetry seems to be on the point of breaking the circle of its own paradoxical desire, it never actually does, like in a Möbius strip.[48] That is even true for *Rvf* 264, which Petrarch placed in the pivotal position between the first and second parts of his collection, or for the final penitential sequence of poems that concludes with the *canzone* 'Vergine bella' (*Rvf* 366).[49] Numerologically speaking, and within the calendrical and cyclical structure of the *Rvf*, which seems to contain one poem for every day of the year, this final poem leads back to *Rvf* 1 and to its paradoxical status as a proemial poem that is meant to abjure everything that follows and so already hints at the inverted and non-linear temporality that is the hallmark of lyric desire in Petrarch.[50] In this way, rather than seeing *Rvf* 366

resulting from continual distraction of the subject under the influence of desire and the impossibility of finding a foothold in the circulation of transcendence that passes from Laura to himself (p. 107).

48   On the concept of 'form of desire', cf. Manuele Gragnolati, *Amor che move. Linguaggio del corpo e forma del desiderio in Dante, Pasolini e Morante* (Milan: il Saggiatore, 2013).

49   On the irresolution of the *Rvf*'s ending, cf. Natascia Tonelli, 'Vat. Lat. 3195: Un libro concluso? Lettura di *Rvf* 360–366', in her *Per queste orme*, pp. 7–34; and Picone, 'Petrarca e il libro non finito'. For a reading of *Rvf* 366 in light of the desire for conversion and in relation to Dante, see Giuseppe Mazzotta, *The Worlds of Petrarch* (Durham, NC: Duke University Press, 1993), 163–66; Mario Petrini, 'La canzone alla Vergine', *Critica letteraria*, 23 (1994), pp. 33–42; Cervigni, 'The Petrarchan Lover's Non-Dialogic and Dialogic Discourse'; and Moevs, 'Subjectivity and Conversion', p. 231 and pp. 238–39.

50   See especially Moevs, 'Subjectivity and Conversion', pp. 231–34. On the relationship between *Rvf* 1 and *Rvf* 23 specifically, both afforded the status of 'incipit', see Rabitti, pp. 102–08.

as a final and successful conversion, which completes or
enacts a linear progression from Laura to God, one could
argue that it replicates the feeding of *canzone* 70 into 23, in
an endless feedback loop.[51]

---

51   For a recent study of *Rvf* 366 in relation to the 'ends' of Petrarch's desire,
     see John Ochoa, 'The Poet Becomes the Poem: The Missing Object and
     Petrarch's Ends in the *Canzoniere*', *Romance Quarterly*, 65.1 (2018), pp.
     38–48.

2. Openness and Intensity
Petrarch's Becoming Laurel in *Rvf* 23 and *Rvf* 228

THE PLANT WORLD

This chapter explores the relationship between Petrarch, poet of the *Rerum vulgarium fragmenta*, and the laurel tree, a symbol that usually stands for the poet's beloved Laura, but in the two poems we will look at comes to be connected also with the lyric 'I'. In other words, while the laurel is a pervasive symbol in Petrarch's *Rerum vulgarium fragmenta*, in keeping with the Ovidian myth of Apollo and Daphne, it is the *beloved* who is usually transformed into the laurel, frustrating the poet's desire to possess her and making that frustration the root of poetry. This scenario corresponds to Freud's idea of sublimation as the diversion of libidinal energies towards nonsexual aims — like artistic creation, intellectual pursuits, or in general, objects of higher social value. The body of Laura/Daphne that her lover fails to possess is 'transferred' into the poetic sign, and desire is 'sublimated' into verse.[1]

In keeping with Leo Bersani's concept of aesthetics and the way in which we have thought of Petrarch in the previous chapter, our approach here is to read Petrarch's lyric textuality not as transcending or 'taming' eros but as replicating the movement of desire, extending it to text, and allowing the reader to experience it. We have already looked at one of the poems we will analyse here, *canzone* 23, the so-called '*canzone* of metamorphoses', and have argued that it is centred on the poet's impossibility, or unwillingness, to relinquish sensual desire and culminates with the suggestion that this experience encompasses a form of paradoxical pleasure. In this chapter, we return to *Rvf* 23 and look at it together with another poem from Petrarch's collection, sonnet 228, and consider both from the perspective of the poet's fusion with the laurel. The 'becoming laurel' of our title is to be taken literally, since in these texts the Petrarchan subject *becomes* the laurel tree in *Rvf* 23 and has the laurel implanted into him in *Rvf* 228, then proceeding to beautify it with his tears and sighs. In looking at *Rvf* 23 and *Rvf* 228, we are interested in the kind of subjectivity and desire — or even sexuality — that might correspond to Petrarch's 'becoming' a laurel tree and that we might locate in relation to the plant world more broadly. Our sense is that the 'becoming tree' entails a loss of self,

---

1   On this dynamic in Petrarch, see Lynn Enterline, 'Embodied Voices: Petrarch Reading Himself Reading Ovid', in *Desire in the Renaissance: Psychoanalysis and Literature*, ed. by Valeria Finucci and Regina Schwartz (Princeton, NJ: Princeton University Press, 1994), pp. 120–45; on Freudian sublimation, see Jean Laplanche and Jean-Bertrand Pontalis, *The Language of Psycho-Analysis*, trans. by Donald Nicholson-Smith (London: Hogarth Press and Institute of Psycho-Analysis, 1973), pp. 431–33.

a kind of dispossession and opening to the outside that conveys a sense of desire not as lack but as intensity.

Our reading is shaped in dialogue with writers who have thought about plants and their modes of existence and have thereby suggested new ways to think about subjectivity — ways that we propose to connect with the concept of openness in the work of Rosi Braidotti. Specifically, we want to relate these ways of thinking about plants with Braidotti's concept of 'polymorphous vitalism', a means of experiencing desire not as a state of lack but as intensity and excess, which she has developed through Gilles Deleuze and Félix Guattari's notion of 'becoming'[2] — and that is the reason why the title of our chapter includes the idea of 'becoming'. For Braidotti, 'Becoming has to do with emptying out the self, opening it out to possible encounters with the "outside"', thereby expanding the possibilities of subjectivity and envisioning a self that can be 'joyfully discontinuous, as opposed to being mournfully consistent.'[3] In other words, becoming entails a loss of autonomy that is 'non-unitary' but not destructive. Insofar as 'the firm boundaries between self and other' dissolve, there is 'an enlargement of one's fields of perspective and capacity to experience', and this enlargement entails a space of becoming which does not limit love to the human subject but instead opens to a 'whole territory' around it.[4]

Some of the philosophers and theorists who have thought about plants have envisioned a similar kind of

---

2   See Rosi Braidotti, 'Intensive Genre and the Demise of Gender', *Angelaki*, 13.2 (2008), pp. 45–57, where she engages in depth with Deleuze and Guattari's *A Thousand Plateaus: Capitalism and Schizophrenia*, trans. by Brian Massumi (Minneapolis: University of Minnesota Press, 1987).

3   Braidotti, 'Intensive Genre', p. 47.

4   Ibid., esp. pp. 55–56.

openness to the outside, like for instance Emanuele Coccia in his 2016 book *La Vie des plantes: Une métaphysique du mélange* and Hélène Cixous in her novels *La* and *Illa*, especially as studied by Sarah-Anaïs Crevier Goulet.[5] The main idea here is the interconnectedness of plants, that is, the idea that they are porous organisms, and that there is a fluid boundary between inside and outside such that the two become hard to differentiate. Plants' natural tendency is to spread: in *La*, Cixous's narrator describes how when she is in a garden to which she feels connected 'vegetally' (J'ai toujours eu la certitude que j'étais liée à un vrai jardin par... Parenté archivégétale?), her body fuses with the earth and surrounding flora such that it is 'étendu partout', as stretched out and vast as the earth itself.[6] And plants are related to each other through an interconnectivity that is also evident in their spreading *across* the earth. According to Coccia, this spreading connotes an ultimate form of openness in the sense that the borders are undone between what we think of as 'the subject' and the *milieu*: 'One cannot separate the plant — *neither physically nor metaphysically* — from the world that accommodates it. It is the most intense, radical, and paradigmatic form of being in the world'.[7] This sort of 'being together', this co-existing, of plants is, as the title of Coccia's study indicates,

---

5   See Emanuele Coccia, *La Vie des plantes* (Paris: Éditions Payot & Rivages, 2016), in English as *The Life of Plants: A Metaphysics of Mixture*, trans. by Dylan J. Montanari (Cambridge: Polity, 2019), from which quotations are taken; Hélène Cixous, *La* (Paris: Gallimard, 1976) and *Illa* (Paris: Des Femmes, 1980), the latter two discussed in detail by Sarah-Anaïs Crevier Goulet, 'Du jardin d'essai / *esse* à l'hortus conclusus: Figures de la naissance et du végétal dans l'oeuvre de Hélène Cixous', in *Des jardins autres*, ed. by Paolo Alexandre Néné and Sarah Carmo (Paris: Archives Karéline, 2015), pp. 257–80.

6   Cixous, *La*, pp. 57–58.

7   Coccia, *The Life of Plants*, p. 5.

a 'métaphysique du mélange' (metaphysics of mixture). In an even more open sense, this state of coexistence of plants is also a 'jumble' of things, for they are conjoined and yet still distinct from one another, in the way that things in an ecosystem are fundamentally entwined, but their particularity and distinctions are nonetheless maintained.[8]

Thinking about the sort of subjectivity to which this kind of 'mélange' might correspond we find suggestive the following lines from Braidotti's essay on Virginia Woolf's relationship with Vita Sackville-West: a 'field [...] of perpetual becomings' in which 'What happens is vitalist erotics, which includes intensive de-territorializations, unhealthy alliances, hybrid cross-fertilizations, productive anomalies and generative encounters — allowing 'the unfolding of ever-intensified affects'.[9] In Braidotti and in some other works that consider plants in relation to eros, this sort of openness and becoming relates to sexuality and not just desire. For example, Natania Meeker and Antónia Szabari have analysed the treatment of plants as modes for human sexuality in the seventeenth-century writings of Guy de la Brosse and Cyrano de Bergerac. Within those works, Meeker and Szabari have traced what they term 'a scene of queer animacy [a term they take from Mel Chen], in which affects and sensations are mobilized across different kinds of bodies and diverse modes of being'. This phenomenon is all the more surprising given that plants are usually considered asexual and yet become an (imagined) site of 'flexible and formally inventive pleasures', 'multiplying pleasures at the limit of what we might recognize as subjectivity itself'. Meeker and Szabari

---

8   As Coccia writes, 'In order for a climate to exist, all the elements within a given space must be at once mixed and identifiable' (ibid., p. 27).

9   Braidotti, 'Intensive Genre', p. 55.

also cite Timothy Morton on tree hugging as a form of eroticism, which suggests that 'To contemplate ecology's unfathomable intimacies is to imagine pleasures that are not hetero-normative, not genital, not geared towards where the body stops and starts'.[10]

This line of thought has been suggestive for our thinking about the Petrarchan subject's 'becoming laurel' in *Rvf* 23 and *Rvf* 228, where that opening to the *végétal* seems intimately bound to the question of pleasure for him.[11] In particular we would like to develop the connection between Braidotti's concept of the 'di-vidual' or open subject, the vegetal, and the idea that it represents an intensification of desire.[12] In this sense, passivity is the possibility of 'an affective, de-personalized, highly receptive subject',[13] which is the closest Petrarch's 'I' gets to a form of dispossession (which the ego usually resists) and corresponds, as we have begun to suggest, to an experience of desire not so

---

10   Natania Meeker and Antónia Szabari, 'Libertine Botany: Vegetal Sexuality and Vegetal Forms', *Postmedieval: A Journal of Medieval Cultural Studies*, 9.4 (2018), pp. 478–89. The quotation from Morton is taken from his article, 'Guest Column: Queer Ecology', *PMLA*, 125.2 (2010), pp. 273–82 (p. 280).

11   On the concept of *végétal*, see Crevier Goulet; and for the way in which becoming-plant has been theorized in Deleuze and Guattari's *Mille plateaux*, see Hannah Stark, 'Deleuze and Critical Plant Studies', in *Deleuze and the Non/Human*, ed. by Jon Roffe and Hannah Stark (London: Palgrave Macmillan, 2015), pp. 180–96. See also Luce Irigaray and Michael Marder, *Through Vegetal Being: Two Philosophical Perspectives* (New York: Columbia University Press, 2016) and Michael Marder, *Plant-thinking: A Philosophy of Vegetal Life* (New York: Columbia University Press, 2013) and *The Philosopher's Plant: An Intellectual Herbarium*, with illustrations by Mathilde Roussel (New York: Columbia University Press, 2014).

12   See Braidotti, 'Writing as a Nomadic Subject', *Comparative Critical Studies*, 11.2–3 (2014), pp. 163–84, where she defines the 'dividual' as 'a singularity bounded by its own powers to endure intensities and relations to others' (n. 9, p. 183).

13   Braidotti, 'Intensive Genre', p. 46.

much as lack but as intensity, or as Braidotti has called it, the 'intensive multipli[cation] of affects'.[14]

OPENING TO LOVE

Our analysis begins with *canzone* 23, where the poetic subject undergoes a series of transformations explicitly modelled on Ovid. As discussed in Chapter 1, the poem is a blueprint of Petrarch's early poetry, one centred on the unrequited love of the troubadour and the Ovidian traditions. In view of the latter, the poem focuses on the transformations of the 'I' through the effects of love — first into a laurel and then into a swan, stone, fountain, flint, voice and stag, evoking respectively the Ovidian myths of Daphne, Cygnus, Battus, Byblis, Echo and Actaeon. All these are imposed on a helpless subject who has no choice but to yield to the force of sensual desire.

Here we are interested in the first three stanzas, which articulate the first metamorphosis of the 'I' — the one into a laurel — and situate it as the turning point in the subject's affective history. In particular, the poem opens with the idea that in his youth, a time defined in terms of freedom, or 'libertade', the poet was not subject to love. What is significant is that this state of not being touched by love is described in terms of enclosure and of a stone-like protection, which was tearless and unbending:

> Nel dolce tempo de la prima etade,
> che nascer vide et anchor quasi in herba
> la fera voglia che per mio mal crebbe,
> perché cantando il duol si disacerba,
> canterò com'*io vissi in libertade*,
> *mentre Amor nel mio albergo a sdegno s'ebbe.*

---

14   Ibid., p. 48.

[...]
I' dico che dal dí che 'l primo assalto
mi diede Amor, molt'anni eran passati,
sí ch'io cangiava il giovenil aspetto;
e *d'intorno al mio cor pensier' gelati*
facto avean quasi adamantino smalto
ch'allentar non lassava il duro affetto.

(In the sweet season of my first youth, | which saw
the birth and budding growth | of the wild de-
sire that grew to torment me, | I will sing, because
singing renders grief | less bitter, *of how I lived in*
freedom then, | *while Love was still scorned in my*
heart. [...] I say, then, that many years had passed
| since the day of Love's first assault, | so that my
youthful aspect was changing; | and *icy thoughts*
around my heart | *had made it almost as hard as dia-*
mond, | *giving no rein to my obstinate desire.*) (*Rvf* 23,
1–6, 21–26; our emphasis)

It is in this context that Love intervenes, and with the help
of a 'powerful lady', Amor turns the subject into the laurel:

Lagrima anchor non mi bagnava il petto
né rompea il sonno, et quel che in me non era,
mi pareva un miracolo in altrui.
[...]
Ché sentendo il crudel di ch'io ragiono
infin allor percossa di suo strale
non essermi passato oltra la gonna,
prese in sua scorta una possente donna,
ver' cui poco già mai mi valse o vale
ingegno, o forza, o dimandar perdono;
e i duo mi trasformaro in quel ch'i' sono,
facendomi d'uom vivo un lauro verde,
che per fredda stagion foglia non perde.

(No tear yet stained my breast | or woke me from
my sleep, and what I lacked | seemed miraculous in
others. [...] For that pitiless foe of whom I speak,

| seeing that none of his darts had yet | pierced be-
neath my clothing, | took into his service a powerful
lady, | against whom neither cunning, nor force, |
nor begging for mercy ever was (or is) much use;
| and these two transformed me into what I am, |
making of me, a living man, a laurel tree, | which,
though winter come, never sheds a leaf.) (*Rvf* 23,
27–29; 32–40)

This first metamorphosis is thus set up as loss of autonomy,
yet strangely it is not something merely negative but rather
a softening. In other words, there is a twist in this part of the
poem, and the twist with respect to the idea of wounding,
penetrability, and porosity is seen as more positive. In *Rvf*
23, therefore, the idea of *libertade* and autonomy appears
as something more limiting and the poem resonates with
Braidotti's stress on the open subject and what she calls
the 'di-vidual': a 'subject-in-becoming' whose processes
are 'collective, intersubjective and not individual or isol-
ated'.[15] In other words, becoming the laurel really means
an opening up to affect. Following Braidotti, who herself is
in dialogue with Baruch Spinoza's *Ethics*, we can say that
relinquishing *potestas* — the forms of restrictive and in-
stitutionalized power — allows for finding one's *potentia*,
a state of creative potentiality and possibility that is the
foundation of vitalist erotics.[16]

The actual metamorphosis is described in detail in
stanza 3 of Petrarch's poem, in which the poet rewrites
Ovid's description of Daphne turning into the laurel as his
own transformation:

Qual mi fec'io quando primier m'accorsi
de la trasfigurata mia persona,

---

15   Braidotti, 'Writing as a Nomadic Subject', p. 173.
16   Ibid., p. 171 and pp. 174–75.

> e i capei vidi far di quella fronde
> di che sperato avea già lor corona,
> e i piedi in ch'io mi stetti, et mossi, et corsi,
> com'ogni membro a l'anima risponde,
> diventar due radici sovra l'onde
> non di Peneo, ma d'un più altero fiume,
> e n' duo rami mutarsi ambe le braccia!

> (Imagine my surprise when first I took note | of
> my transfigured person, | and saw my hair become
> the very leaves | with which I had hoped to be
> crowned, | and my feet, with which I stood and
> walked and ran, | become two roots (since every
> member | answers to the soul) beside the rippling
> waters, | not of Peneus, but of a nobler river, | and
> both my arms transform into two branches!) (*Rvf*
> 23, 41–49)

Critics have pointed out that the poet's transformation
into the laurel in lines 38–40 (beautifully illustrated in a
1470 Venetian incunabulum now in the Biblioteca Queriniana in Brescia)[17] is connected to a passage from the
Triumphus Cupidinis that describes love as complete loss
of control and autonomy and as all consuming: 'e so in
qual guisa | l'amante nell'amato si transforme' (and I know
in what way | the lover turns into the beloved; III, 161–
62).[18] Love is an experience of dispossession: for instance,
Santagata talks of the poet being 'dispossessed of his own

---

17   The Petrarca Queriniano incunable is one of the most richly decor-
     ated examples of Petrarch's works produced in the 15th century. It
     can be viewed digitally at <http://www.misinta.it/biblioteca-digitale-
     misinta-2/1400-2/1470-petrarca-canzoniere-e-trionfi-miniato> [ac-
     cessed 20 August 2020]. For further detail on this incunable, see
     Francesco Petrarca, *Canzoniere, Trionfi: l'incunabolo veneziano di
     Vindelino da Spira del 1470 nell'esemplare della Biblioteca civica Quer-
     iniana di Brescia con figure dipinte da Antonio Grifo, INC. G V 15*,
     ed. by Giuseppe Frasso, Giordana Mariani, and Ennio Sandal (Rome:
     Salerno, 2016).

18   See Chapter 1, n. 19.

identity' (spossessato dalla propria identità) to the degree
that he 'loses consciousness of himself' (perde coscienza
di sé). The experience is a form of 'ecstatic forgetfulness'
(smemoramento estatico).[19] Moreover, the concept of the
lover's transformation into the beloved seems to displace
into a lyric context the theological concept of 'compassion',
that is, the idea that Mary's love for Christ during His Passion transformed her into an image of her Son because, as
Bonaventure writes, 'the power of love transforms the lover
into an image of the beloved' (vis amoris amantem in amati
similitudinem transformat).[20]

If we want to understand better what it means to *become laurel* in *Rvf* 23, we could look at the metamorphoses
that follow, but as we saw in Chapter 1, all that matters
is the first metamorphosis: the following ones are either
temporary or a fantasy and didn't actually happen. What
this means is that the poet never got out of being a laurel,
and indeed line 38 states 'i duo mi trasformaro *in quel ch'i'
sono*' (and these two transformed me *into what I am*), so
it is clear that the actual permanent condition of the lyric
'I' is the one described in lines 17–20: 'et un penser che
solo angoscia dàlle, | tal ch'ad ogni altro fa voltar le spalle,
| e mi face obliar me stesso a forza: | che tèn di me quel
d'entro e io la scorza' (and a single thought which causes
only anguish, | and makes me deaf to all other thoughts,
| and forces me to forget myself entirely: | for it governs
all that is in me, and I only the shell). The image of the
'scorza' (literally the bark of the tree) makes it clear that

19   See Santagata's note in Petrarca, *Canzoniere*, p. 105.

20   Bonaventura, *De assumptione B. Virginis Mariae*, sermo 2, in *Bonaventurae
      opera Omnia*, ed. by PP. Collegii S. Bonaventurae, 11 vols (Quaracchi:
      Collegium S. Bonaventurae, 1882–1902), ix (1901), p. 161; see also:
      Otto G. von Simpson, '*Compassio* and *Co-redemptio* in Roger van der
      Weyden's *Descent from the Cross*', *The Art Bulletin*, 25 (1953), pp. 9–16.

here the poetic subject really *is* a tree: he's only thinking
of Laura, and that thought alienates him from himself as a
sense of fusion into the beloved that dispossesses the lover
of his identity. *That* seems to be the state of being turned
into Laura. That condition, after all, is the result of a violent
transformation — but at the end of the poem it is also
revealed to be a pleasurable one:

> né per nova figura il primo alloro
> seppi lassar, ché pur la sua dolce ombra
> ogni men bel piacer del cor mi sgombra.
>
> (nor could I ever leave the first laurel behind | for
> a new form, for its sweet shade | expels all lesser
> pleasure from my heart.) (*Rvf* 23, 167–69)

In these lines too there is a striking combination of identity
and alterity in the relationship between the poetic subject
and the laurel tree. On the one hand, as Carla Freccero
has argued, there seems to be an irreducible 'masculinized
identification' between the poet and the 'alloro', which re-
iterates the initial dynamic of the transformation into the
'lauro verde'.[21] On the other hand, with the 'nova figura',
the gender of the subject shifts between masculine and
feminine, and as Marguerite Waller, has noted, the 'ombra'
itself is both double and a locus of instability: 'The shadow
of the laurel is his shadow and he is, in some sense, its
shadow [...], but his awareness of that fact prevents reification of himself in the image of some seemingly more
substantial counter'.[22] Santagata glosses the final line, on
the effects of this shadow, 'it chases from my heart all
other passion as less beautiful' (mi scaccia dal cuore ogni

---

21   See Carla Freccero, 'Ovidian Subjectivities', esp. pp. 27–30.
22   See Marguerite Waller, *Petrarch's Poetics and Literary History* (Amh-
     erst: University of Massachusetts Press, 1980), p. 104.

altra passione, come meno bella), where passion is pleasure and carries this paradoxical tone that for us is a cipher of Petrarchan desire and pleasure.[23]

MÉLANGE

While *canzone* 23 stages the poet's transformation into the laurel, in *Rvf* 228 Love opens the left side of the lyric subject and plants the laurel tree in the middle of his heart. In this poem we find an opening and a wound, which are followed by an act of nurturing, and indeed critics such as Nicholas Mann have spoken of Petrarch as 'gardener' in relation to this sonnet, one who 'cultivates' the laurel in the double sense of the Latin *cultus* meaning both to 'cultivate' and 'to worship':[24]

> Amor co la man dextra il lato manco
> m'aperse, e piantòvi entro in mezzo 'l core
> un lauro verde sí che di colore
> ogni smeraldo avria ben vinto et stanco.
>
> Vomer di pena, con sospir' del fianco,
> e 'l piover giú dagli occhi un dolce humore
> l'addornâr sì, ch'al ciel n'andò l'odore,
> qual non so già se d'altre frondi unquanco.
>
> Fama, Honor et Vertute et Leggiadria,
> casta bellezza in habito celeste
> son le radici de la nobil pianta.
>
> Tal la mi trovo al petto, ove ch'i' sia,
> felice incarco; et con preghiere honeste
> l'adoro e 'nchino come cosa santa.

23   See Santagata's note in Petrarch, *Canzoniere*, p. 123.

24   Nicholas Mann, 'Petrarca giardiniere (a proposito del sonetto ccxxviii)', *Letture Petrarce*, 12 (1992), pp. 235–56. On the broader topic of Petrarch and gardens, see also William Tronzo, *Petrarch's Two Gardens: Landscape and the Image of Movement* (New York: Italica Press, 2014), pp. 1–23. This image of Love as 'gardener' is also present in *Rvf* 64, 6–7, 'del petto ove dal primo lauro innesta | Amor più rami'.

(Love opened my left side with his right hand | and planted, in the middle of my heart, | a laurel tree so green in colour | that it would far outshine any emerald. || The ploughshare of pain, the sighs of my heart, | and the raining down of sweet tears from my eyes | have so embellished it that its fragrance wafted heavenward; | I do not think that other leaves have ever equalled it. || Fame, honour, virtue, grace, | chaste beauty with celestial demeanour: | these are the roots of the noble plant. || Wherever I am, I find it a happy burden | on my chest; and with honest prayers | I adore and bow to it as a sacred thing.) (*Rvf* 228)

A wound that is opened by Love is a common image in the lyric tradition, but here it also alludes to the Christian trope of receiving the stigmata. Yet with Coccia's earlier suggestion in mind, it is impossible to read the poem and consider the plant as separate from the world that accommodates it. So while the 'I' does not *become* the laurel in this poem (as it did in *Rvf* 23), there is a mixing of the 'I' with the tree. In the case of the Petrarchan sonnet the 'I' is the 'world that receives' the plant, and as in *Rvf* 23, we find an 'impossible separation' between the subject and the laurel. In *Rvf* 23 it is a result of transformation, and in *Rvf* 228 it is in Coccia's sense of 'mélange'.

Sonnet 228 opens by reiterating the beginning of *Rvf* 23 and describes the origin of the poet's love for Laura: Love, Amor, takes hold of the subject and literally opens ('m'aperse') his left side and implants the laurel into the very centre of his heart ('in mezzo al core'). Then the poet cultivates the plant with his suffering and by watering it with tears, which in a very Petrarchan way are defined oxymoronically as 'dolce humore' (sweet water). This bodily act of nurturing the plant makes it special and unique, and the word 'odore', relating to the fragrance of the tree, indicates the sensual character of the poet's desire. Yet 'odore' also evokes the 'arbor odorifera' (fragrant tree) of Petrarch's *Coronation Oration* (*Collatio laureationis*), where the laurel is the symbol of poetic fame and glory, as well as the *dolce lignum* of the Cross and the sweet fragrance linked to God.[25] Indeed, as Manuela Boccignone has shown, if the beloved's presence in the poet's heart is a common, well-established motif of the lyric tradition, the image of the tree implanted in the heart corresponds to the Cross and has a strong Christological connotation in medieval allegorical tradition that we might also perceive in poems in which Petrarch consciously sets the laurel tree, associated with Laura, against the tree of the Cross (see especially *Rvf* 142).[26]

The following tercet describes the laurel, that is, the beloved Laura, as a 'nobil pianta', suggesting that she is a noble and even pure being, and it is therefore different from the way in which Laura is often described as incom-

---

25   On these intertexts see Rosanna Bettarini's commentary of line 7 of the poem, in Petrarca, *Canzoniere*, p. 1056. The reference to the sweet fragrance of the Lord comes in Gen. 8.21 ('Odoratusque est Dominus odorem suavitatis', as Castelvetro notes in his commentary (also cited in Bettarini). On *dulcedo* and *suavitas* as characteristics of God see also Mary Carruthers, *The Experience of Beauty in the Middle Ages* (Oxford: Oxford University Press, 2013), pp. 80–107. Petrarch's *Collatio laureationis* is available in English as 'Petrarch's Coronation Oration', trans. by Ernest Hatch Wilkins, *PMLA*, 68.5 (Dec. 1953), pp. 1241–50. The Latin text is in *Opere latine di Francesco Petrarca*, ed. by Antonietta Bufano, 2 vols (Turin: UTET, 1975), II, pp. 1255–83. According to Mann ('Petrarca giardiniere', pp. 244-45), the perfume of the tree can also be connected to the fame and immortality the poet seeks to bestow on Laura and he cites the Song of Songs 1.3 ('unguentum effusionis nomen tuum') and Catullus (VI, 16–17) as possible sources.

26   Manuela Boccignone, 'Un albero piantato nel cuore (Petrarca e Iacopone)', *Lettere italiane*, 52.2 (April–June 2000), pp. 225–64. On the image of the tree in Petrarch and Jacopone, see Lina Bolzoni, *La rete delle immagini: predicazione in volgare dalle origini a Bernardino da Siena* (Turin: Einaudi, 2002), pp. 103–44.

patible with God and even His enemy. Laura would seem to be not an evil distraction but rather depicted in the lyric mode associated with the divinization of the *donna*, more in line with a certain *stilnovo* mode that runs from Guinizzelli to Dante. At this point it would seem that there is nothing problematic in this love — and indeed critics have even read the poem as signalling 'the protagonist's progress on the arc of his spiritual journey' insofar as it stages 'the ordering of the inchoate matter of the passions into a new textual body of the virtues'.[27] Instead, we argue that a real turn takes place in the following and final tercet, actually in the last line and its vertiginous twist: up to 'preghiere oneste' the reader expects the sonnet to culminate with a sort of moral climax, but instead suddenly we are presented with an image of idolatry: 'l'adoro e inchino come cosa santa' (I adore and bow to it as a sacred thing). The verb 'adoro' signals the conflation, since it means both to show devotion to a divinity and, in courtly lyric, to worship the beloved lady as though she were divine. (It is, for example in Giacomo da Lentini, Chiaro Davanzati, and in Cino da Pistoia.)

A suggestive antecedent for this conflation may be found in the final stanza of Guido Cavalcanti's *ballata* 'Perch'i' no spero di tonar giammai', which we shall discuss at length in Chapter 5:

> Tu, voce sbigottita e deboletta
> ch'esci piangendo de lo cor dolente,
> coll'anima e con questa ballatetta
> va' ragionando della strutta mente.
> Voi troverete una donna piacente,
> di sì dolce intelletto

---

27   See most recently Thomas E. Peterson, '"Amor co la man dextra il lato manco" (*Rvf* 228) as Allegory of Religious Veneration', *MLN*, 135.1 (January 2020), Italian Issue, pp. 17–33 (pp. 31–32).

che vi sarà diletto
starle davanti ognora.
Anim', e tu l'adora
sempre, nel su' valore.

(Bewildered and frail voice, | you who weeping
leave my grieving heart, | with my soul and this little
ballata | tell her of my fractured mind. | You will
find a dazzling lady, | with such sweet intellection
| that it will delight you | to remain eternally in her
presence. | Then, my soul, adore her | always, in all
her valour.) ('Perch'i' no spero di tonar giammai',
37–46)[28]

As Claudio Giunta has observed, Cavalcanti's poem is
constructed upon the model of contemporary will and
testaments and, in particular, reproduces the motif of the
commendatio anime, that is, the recommendation of one's
soul to God with the hope that after death it may succeed
in enjoying the beatific vision. Significantly, though, Cavalcanti's text replaces God with the lady and concludes by
making the wish that the poet's soul dwell in an eternal contemplation of his beloved, where the verb 'adora', which
resonates with the Biblical line 'quia ipse est dominus tuus
et adora eum' (*Psalms* 44.12), suggests a love that is experienced with the intensity of faith.[29]

Petrarch's sonnet undertakes a similar operation and
concludes by staging what in Augustinian terms can be

28   Quotations of Cavalcanti's poems are taken from Guido Cavalcanti,
     Rime, ed. by Roberto Rea and Giorgio Inglese (Rome: Carocci, 2011).

29   Claudio Giunta, 'Guido Cavalcanti, "Perch'i' no spero di tornar
     giammai"', in *Codici. Saggi sulla poesia del Medioevo* (Bologna: il
     Mulino, 2005), pp. 45–61. The Biblical reference is noted by Roberto
     Rea in his commentary to the poem in Cavalcanti, *Rime*, p. 199. On
     Cavalcanti's ironic use of Biblical intertexts, see Paola Nasti, 'Nozze
     e vedovanza: dinamiche dell'appropriazione biblica in Cavalcanti e
     Dante', *Tenzone*, 7 (2006), pp. 71–110.

understood as a form of idolatry, that is, the act of turning the creature into the Creator and thereby perverting
the *ordo amoris*, according to which worldly, mortal things
are not to be desired or enjoyed per se but used as instru-
ments (objects of use, *uti*) that move the soul towards God,
who alone represents the ultimate object of desire and
the only object of enjoyment (*frui*).[30] In John Freccero's
reading, this kind of idolatry, which is a recurrent feature
of Petrarch's *Rerum vulgarium fragmenta*, corresponds to
a reification of the sign and of desire, both of which are
emblematized in the figure of the laurel, which Petrarch
makes into a self-sufficient symbol of poetic autonomy: 'a
poetry whose real subject matter is its own act and whose
creation is its own author' with no reference to the world
beyond the one the *Rerum vulgarium fragmenta* create. For
Freccero, this project risks stripping both the poet's beloved (Laura) and desire of their vitality in order to arrive
at immortality and the illusion of substance, when really
the object the poet pursues is a mirage, and the sign, in
the absence of an external referent, remains opaque and
unknowable.[31] In contrast, while our reading of the two
poems acknowledges the presence of the idea of desire as
non-progression as well as the presentation of the poet's
fidelity to love as wrong in Augustinian terms, we contend
that ultimately the poems do not present the steadfastness
of the poet's desire for Laura as mere reification or fixation

---

30   See Augustine, *De doctrina Christiana* (PL 34), I, 4 <http://www.
      augustinus.it> [accessed 15 September 2020]. On this distinction, see
      also Lombardi, *The Syntax of Desire*, p. 15.

31   John Freccero, 'The Fig Tree and the Laurel: Petrarch's Poetics', *Dia-
      critics*, 5.1 (Spring 1975), pp. 34–40 (esp. pp. 38–39). On petrified
      immobility as the hallmark of *canzone* 23, see also Barolini, 'The Making
      of a Lyric Sequence', p. 30.

but rather as a paradoxical openness to passion and the susceptibility to being moved.

The proposition with which we would like to conclude this chapter is that the connection between the poet and the laurel, which is unusual not in terms of frequency but in terms of modality, is a sign of a profound intimacy between *canzone* 23 and sonnet 228 — an intimacy that is certainly related to the poet's unwavering sensual desire but that also helps us to appreciate an aspect that is usually less perceived in Petrarch's poetry: the paradoxical pleasure deriving from dispossession and softening the boundaries with the other.[32] Sonnet 228 may even convey a sense of commingling at the level of sound, in the linguistic texture of the words, since according to Mann we might see in the 'core' (heart) of line 2 a fusion of 'or' and 'co' sounds, the first of which runs from 'Am*or*' (1) through to 'ad*oro*' (14) and the last of which is especially prominent in the final line, 'l'ad*oro* e 'nchino *co*me *co*sa santa'.[33] In the case of both poems, pleasure comes from the subject's passivity, which enables it to be penetrated and affected from the outside and after to remain in that state as one of unparalleled 'sweetness' (dolcezza, *Rvf* 23) and 'happy burden' (felice incarco, *Rvf* 228). Our hypothesis is that this paradoxical pleasure is connected to the plant imagery informing the two poems and that if read with the works that have recently focused on the plants' mode of existence, our two texts vibrate with a desire that makes the subject boundless and expands it into the experience of intensity.

---

32   On paradoxical pleasure, see Chapter 1.

33   See Mann, 'Petrarca giardiniere', p. 252.

3. 'Lust in Action'
Control and Abandon in Dante, Petrarch, and Shakespeare

This chapter proposes a reading of three sonnets that explore the relationship between will, knowledge, and desire: Dante's 'Io sono stato con Amore insieme', Petrarch's 'S'amor non è, che dunque è quel ch'io sento?' (*Rvf* 132), and Shakespeare's 'Th'expense of spirit in a waste of shame' (sonnet 129). Our decision to read these three texts together derives from the fact that they are all 'mini-treatises' on passion in the sonnet form that analyse desire from a physiological perspective and define it as a sensual force overcoming the will and rendering the subject passive.

In this undertaking, as we have mentioned in the introduction, our aim is not to put forward a genealogical link between the texts or to suggest that one is the source of the other. As far as we are aware, it is not known whether Shakespeare knew Dante, even though it has been suggested that Petrarch may work as an intermediary between the two given that Shakespeare would have been familiar with at least some of Petrarch's poems in Thomas Wyatt's and

Surrey's translations/adaptations. Moreover, in the specific case of *Rvf* 132, that poem came into the English tradition as early as Chaucer, when he incorporated a translation/expansion of it in his *Troilus and Criseyde*, providing an authoritative link to the English context.[1] We are also aware that the transversal reading we are attempting could risk abstracting the three poems under discussion from their original context. In a way, this is a stronger gesture in the case of Petrarch and Shakespeare since they wrote lyric sequences in which the placement of a particular poem is very much part of the meaning of the poems themselves (and, as we shall indicate later, *Rvf* 132 and sonnet 129 are not only each within a 'sequence' but also in a 'subsequence').[2] Yet as will become clear, Dante's sonnet also points to a larger context within the poet's *oeuvre* and as such is embedded in its own way in a field of textual relationships.

---

1   On the relationship between Shakespeare and Petrarch, also in the context of English Petrarchism, see Thomas P. Roche, Jr, *Petrarch and the English Sonnet Sequences* (New York: AMS Press, 1989), esp. chapter 8; Heather Dubrow, *English Petrarchism and its Counterdiscourses* (Cornell, NY: Cornell University Press, 1995), esp. chapter 4; Ronald L. Martinez, 'Francis, Thou Art Translated: Petrarch Metamorphosed in English, 1380–1595', *Humanist Studies & the Digital Age* 1.1 (2011), pp. 80–108; Linda Gregerson, 'Open Voicing: Wyatt and Shakespeare', in *The Oxford Handbook of Shakespeare's Poetry*, ed. by Jonathan Post (Oxford: Oxford University Press, 2013), pp. 151–66.

2   On the notion of lyric sequence see Barolini, 'The Making of a Lyric Sequence'. See also Michael R. G. Spiller, *The Sonnet Sequence: A Study of its Strategies* (New York: Twayne, 1997); Olivia Holmes, *Assembling the Lyric Self: Authorship from Troubadour Song to Italian Poetry Book* (Minneapolis: University of Minnesota Press, 2000); Marco Santagata, *Dal sonetto al canzoniere: Ricerche sulla preistoria e la costituzione di un genere* (Padua: Liviana, 1979); Marisa Galvez, *Songbook: How Lyrics Became Poetry in Medieval Europe* (Chicago: University of Chicago Press, 2012); and Roland Greene and Bronwen Tate, 'Lyric Sequence', in *The Princeton Encyclopedia of Poetry and Poetics*, ed. by Roland Greene and others, pp. 834–36, including the bibliography listed at the end of the entry.

As in the rest of this book, the experiment that we propose carrying out is to bring the poems into dialogue and see what they share and where they differ from one other, with the hypothesis that they can illuminate each other in productive ways. Pivotal to our reading is an attention to poetic form, specifically the way in which each poet appropriates — or transgresses — the constraints of the sonnet form in order to express or even master the uncontrollable nature of desire by exhibiting differing degrees of control in or over his texts. In this case, too, our attention to form is indebted to Bersani's concept of 'aesthetics', which acknowledges textuality's capacity to replicate the movement of desire and have the reader experience it.[3]

LUCIDITY

Dante's 'Io sono stato' is a sonnet written to Cino da Pistoia most likely between 1303 and 1306 and, as such, is one of the author's latest lyrics. It is accompanied by a Latin epistle in reply to Cino's sonnet 'Dante, quando per caso s'abbandona', which opens by posing in an obscure way the question of whether it is licit to abandon an old love for a new one:

> Dante, quando per caso s'abbandona
> lo disio amoroso della speme
> che nascer fanno gli occhi del bel seme
> di quel piacer che dentro si ragiona,
>
> i' dico, poi se morte le perdona
> e Amor tienla più delle due estreme,
> che l'alma sola, la qual più non teme,
> si può ben trasformar d'altra persona.

---

3   See Chapter 1.

(Dante, when by chance it happens that the love-
desire despairs of that hope which the eyes cause
to grow from the fair seed of beauty revolved in the
mind, then I say that — if death reprieves her, and
if Love controls her more than the two extremes
— the soul, left to herself and fearing nothing more
now, is fully at liberty to change to another person.)
(1–8)[4]

A reply to this proposition by Cino, Dante's sonnet can be
considered a *quaestio de amore*. It reads as follows:

Io sono stato con Amore insieme
de la circulazion del sol mia nona,
e so com'egli affrena e come sprona
e come sotto lui si ride e geme.

Chi ragione o virtù contra gli sprieme,
fa come que' che 'n la tempesta sona
credendo far colà dove si tona
esser le guerre de' vapori sceme.

Però nel cerchio de la sua palestra
liber arbitrio già mai non fu franco,
sì che consiglio invan vi si balestra.

Ben può con nuovi spron punger lo fianco,
e qual che sia 'l piacer ch'ora n'addestra,
seguitar si convien, se l'altro è stanco.[5]

---

4   Cino's sonnet and its translation are cited from *Dante's Lyric Poetry*, ed.
     by Kenelm Foster and Patrick Boyde, 2 vols (Oxford: Oxford Univer-
     sity Press, 1967), I, pp. 198–99. On Dante's correspondence with Cino,
     see André Pézard, 'De passione in passionem', *L'Alighieri*, 1 (1960), pp.
     14–26; Natascia Tonelli, 'Amor da che convien ch'io mi doglia', in
     Dante: Le quindici canzoni. Lette da diversi (Lecce: Pensa Multimedia,
     2012), pp. 255–83; Enrico Fenzi, 'Ancora sulla *Epistola* a Moroello e
     sulla "montanina" di Dante (*Rime*, 15)', *Tenzone*, 4 (2003), pp. 43–84;
     and Sabrina Ferrara, 'Io mi credea del tutto esser partito: il distacco di
     Dante da Cino', in *Cino nella storia della poesia italiana*, ed. by Rossend
     Arqués Corominas and Silvia Tranfaglia (Florence: Cesati, 2016), pp.
     99–111.

5   Dante's sonnet is cited from Dante Alighieri, *Rime*, ed. by Domenico
     de Robertis (Tavarnuzze [Florence]: SISMEL · Edizioni del Galluzzo,
     2005).

(I have been together with Love | since my ninth
rotation of the sun, | and I know how he tightens
his reins and digs in his spurs | and how under his
sway you laugh and groan. || Trying to use reason
or power against him | is like ringing church bells
in a storm, | thinking they will calm the clashing va-
pours | where the thunder sounds. || For on Love's
battleground | free will has never truly been free, |
and reason shoots there in vain. || He can spur you
on again, rest assured; | and whatever new passion
is leading you, | you must pursue it, if the old one is
spent.)

Dante's sonnet responds 'per le rime', that is, it reprises
the same rhymes of the *envoi* of Cino's poem and states
that there is no choice: if an old passion is extinguished
and a new attraction arises, one cannot but follow it. In
particular, Dante's poem asserts that the lover has no control over passion because it hinders reason and its ability to exert free judgment (9–11). This idea reaffirms a
well-established courtly topos, which in Italy had been ex-
pounded by the Sicilians and recently reaffirmed by Guido
Cavalcanti's tragic and grand exemplum, in particular in
the doctrinal *canzone*, 'Donna me prega, per ch'eo voglio
dire', which is also a treatise on love. In this poem, Cavalcanti declares that in love, which he regards as a passion of
the sensitive soul, 'la 'ntenzione – per ragione vale' (33),
effectively expressing the same concept that we later find
in Dante's sonnet. Yet if the motif is common in the lyric
tradition, it is interesting to note its untimeliness with respect to Dante's meditation on love insofar as it contradicts
both the previous project of the *Vita Nova* to integrate
desire and reason and the *Commedia*'s ethics of desire. In
the former, the poet claims that his love for Beatrice happens with 'lo fedele consiglio della ragione' (the faithful

counsel of reason; II, 9/1.10),[6] and in the central cantos of
the *Purgatorio*, desire is explained in precisely the opposite
terms of Dante's 'Io sono stato'. One could also contrast
the sonnet's claim with Dante's almost-contemporary self-
presentation in the *De vulgari eloquentia* as 'cantor rectitu-
dinis' (II, ii, 9), i.e., as a moral poet as exemplified by his
canzone 'Doglia mi reca ne lo core ardire'. In other words,
Dante's journey as a poet is usually seen as a progressive
transformation of eros into *caritas*, yet 'Io sono stato' contradicts and destabilizes that linearity and progression by
reaffirming the supremacy of eros over reason. Not only
does Dante, even at a later stage, theorize desire in terms of
compulsion,[7] but as Kenelm Foster and Patrick Boyde have
remarked, in the first quatrain he even admits to a 'carnal
love' for Beatrice (1–2).[8]

As Dante's accompanying Latin epistle to Cino confirms, here love is a passion of the sensitive soul: 'Cum
igitur potentia concupiscibilis, que sedes amoris est, sit po-

---

6   We quote Dante's *libello* from Dante Alighieri, *Vita Nuova*, ed. by
    Domenico De Robertis, (Milan–Naples: Ricciardi, 1980), which uses
    the text by Michele Barbi (Dante Alighieri, *Vita Nuova*, Florence:
    Bemporad, 1932). The reference to the text according to its tradi-
    tional subdivision into forty-two chapters is followed by the reference
    according to the subdivision into thirty-one paragraphs proposed by
    Gugliemo Gorni (Dante Alighieri, *Vita Nova*, ed. by Guglielmo Gorni
    (Turin: Einaudi, 1996)).

7   See Barolini, 'Dante and the Lyric Past', pp. 23–45, and her 'Dante and
    Cavalcanti (On Making Distinctions in Matters of Love): *Inferno* 5 in
    its Lyric and Autobiographical Context', in her *Dante and the Origins
    of Italian Literary Culture*, pp. 70–101. One of the reasons for Dante's
    return to a more traditional courtly mode could be that he was at this
    point close to the court of the Malaspina, which was one of the most
    important centres for troubadour poetry in Occitan. See Gilda Caiti
    Russo, *Les Troubadours et la Cour des Malaspina* (Montpellier: Presses
    Universitaires de la Meditérrané e, 2005), and 'Il marchese Moroello
    Malaspina testimone ideale di un dibattito tra Dante e Cino sull'eredità
    trobadorica', *Dante Studies*, 124 (2006), pp. 137–48.

8   See *Dante's Lyric Poetry*, ed. by Boyde and Foster, II, p. 323.

tentia sensitiva, manifestum est quod post corruptionem unius passionis qua in actum reducitur, in alium reservatur' (Since, then, the appetitive faculty, which is the seat of love, is a faculty of sense, it is manifest that after the exhaustion of the passion by which it was brought into operation it is reserved for another; III, 5).[9] As in Cavalcanti, we are in the domain of natural philosophy and medical discourse, which considers the subject as fully submerged in the realm of matter and sensual appetite, which paralyzes the faculty of judgment and its ability correctly to advise the will whether an object of desire is good or bad.[10] This is the precise and technical way one should understand the only-apparent paradox that is put forward in lines 9–11: in matters of love 'free will has never truly been free' (liber arbitrio già mai non fu franco).[11] In the poem this defeat of reason in Love's arena is expressed through two

---

9   The Latin epistle to Cino is cited from Dante Alighieri, *Rime*, ed. by Claudio Giunta (Milan: Mondadori, 2018), pp. 517–19. The translation comes from *Dante Alagherii epistolae = The letters of Dante*, trans. by Paget Toynbee, 2nd edn (Oxford: Clarendon Press, 1966).

10 On will and the faculty of judgment in Dante, see Giorgio Stabile, 'Volontà', in *Enciclopedia dantesca*, ed. by Umberto Bosco, 6 vols (Roma: Istituto della Enciclopedia Italiana, Fondata da Giovanni Treccani, 1970–78), V, cols 1134–40; and also the definition that Dante gives in *Monarchia* I, xii, 4: 'Si ergo iudicium moveat omnino appetitum et nullu modo preveniatur ab eo, liberum est; si vero ab appetitu quocunque modo preveniente iudicium moveatur, liberum esse non potest, quia non a se, sed ab alio captivum trahitur'. Quoted from Dante, *Monarchia*, ed. and trans. by Prue Shaw (Cambridge: Cambridge University Press, 1995).

11 This paradox is only apparent because it can actually be explained through contemporary Scholastic philosophy. On the distinction between free will and free choice in the Scholastic context, see J. B. Korolec, 'Free Will and Free Choice', in *The Cambridge History of Later Medieval Philosophy: From the Discovery of Aristotle to the Disintegration of Scholasticism 1100–1600*, ed. by Norman Kretzmann and others (Cambridge: Cambridge University Press, 1982), pp. 629–41 and Alain De Libera, *Volonté et action: Cours du Collège de France 2014/2015* (Paris: Vrin, 2017).

main metaphors: the lover being ridden by Love as a horse (which recalls the common image of old Aristotle being ridden by Phyllis), and the useless ringing of bells during a storm (which anticipates the 'bufera infernal' of *Inferno* v).[12] This passivity culminates in the necessary acquiescence to Love's power that is expressed in the final tercet, where the noun 'piacere' hints that there is nonetheless something pleasurable in this abandon.[13]

So while everything in Dante's sonnet is about compulsion and submission to love, what we find interesting is that there is not much room for overwhelming angst. This is in contrast to the near-contemporary 'canzone montanina', which, as scholars have pointed out, shows several connections, both formal and thematic, with our sonnet, but in a more tormented and heightened mode, which stresses the lover's anguish in being completely dominated by passion.[14] Our sonnet is instead a space of knowledge. The poetic subject has proved the contradictory and destabilizing effects of love, which restrain and goad, provoking laughs and groans, but there is a kind of lucidity in the answer to Cino's question, 'Io sono stato con amore insieme [...] e *so* com'egli affrena e come sprona | e come sotto lui si ride e geme' (1; 3–4; our emphasis). Phrases like 'so' in l. 3 or 'ben può' in l. 12 leave no space to doubt and correspond to the deductive reasoning of the discourse of science and

---

12   See Barolini, 'Dante and Cavalcanti,' p. 89.

13   Claudio Giunta, in his notes on Dante's sonnet, has glossed 'piacere' not as 'bellezza' but as 'sentimento piacevole della passione amorosa', whereas in Cino's sonnet to which Dante is replying, 'quel piacer che dentro si ragiona' (4) refers to the introjected image of the lady, in her beauty, that the lover turns over in his mind. See Giunta's commentary in Dante, *Rime*, p. 516.

14   On Dante's *Canzone montanina* see Tonelli, 'Amor d che convien'; and John C. Barnes and Zygmunt G. Barański, 'Dante's *Canzone montanina*', *The Modern Language Review*, 73.2 (April 1978), pp. 297–307.

its accurate Scholastic substrate: as we shall see, things are very different in Petrarch. Although Dante's sonnet begins with a series of contrasts, it maintains a kind of consequential, rational movement that culminates with the irrefutable clarity of 'si convien' in the last line. This clear knowledge allows the 'I' to affirm itself so prominently at the beginning of the sonnet: '*Io* sono stato con Amore insieme'. Put another way, even if the onslaught of passion is described in a way that could suggest an annihilation of the 'I' under the force of Love, the matter-of-fact tone is maintained, and there is still a subject that commentates on that experience with authority and lucidity.

(IM)BALANCE

Such lucidity is lacking in Petrarch's *Rvf* 132. It is the first sonnet in a triptych on the question of the nature of love, which privileges oxymoron, antithesis, and paradox.[15] It reads:

> S'amor non è, che dunque è quel ch'io sento?
> Ma s'egli è amor, perdio, che cosa et quale?
> Se bona, onde l'effecto aspro mortale?
> Se ria, onde sí dolce ogni tormento?
>
> S'a mia voglia ardo, onde 'l pianto e lamento?
> S'a mal mio grado, il lamentar che vale?
> O viva morte, o dilectoso male,
> come puoi tanto in me, s'io no 'l consento?

---

15 Michelangelo Picone has located the poem after the cinque 'canzoni sorelle' (*Rvf* 125–29) — largely set in Vaucluse and centred on the search for the image of the beloved — and just before the sonnets that denounce the Babylonian captivity of the Church in Avignon (*Rvf* 136–38): 'I paradossi e i prodigi dell'amore passione (*Rvf* 130–140)', in *Il Canzoniere: Lettura micro e Macrotestuale*, ed. by Michelangelo Picone (Ravenna: Longo, 2007), pp. 313–33.

Et s'io 'l consento, a gran torto mi doglio.
Fra sí contrari vènti in frale barca
mi trovo in alto mar senza governo,

sí lieve di saver, d'error sí carca
ch'i' medesmo non so quel ch'io mi voglio,
et tremo a mezza state, ardendo il verno.

(What is this feeling, if not love? | And if love, by
God, what is its essence, and what its quality? |
If it is good, then why this fatal agony? | If it is
wicked, then why is every torment so sweet? || If
I burn of my own volition, then why such tears and
lamentation? | If against my will, then what sense
does lamenting have? | O living death, o delightful
anguish, | how can you do so much to me without
my consent? || And if I consent, then I have no right
to complain. | Buffeted by such opposing winds in a
flimsy vessel, | I find myself in rough water without
a rudder, || so light of knowledge and heavy with
error | that I myself don't know what I want, | and
I tremble in mid-summer and burn in winter.) (*Rvf*
132)

Petrarch's sonnet is a veritable mini-treatise on love that
situates itself in a line that begins with Guillaume IX
d'Aquitaine and extends to Italy through the *tenzone*
between the Sicilian poets, Jacopo Mostacci, Pier della
Vigna, and Giacomo da Lentini.[16] The poem is one of

---

16   On the link with Guillaume IX d'Aquitaine, the earliest troubadour
     poet whose texts have survived, see Marco Santagata's notes to
     Petrarch's poem, in Petrarca, *Canzoniere*, in relation to the poetic
     technique of the *devinalh*, 'ovverosia della costruzione di enigmi per
     addizioni di contrari' (p. 648). The *tenzone* among the Sicilian poets
     Jacopo Mostacci, Pier della Vigna, and Giacomo da Lentini is made up
     of three sonnets that debate the nature of love, specifically whether love
     is, in Aristotelian terms, an 'accident' or a 'substance'. See Michelan-
     gelo Picone, 'La tenzone "de amore" fra Jacopo Mostacci, Pier della
     Vigna e il Notaro', in his *Percorsi della lirica duecentesca* (Florence:
     Cadmo, 2003), pp. 47–67, and Bettarini's introductory note to *Rvf* 132,
     in Francesco Petrarca, *Canzoniere. Rerum vulgarium fragmenta*, ed. by
     Rosanna Bettarini, 2 vols (Turin: Einaudi, 2005), I, p. 641.

the most Scholastic texts of the collection and opens
with the question about the essence of love: 'S'amor non
è, che dunque è quel ch'io sento?', in which the feeling
of love is established as the object of an intellectual
investigation. As Piero Boitani has underscored, the rest
of the octave continues by asking six more questions
that stem from the first, according to 'a scholasticizing
process of *divisio*'.[17] Thus the octave appears to follow the
rational and investigative mode of the medieval *quaestio*,
addressing not only the nature of love but also the role
of the will and opening up several possibilities ranging
from total passivity ('Come puoi tanto in me, s'io nol
consento?') to responsibility ('E s'io 'l consento, a gran
torto mi doglio') and even to paradoxical pleasure ('S'a
mia voglia ardo, onde 'l pianto e lamento?').[18] And yet
the sestet provides no answer to these questions and,
in a quintessentially Petrarchan move, proposes instead
the impossibility of knowing due to being prey to love
sickness.

Indeed, this poem is not only one of the most Scholastic of Petrarch's collection but also one of the most
physiological in its display of the symptoms of the *malattia d'amore*. Bettarini has recalled Andreas Capellanus's
treatise *De amore* and stated that in this poem love 'is a
pathology of sensation, a feverish disturbance, like the condition of the one who shivers with cold "in mid-summer"
and burns in heat in the depths of winter'.[19] These are
the same symptoms that, as Natascia Tonelli has shown,

---

17 Piero Boitani, '*O quike deth*: Love, Melancholy, and the Divided Self',
    in *The Tragic and the Sublime in Medieval Literature* (Cambridge: Cam-
    bridge University Press, 1989), pp. 56–74 (p. 57).

18 On masochistic pleasure in Petrarch see Chapters 1 and 2.

19 See Rosanna Bettarini's gloss in Petrarca, *Canzoniere*, I, p. 641; our
    translation.

inform much of Duecento love poetry, especially Cavalcanti's, with its emphasis on love as a passion of the sensitive soul that affects the body and paralyzes the mind.[20]

Even though the concept of love is the same as that
in Dante's 'Io sono stato', the movement of Dante's and
Petrarch's sonnets is different. As we have already hinted,
while Dante's sonnet conveyed the poetic subject's grasp of
the matter of love and provided a lucid dissection of desire
and its consequences with Scholastic precision, Petrarch's
sonnet transitions back from the theoretical quest to the
poetic subject's feeling and experience of love. The result is
that the subject's knowledge is completely hindered and replaced by the typically Petrarchan condition of error — his
boat is light on knowledge and heavy on error — which in
turn becomes an existential impasse: 'Fra sì contrari venti
in frale barca, | mi trovo in alto mar senza governo, | sì
lieve di saver, d'error si carca, | ch'i' medesmo non so quel
ch'io mi voglio, | e tremo a mezza state, ardendo il verno'
(10–14).[21] The Petrarchan 'I' is even more present than
the already prominent 'I' that opened Dante's sonnet, but
it stops being concerned with the theoretical understanding of love and capitulates instead to a state of confusion

---

20   See Tonelli, *Fisiologia della passione*.

21   'Errore' is a quintessentially Petrarchan term and key also in *Rvf* 129,
      where it designates a state of self-forgetting that stems from a fixation
      on the beloved's image and Love's control over the 'I', which desires
      nothing else: 'Ma mentre tener fiso | posso al primo pensier la mente
      vaga, | et mirar lei, et oblïar me stesso, | sento Amor sí da presso, |
      che del suo proprio error l'alma s'appaga: | in tante parti et sí bella la
      veggio, | che se l'error durasse, altro non cheggio'. 'Voglia', meanwhile,
      is a key concept in *Rvf* 118, a sonnet that expresses the impasse that
      comes from non-decision and is summarized in the lines 'Or qui son,
      lasso, et voglio esser altrove; | et vorrei piú volere, et piú non voglio;
      [...] né per mille rivolte ancor son mosso' (9–11; 14). On errancy
      in Petrarch see Philippe Guérin, 'Pétrarque, ou de l'écriture comme
      odyssée', in *Voyages de papier: Hommage à Brigitte Urbani*, ed. by Perle
      Abbrugiati and Claudio Milanesi (= *Italies*, 17/18 (2014)), pp. 31–57;
      and Southerden, 'The Art of Rambling'.

that takes it back to the sensations that gave rise to the investigation in the first place. In other words, if the first line asked the question 'S'amor non è, che dunque è quel ch'io sento?', at the end of the sonnet knowledge is gone, and only the 'sentire', i.e. sensation, remains. In a similar way, as Warren Ginsberg has indicated, the Aristotelian principle of non-contradiction collapses, and the binary Scholastic mode of reasoning is replaced by paradox, which is the Petrarchan mode of desire and already present in the octave with the oxymora 'dolce [...] tormento' and 'dilectoso male' in lines 4 and 7.[22]

One also finds paradox in the status of the 'I', which is hindered in its knowledge and reduced to pure sensation but not annihilated. The last two lines reaffirm the poetic subject through the repeated personal pronouns as a coexistence of opposites. Similarly, the epistemological instability ('non so') is replicated formally, for example in the imbalance between octave and sestet, in the sense that line 9 seems to logically belong with the quatrains as also indicated by the structure of the *coblas capfinidas* of 'consento' in lines 8–9; or, in the last line, where one could expect a parallelism between indicatives, one finds instead the indicative 'tremo' followed by the gerund 'ardendo'. John Kerrigan has spoken of a 'calculated asymmetry' that characterizes almost all of Petrarch's poetry in the *Rerum vulgarium fragmenta*, and in *Rvf* 132 what we might call a 'harmony without symmetry' conveys the masterly control through which the unstable 'I' reaffirms itself and relishes in the pleasure of cultivating that imbalance.[23]

---

22 Warren Ginsberg, 'Chaucer and Petrarch: "S'amor non è" and the *Canticus Troili*', *Humanist Studies & the Digital Age*, 1.1 (Winter 2011), pp. 121–27 (p. 122).

23 See John Kerrigan, 'Between Michelangelo and Petrarch: Shakespeare's Sonnets of Art', in *On Shakespeare and Early Modern Literature: Essays*

EXCESS

The question of pleasure is also at stake in Shakespeare's sonnet 129, which is the third of the Dark Lady sequence that follows the sonnets written about the Young Man (1–126). In particular, sonnets 127 and 128 signal an aesthetic shift towards that which the poet calls 'blackness' and which corresponds to a journey into the most obscure recesses of sexual appetite.[24]

Like the poems by Dante and Petrarch we have already analysed, sonnet 129 puts forward a physiological concept of desire as an annihilation of the will. Crucially, however, there is an enormous difference with respect to what we have seen in the case of Dante and Petrarch insofar as this physiological concept of desire and the corresponding form of the text are taken to another level with respect to what comes before. Indeed, if we wanted to use an adjective that itself recurs twice in the sonnet, we could say that the cipher of the poem is its 'extreme' character: exaggerated, without control or limits. In this respect, sonnet 129 corresponds well to the way in which Linda Gregerson has suggested that Shakespeare intensifies the agitation and torment of Petrarch's sonnets, which he would have encountered in Wyatt's translation, and in relation to which

---

(Oxford: Oxford University Press, 2011), pp. 23–40 (p. 25). See also Peter Hainsworth's reading of the sonnet in *Petrarch the Poet: An Introduction to 'Rerum vulgarium fragmenta'* (New York: Routledge, 2014), p. 209, in which he acknowledges a certain 'game'-like aspect and a lighter tone.

24 On the relationship between the two sequences, see Michael Schoenfeldt, 'The Sonnets', in *The Cambridge Companion to Shakespeare's Poetry*, ed. by Patrick Cheney (Cambridge: Cambridge University Press, 2007), pp. 125–43, and his 'Friendship and Love, Darkness and Lust: Desire in the Sonnets', in his *The Cambridge Introduction to Shakespeare's Poetry* (Cambridge: Cambridge University Press, 2010), pp. 88–111.

she remarks that this is 'Petrarch with a vengeance'.[25] Sonnet 129 reads as follows:

> Th'expense of spirit in a waste of shame
> Is lust in action; and till action, lust
> Is perjur'd, murderous, bloody, full of blame,
> Savage, extreme, rude, cruel, not to trust;
> Enjoy'd no sooner but despised straight;
> Past reason hunted; and no sooner had,
> Past reason hated, as a swallow'd bait,
> On purpose laid to make the taker mad:
> Mad in pursuit, and in possession so;
> Had, having, and in quest to have, extreme;
> A bliss in proof, and prov'd, a very woe;
> Before, a joy propos'd; behind, a dream.
>> All this the world well knows; yet none knows well
>> To shun the heaven that leads men to this hell.[26]

One immediately notices a striking feature of this text. Unlike in Dante and Petrarch's sonnets, there is no grammatical 'I' in Shakespeare's sonnet — indeed, this poem is one of only two instances in Shakespeare's sonnets in which the 'I' is missing, in this case because of its complete annihilation by the self-destructive and violent impulse of sexual desire.[27] Lines 1–2 already say it all in the sense that there is no space for love in this sonnet, only lust. The reader is immediately introduced to the obscurity of bodily matter and the most degrading and humiliating aspects of the sexual impulse, which is represented as a disease. As in Dante and Petrarch's sonnets, we are dealing with lovesickness, but here the reference is specifically to the medical

---

25   Gregerson, 'Open Voicing', p. 159.

26   We cite the poem from William Shakespeare, *Shakespeare's Sonnets*, ed. by Katherine Duncan-Jones (London: Methuen Drama, 2010).

27   The other sonnet from which the 'I' is absent is 94, 'They that have power to heart and will do none'. See Schoenfeldt, 'Friendship and Love', pp. 96–97.

theory that orgasm diminishes the vital force and leads the subject closer to death. The physicality of that experience has been aptly described by Don Paterson with reference to the contemporary understanding of the chemical and hormonal changes that occur in the (male) brain before, during, and after sex:

> [I]t's too irrational and disproportionate a response to explain by anything but a bizarre reaction to a sudden flood of post-orgasmic transmitters. Your anticipatory thrill-dopamine goes through the roof during arousal, but the proclatin secreted during orgasm suddenly suppresses it, so you get a mood plummet […] driv[ing] you into your limp 'refractory period'.[28]

In Shakespeare, as the references to shame and lust make clear, love sickness brings 'physical as well as moral degradation'.[29] Indeed, like many other words in Shakespeare's poetic language, 'spirit' is a polyvalent word and stands here for the vital force, the soul, and also 'semen'.

The remainder of the sonnet, up to the final couplet, offers a veritable anatomy of desire, describing the different phases of 'lust in action' in terms of a before, during, and after. And it is arguably the time before that is most emphasized, to which are dedicated the chaotic accumulation of lines 3–4 and 6–8; the first hemistich of line 9 ('mad in pursuit'); the second hemistich of line 10 ('in quest to have, extreme'); and the first of line 12 ('before a joy proposed'). The idea that is continually repeated in the poem is that of pre-orgasmic desire as a trick or 'bait', 'laid to make the taker mad', i.e. compulsive and obsessive. The moment

---

28   Don Paterson, *Reading Shakespeare's Sonnets: A New Commentary* (London: Faber and Faber, 2010), pp. 388–89.

29   See Katherine Duncan-Jones's notes to this poem, in *Shakespeare's Sonnets*, pp. 272–73.

of 'action' itself, the 'now' of desire (a concept to which we will return in the following chapter), is remembered only very briefly: in addition to the phrase 'lust in action' in line 2, we have in line 9 'mad in possession', and in line 11, 'a bliss in proof', which is perhaps the only positive note of the whole poem, if we can call it that. Instead, the idea of the 'after' is that of scorn, hatred, suffering and self-abasement, experienced as shame and self-loathing. Yet notwithstanding the repellent and demeaning nature of the sexual impulse, the subject — which is no longer a subject, annihilated as it is by desire — cannot but continue to want it. The overall message of the sonnet is the impossibility of resisting the attraction that sexual appetite continues to exert, even nostalgically, in the phrase 'behind a dream'. It indicates the self-delusion, as well as the susceptibility of being lured into its power and fascination over and again.

The impossibility of controlling desire with reason is repeated in the anaphora of 'past reason' in lines 6 and 7 and returns in the final couplet, which is a sort of aphorism. Here the concept of knowing (and not knowing), which was present in Dante and Petrarch's sonnets, also returns: 'All this the world well knows, yet none knows well | to shun the heaven that leads men to this hell' (13–14). Here there is a split between a theoretical knowledge of the neg-ativity of the sexual impulse and the concrete impossibility of refusing it even knowing what it truly is, where 'hell' reiterates the negative and misogynistic drive of the sonnet since 'hell', in this case, stands not only for all 'the shame and hatred described in the previous lines' but also for the vagina.[30] In other words, Shakespeare's impersonal state-ment recovers the lucidity in the matter of love (here lust) of the Dantean subject and turns the Petrarchan not know-

---

30   See Duncan-Jones, *Shakespeare's Sonnets*, pp. 372–73.

ing into the impossibility of resisting a truly masochistic, self-destructive impulse. Moreover, if we consider that 'to lead' is the equivalent of the Italian 'menare', we cannot but be reminded of canto v of *Inferno* and of the entire lyric tradition that subtends it, and we could say therefore that with Shakespeare, the hell of passion is found on earth.[31]

As in Dante's and Petrarch's sonnets, irrational compulsion is consequently at the centre of Shakespeare's poem, but while Dante and Petrarch's sonnets maintain a sense of self, no matter how impaired by desire, in sonnet 129 the poetic subject disappears from the text, destroyed by the strength of its sexual impulse. As in Dante and Petrarch, we would say that lyric textuality perfectly corresponds to the desire that it expresses, in this case through its formal exaggeration, lack of control, and disjointedness. Michael Schoenfeldt has commented that the sonnet's 'headlong syntax and rushed enjambment brilliantly enact the rash, impulsive action the poem describes' and that 'The emphatic but progressively exhausted stresses of line 4 effectively produce one of Shakespeare's least metrical lines'.[32] In addition, and this is particularly interesting having read Petrarch's sonnet, the *coblas capfinidas* structure that sees the adjective 'mad' repeated between the end of line 8 and the beginning of line 9 is placed in the same position as the repetition of 'consento' in Petrarch's sonnet, notwithstanding the different organization of the Elizabethan sonnet into three quatrains and a final rhym-

---

31   Cf. *Inferno* v's description of the lustful souls as buffeted by the infernal storm, 'La bufera infernal, che mai non resta, | mena li spiriti con la sua rapina | voltando e percotendo li molesta (31–33); 'di qua, di là, di giù, di sù li mena' (43). Text is cited from Dante Alighieri, *La Commedia secondo l'antica vulgata*, ed. by Giorgio Petrocchi, 4 vols (Milan: Mondadori, 1966–67). On the verb 'menare', see Barolini, 'Dante and Cavalcanti'.

32   Schoenfeldt, 'The Sonnets', p. 133.

ing couplet. The big difference from Petrarch is that here the poem builds not through antithesis but via accumulation, which creates the feeling of excess noted above. Any sense of control, no matter how asymmetrical or paradoxical, is gone, and this formal imbalance replicates well the destructive and uncontrollable nature of sexuality, which produces only a moment of pleasure, which, for Shakespeare, is inextricable from disgust and self-loathing and traumatizes the self (or what remains of it) into repetition compulsion.[33]

Thus in Shakespeare's sonnet there is no room for balance or control of any sort, and with the destitution of the subject, everything else falls apart. Simultaneously, the sonnet form itself is altered, not merely in the turn from the Italianate to the Elizabethan form but in the sense that the many caesuras in the verse lines, combined with the enjambments, create a totally different rhythm: at moments furious, at other times nearly broken, in keeping with the unstoppable drive of the sexual impulse and the downfall to which it leads. Rather than Dante's lucidity or Petrarch's confusion, in Shakespeare's sonnet we find obsession that may even devolve into hallucination. Abandoning oneself to repetition compulsion is staged as entering a black hole that absorbs all light and subsumes everything to sheer intensity. And even though at the end of the sonnet, the aphorism in the final couplet would seem to open up towards a more detached or universal statement, the final, misogynistic reference to '*this* hell' hits the readers with affective violence. An analogous experience occurs

---

33 Repetition compulsion is a Freudian notion. See Sigmund Freud, 'Beyond the Pleasure Principle' (1920), in *The Standard Edition to the Complete Psychological Works of Sigmund Freud*, ed. and trans. by James Strachey, 24 vols (London: Hogarth Press, 1953–74), XVIII (1955), pp. 7–64.

when reading some of the most scatological lyrics of the troubadour Arnaut Daniel, where, as Bill Burgwinkle has noticed, the sexual and somatic details are such that 'we cease even to consider what pleasure might be had from the operation and instead relish the poet's delight in wiping our faces in the abject'.[34] In Shakespeare's sonnet too a paradoxical space of pleasure is opened up for readers, who are left both shocked and amazed by the force of what the poem's aesthetics has made them experience.

---

34 See William Burgwinkle, 'Modern Lovers: Evanescence and the Act in Dante, Arnaut, and Sordello', in *Desire in Dante and the Middle Ages*, ed. by Manuele Gragnolati and others (Oxford: Legenda, 2012), pp. 14–28 (pp. 19–21).

4. Declensions of 'Now'
Lyric Epiphanies in Cavalcanti, Dante, and Petrarch

This chapter continues to explore the risks and pleasures of passivity by reading together three sonnets by Cavalcanti, Dante, and Petrarch: 'Chi è questa che vèn ch'ogn'om la mira'; 'Tanto gentile e tanto onesta pare', and 'Erano i capei d'oro a l'aura sparsi' (*Rvf* 90). All three sonnets engage with the notion of epiphany, understood as an event in time that is focused on an experience of instantaneity and implies a showing forth.[1] In this sense, epiphany (etymologically derived from the Greek, ἐπιφάνεια, meaning 'manifestation')

---

1   On the notion of epiphany, see Paul Friedrich, 'Lyric Epiphany', *Language in Society*, 30 (2001), pp. 217–47; and Rainer Warning, 'Seeing and Hearing in Ancient and Medieval Epiphany', in *Rethinking the Medieval Senses: Heritage, Fascinations, Frames*, ed. by Stephen G. Nichols, Andreas Kablitz, and Alison Calho (Baltimore, MD: Johns Hopkins University Press), pp. 102–16, which includes a comparative reading of poems by Dante and Petrarch. He argues that relative to Dante, Petrarch's epiphanies are more 'subjective' and 'psychologizing'; in a poem like *Rvf* 111 (and arguably in *Rvf* 90 too), Petrarch 'allows a specific temporal moment to break into the language with the fugacity

is a kind of presencing: a way both to make presence visible
and to experience it in the 'now'.

In all three sonnets, the manifestation is that of the
beloved, and they all register the effects that her appearing
has on the poetic subject. Yet they are far from homogen-
ous in their attempts to capture the particular temporality
of the lady's epiphany and of its effects in the present.
Our analysis of these temporal differences in the lyrics
has led us to consider them in relationship to non-linear
temporality, especially queer temporality. For the last few
decades, queer theory has been interested in exploring how
in its entanglement with desire and embodiment, temporality can take many different forms that challenge the
normativity of progression, linearity, and teleology.[2] For
instance, both Lee Edelman and Jack/Judith Halberstam
have criticized, in very different ways, the heteronormative
structure of progressivist visions of futurity, and Heather
Love has shown the significance of looking backwards.[3]
Scholars like Carolyn Dinshaw and Carla Freccero have
also destabilized linear ways of understanding the past and

---

of an appearance' (p. 112). See also Warning, 'Imitatio und Intertextualität. Zur Geschichte lyrischer Dekonstruktion der Amortheologie:
Dante, Petrarca, Baudelaire', in *Lektüren romanischer Lyrik. Von den
Trobadors zum Surrealismus* (Freiburg: Rombach, 1997), pp. 104–41.
For a discussion of epiphany's sacramental charge, and an argument for
its cautious use in relation to broader notions of lyricism, see Robin
Kirkpatrick, 'Polemics of Praise: Theology as Text, Narrative, and Rhet-
oric in Dante's *Commedia*', in *Dante's 'Commedia': Theology as Poetry*,
ed. by Vittorio Montemaggi and Matthew Treherne (Notre Dame, IN:
University of Notre Dame Press, 2010), pp. 14–35 (pp. 17–21).

2   See for instance, *Queer Temporalities*, ed. by Elizabeth Freeman
     (=*GLQ: A Journal of Lesbian and Gay Studies*, 13.2–3 (2007)).

3   Lee Edelman, *No Future: Queer Theory and the Death Drive* (Durham,
     NC: Duke University Press, 2004); Judith Halberstam, *In a Queer Time
     and Place: Transgender Bodies, Subcultural Lives* (New York: New York
     University Press, 2005); Heather Love, *Feeling Backward: Loss and the
     Politics of Queer History* (Cambridge, MA: Harvard University Press,
     2009).

relating to it.[4] In this chapter, we dialogue in particular with Carolyn Dinshaw's interest in the different possibilities of the present and the 'now'. Dinshaw has shown that '[t]he present moment is more heterogeneous and asynchronous than the everyday image of *now* [...] would allow'.[5] Through her analysis of mainly middle English narrative texts, Dinshaw has shown that 'desire can reveal a temporally multiple world in the *now* (a queer world, that is)'.[6] In looking at our three Italian lyric epiphanies, we are also interested in the relationship between temporality and desire, in particular how 'now' is declined differently and thereby articulates diverse subjectivities.

QUESTIONING

The first sonnet of our trilogy, 'Chi è questa che vèn', is by the Florentine poet Guido Cavalcanti:

> Chi è questa che vèn, ch'ogn'om la mira,
> che fa tremar di chiaritate l'âre
> e mena seco Amor, sì che parlare
> null'omo pote, ma ciascun sospira?
>
> O Deo, che sembra quando li occhi gira!
> dical' Amor, ch'i' nol savria contare:
> cotanto d'umiltà donna mi pare,
> ch'ogn'altra ver' di lei i' la chiam' ira.

---

4   Carolyn Dinshaw, *Getting Medieval: Sexualities and Communities, Pre-*
      and Post-modern (Durham, NC: Duke University Press, 1999); Carla
      Freccero, *Queer/Early/Modern* (Durham, NC: Duke University Press,
      2006).

5   Carolyn Dinshaw, *How Soon is Now: Medieval Texts, Amateur Readers,*
      and the Queerness of Time (Durham, NC: Duke University Press, 2012),
      p. 7 (italics in the original).

6   Dinshaw, *How Soon is Now*, p. 5 (italics in the original).

Non si poria contar la sua piagenza,
ch'a le' s'inchin' ogni gentil vertute,
e la Beltate per sua dea la mostra.

Non fu sì alta già la mente nostra
e non si pose 'n noi tanta salute,
che propiamente n'aviàn canoscenza.

(Who is she who approaches, on whom everyone gazes, | who makes the air tremble with clarity | and brings Love in her wake, so that | no one can speak but each one sighs? || Oh God, what she seems when she looks my way! | Let Love himself speak of it, for I would not know how: | she appears to me a lady of such humility | that next to her all other women seem proud. || No one could describe her fairness, | for every gracious virtue bows to her, | and Beauty worships her as its goddess. || No mind has reached such heights, | none of us has ever had such perfection | to know her properly.)

As noticed by several commentators, this sonnet is already in a dialogue with what comes before, specifically with Guido Guinizzelli's sonnet 'Io vo'[gliọ] del ver mia donna laudare', which engages with the motif of the *laus mulieris* from the troubadour and early Sicilian tradition but pushes it to a new intensity.[7] Indeed, its main characteristic is the theologization of the lady to the extent that the event of her appearing elevates her to quasi-divine status. 'Io vo'[gliọ]

---

7   See Guido Guinizzelli, *Rime*, ed. by Luciano Rossi (Turin: Einaudi, 2002), p. 50. The poem, which we quote from *Poeti del Dolce stil novo*, ed. by Donato Pirovano (Rome: Salerno, 2012), pp. 43–45, reads as follows: 'Io vo'[gliọ] del ver la mia donna laudare | ed asembrarli la rosa e lo giglio: | piú che stella dïana splende e pare, | e ciò ch'è lassú bello a lei somiglio. || Verde river' a lei rasembro e l'àre, | tutti color di fior', giano e vermiglio, | oro ed azzurro e ricche gioi per dare: | medesmo Amor per lei rafina meglio. || Passa per via adorna, e sí gentile | ch'abassa orgoglio a cui dona salute, | e fa 'l de nostra fé se non la crede; | e non·le pò apressare om che sia vile; | ancor ve dirò c'ha maggior vertute: | null' om pò mal pensar fin che la vede.'

del ver' is one of the poems with which Guinizzelli tried
to revitalize the courtly tradition after it had been viol-
ently denounced by Guittone d'Arezzo in his *canzone* 'Ora
parrà s'eo saverò contare' and in his 'conversion' into Frate
Guittone. In particular, Guittone had fiercely criticized the
immorality of the courtly discourse and its incompatib-
ility with God and the use of reason. The 'solution' that
Guinizzelli proposed consists in contaminating the courtly
register with modes from sacred poetry and in turning the
praise of the lady into the description of an epiphany of a
truly miraculous being, one capable of improving the lover
and making him virtuous.[8]

Cavalcanti's 'Chi è questa che vèn' both alludes to this
contamination and recasts it. The allusion is made expli-
cit through the use of two rhymes (one in each stanza)
and four rhyme words, *âre*, *pare*, *virtute*, *salute*, that also
appear in 'Io vo'[gliọ] del ver'. Cavalcanti's poem opens
with the same airy radiance and lightness of Guinizzelli's
antecedent and also repeats the strategy of contaminating
the erotic and the theological, rewriting as its incipit a verse
from the Song of Songs, 'Quae est ista quae progeditur'
(Who is she that cometh forth; 6.9).[9] The poem opens
by celebrating the splendour of the lady's epiphany and by
conveying the extraordinary effects of her power and radi-

---

8   On the polemical relationship between Guinizzelli and Guittone,
     whose sonnet 'S'eo tale fosse ch'io potesse stare' accuses a fellow poet,
     most likely Guinizzelli, of the 'foul mistake' (laido errore) of replacing
     the technique of 'sopravanzamento' with that of 'equiparazione' and
     thereby introducing modes of sacred poetry into his courtly verses, see
     Paolo Borsa, *La nuova poesia di Guido Guinizzelli* (Fiesole: Cadmo,
     2007), pp. 61–102.

9   As Paola Nasti has noted, there is an additional 'riscrittura' in Caval-
     canti's poem of another verse from the Song of Songs, 'averte oculos
     tuos a me quia ipsi me avolare fecerunt' (6.4). See Nasti, 'Nozze e
     vedovanza', p. 74. Latin text and translation of the Song of Songs come
     from <http://www.latinvulgate.com/> [accessed 18 July 2020].

ance, which even make the air tremble, thereby transposing
into the environment the reaction usually characterizing
the Cavalcantian lover.[10] Her appearing is a manifestation of Love itself, and the only possible response to that
encounter is a silent, powerless sigh. The first quatrain
conveys a sense of fullness in the present, and following
Jonathan Culler's theorization of lyric as an 'event', one
could say that the use of just present tenses up to line 5
makes the immediateness of epiphany and its fulguration
reiterable each time the poem is read.[11] However, a gap is
opened in that fullness by the rhetoric of the poem, which
articulates the description of the epiphany as a question
about the lady that turns out to be unanswerable. In this
way, from the awesome shock of her presence, the lover
passes to a state of consternation and, after, into an awareness of the impossibility of ever truly knowing her for what
she is.

The nature of temporality in the poem registers the
decline from presence to absence. At first we might see the
'now' of epiphany compressed in its fullness between the
'vèn' of line 1 — the coming (to be) and coming to pass
of the lady — and the 'quando' (when) of line 5, when, according to the typical phenomenology of love in Duecento
lyric poetry, the lover's eyes are hit by the lady's gaze.[12] It is

---

10   It is the optical phenomenon of 'scintillation' — see the note to line 2 of
     the poem in Guido Cavalcanti, *Rime. Con le rime di Iacopo Cavalcanti*,
     ed. by Domenico De Robertis (Turin: Einaudi, 1986), p. 17.

11   Culler, *Theory of the Lyric*, pp. 125–31, especially p. 131.

12   See Bruno Nardi, 'Filosofia dell'amore nei rimatori italiani del Due-
     cento e in Dante', in *Dante e la cultura medievale. Nuovi saggi di filosofia
     dantesca*, ed. by Paolo Mazzantini, new edn (Bari: Laterza, 1985), pp.
     9–79, Dana Stewart, *The Arrow of Love: Optics, Gender, and Subjectivity
     in Medieval Love Poetry* (London: Bucknell University Press, 2003),
     and Heather Webb, *The Medieval Heart* (New Haven, CT: Yale Uni-
     versity Press, 2010), pp. 61–82.

as though an entire phenomenology of love is condensed in that instant. The exclamation mark added by editors at the end of line 5 registers the shock of the visual encounter as well as the precipitation that follows, which is at once an erotic fall and a sign that the intensity of the epiphany fades.[13] Line 6, 'dical' Amor, ch'i' nol savria contare', begins to suggest that the subject cannot answer the question he has asked. The overwhelming nature of the lady induces his aphasia and the repeated negation of his ability to speak of her. In this way, the physical and physiological phenomena that register the epiphany, as awe-inspiring and dazzling as they are, give way to an only more ambivalent paralysis that is cognitive and registered by a series of negations: 'Non si poria contar [...] Non fu sì alta già la mente nostra | e non si pose 'n noi tanta salute' (9–13).

Some critics have spoken of apophatic theology in relation to Cavalcanti's insistent negation and have seen it as another way of stressing the miraculous nature of the lady and her ineffability, while others have focused instead on the pessimism conveyed by the sonnet. Paola Nasti has even argued that Cavalcanti's translation of the Song of Songs is potentially parodic and serves to turn a text of positive theology into the basis for a negative metaphysics, 'almost to refute the idea that through the mediation of spiritual love [...] man can get closer to God, and vice versa'.[14] Along these lines, Cavalcanti's appropri-

---

13   Cf. Robert Pogue Harrison, *The Body of Beatrice* (Baltimore, MD: Johns Hopkins University Press, 1988), p. 72.

14   '[Q]uasi a rifiutare l'idea che attraverso la mediazione dell'amore spirituale [...] l'uomo possa avvicinarsi a Dio e viceversa' (Nasti, 'Nozze e vedovanza', p. 82). On the negative theology of Cavalcanti, see for instance De Robertis: 'si giunge qui alla proclamazione d'inconoscibilità e ineffabilità in termini senz'altro di teologia negativa', in his edition of Cavalcanti's *Rime*, p. 17. By contrast, Nasti's argument proceeds along a dual track to emphasize just how 'disconcerting' (sconcertante) Caval-

ation of the Song of Songs negates, in turn, Guinizzelli's theologizing of courtly poetry and recasts his diviniza-tion of the *donna* from a much more pessimistic perspec-tive. Moreover, Cavalcanti's use of the word 'propiamente', which Guinizzelli had employed in his *canzone*, 'Al cor gen-til rempaira sempre amore', to communicate the complete identity of love and the noble soul like heat from a burning flame, is revealing.[15] The adverb is resignified to imply a kind of improper knowledge, an imbalance in nature, in the sense that for Cavalcanti there can be no equivalence between the lady's power and the inability of the lover's mind to comprehend it.

There is no doubt about the lady's splendour, which as we have seen, is beautifully if ambivalently conveyed in the opening of the poem, but it seems to us that another modal-ity begins to emerge and to align 'Chi è questa che vèn' with other poems by Cavalcanti that stress the impossibility of knowledge caused by the power of love. Within the general framework of Cavalcanti's Aristotelian philosophy of pas-sion, this failure of intellection results from an inability to move beyond the particularity of the sensory image that is internalized as a phantasm and meditated upon obsessively

---

canti's allusion to the Song of Songs could have been for his medieval audience. Firstly, she suggests that he engages with the gnoseological dimension of the Song of Songs that, in allegorical interpretations, was centred on the intellectual and moral perfection the soul (Bride) could achieve through divine grace and spiritual union (Bridegroom), mov-ing it in an 'agnostic' direction. Secondly, she considers how Cavalcanti potentially engages with the liturgical context as well. Since the verse he cites was particularly present in forms of Marian devotion and the celebration of the Annunciation, his use of it potentially reverses the positive 'comic' associations it had in Marian liturgy (where it emphas-ized love as the way to reach God). See Nasti, 'Nozze e vedovanza', pp. 81–87.

15   See lines 8–10 of Guinizzelli's *canzone*, 'e prende amore in gentilezza loco | così propïamente | come calore in clarità di foco'.

without the possibility of further abstraction.[16] However, what seems particular in 'Chi è questa che vèn' is the suggestion that the lover, having been struck by the lady's gaze, does not even begin the process of intellecting her image, and the phenomenon of the creation of the phantasm, usually very present in Cavalcanti's poetry, is not mentioned at all.[17] As Robert Harrison has written with reference to the impaired temporality of the process, 'Guido's [sonnet] begins with an explosive eruption of perfect verse, which the rest of the poem cannot sustain. The sigh comes too quickly, the lady vanishes too suddenly, and the poem features an extended anticlimax from the second stanza on'.[18] This may explain why, rather than an obsessive fixation upon the phantasm, we find instead a quite impersonal, distanced, and somewhat external representation of the lady

---

16   See Rea's commentary in his edition of Cavalcanti's *Rime*, p. 59. For an explanation of the cognitive modality expressed by Cavalcanti's poems (especially in his doctrinal *canzone* 'Donna me prega'), see Giorgio Inglese, *L'intelletto e l'amore: Studi sulla letteratura italiana del Due e Trecento* (Florence: La Nuova Italia, 2000), pp. 23–26. Both Rea and Inglese follow the 'Averroistic' interpretation of Cavalcanti's poetry, which sees his anthropology as influenced by the way in which in the late thirteenth-century Aristotle's treatises on the soul were interpreted through Averroes' commentaries. For a recent interpretation of Cavalcanti's poetry that is more interested in its connections with contemporary medicine, see Tonelli, *Fisiologia della passione*, pp. 3–70. Either way, the consequence of love is death, to be understood as an epistemological failure in the former case and as the physical cessation of life in the latter. On the cognitive paralysis of 'Chi è questa che vèn', see also Maria Luisa Ardizzone, *Guido Cavalcanti: The Other Middle Ages* (Toronto: University of Toronto Press, 2002), pp. 17–18, and Paolo Borsa, 'L'immagine nel cuore e l'immagine nella mente: dal Notaro alla *Vita nuova* attraverso i due Guidi', in *Les Deux Guidi: Guinizzelli et Cavalcanti. Mourir d'aimer et autres ruptures*, ed. by Marina Gagliano, Philippe Guérin, and Raffaella Zanni (Paris: Presses Sorbonne Nouvelle, 2016), pp. 75–92 (esp. pp. 83–85).

17   On the significance of the phantasm in Cavalcanti's poetry, see Agamben, *Stanzas*.

18   Harrison, *The Body of Beatrice*, p. 72.

in relation to the hypostatized terms, 'umiltà' (humility), 'piagenza' (fairness), and 'Beltate' (Beauty).

The conditional tense in line 9, 'Non si poria...', together with the emphatic negative, makes a decisive move in the tercets towards the space (and time) of impossibility — the one that is excluded from the lover's experience and ultimately traps him in the fixed condition of *not knowing* ('Non *fu* [...] non si *pose*') while still desiring to know the lady and yet recognizing the futility of that desire. Thus the lady remains out of reach, and by the last tercet, she is completely inaccessible to consciousness and practically absent. We now understand that the choice of articulating the lady's epiphany as a question that cannot (and never will) be answered has introduced a disturbance that reduces the fullness of presence and shifts the focus towards lack and absence. In particular, the end of the poem indicates that, although something could have started, not only is the process of 'canoscenza' negated, it is specifically aborted.

The story the poem tells is ultimately this one of an anticipated and inevitable loss, and there is something quite fatalistic in this perspective, which seems in line with the ineluctability that represents the general mood of Cavalcanti's insistence on physiology governing the subject.[19] Thinking about how Cavalcanti's articulation of temporality creates a space for negativity, we might say that what is at first presented as the 'now' of epiphanic encounter turns out to be an epistemological 'not yet' that corresponds to a 'never there'. This becomes the dominant temporal mode of Cavalcanti's sonnet and qualifies the 'now' of its epi-

---

19   On anticipated loss and the work of mourning, see Jacques Derrida, *The Work of Mourning*, ed. by Pascale-Anne Brault and Michael Naas (Chicago: University of Chicago Press, 2001) and Rushworth, *Discourses of Mourning*.

phany. As a mode, it correlates to what in desiring terms is a moment of 'pre-loss' that emphatically forecloses the possibility of the experience begun at the moment of epiphany ('*quando* li occhi gira') coming to completion insofar as its beginning is also its end.

LIVING

If we can think of the 'now' in Cavalcanti's poem as never getting beyond a state of pre-loss, the 'now' in Dante's 'Tanto gentile e tanto onesta pare', by contrast, coincides with a moment of losslessness. Like Cavalcanti's 'Chi è questa che vèn', Dante's sonnet also refers to Guinizzelli's 'Io vo'[glio] del ver' and restages the lady's epiphany; but whereas Cavalcanti stresses the lover's insufficiency and the lady's unattainability, Dante develops even further Guinizzelli's poetics of praise and theologization of eros and does so in a fully positive way. In the *Vita Nova* the sonnet will exemplify the newly found praise style ('stilo de la loda'), which is staged as a way to break with Cavalcanti's negativity and to embrace instead a self-sufficient form of love that finds perfect happiness in the praise of the lady herself:

> Tanto gentile e tanto onesta pare
> la donna mia quand'ella altrui saluta,
> ch'ogne lingua divien tremando muta,
> e gli occhi no l'ardiscon di guardare.
>
> Ella se ·n va, sentendosi laudare,
> benignamente d'umiltà vestuta;
> credo che sia una cosa venuta
> di cielo in terra a miracol mostrare.
>
> Mostrasi sì piacente a chi la mira,
> che fier per gli occhi una dolcezza al core,
> che 'ntender no·lla può chi no·lla prova:

e par che della suo labbia si mova
un spirito soave pien d'amore,
che va dicendo a l'anima: 'Sospira!'[20]

(My lady appears so graceful and dignified | when
she greets those around her, | that every tongue
turns trembling mute | and eyes dare not look
upon her. || She walks by, hearing herself praised,
| clothed in kind humility. | I believe that she has
come from heaven | to earth to show forth a mir-
acle. || She shows herself so lovely to those who
look upon her | that, through the eyes, the heart is
pierced by a sweetness | known only to those who
have felt it. || And from her lips seems to move |
a gentle spirit, full of love, | that says to the soul:
'sigh!'.)

We can think of Dante's sonnet as an epiphany that begins
from the first word of the opening line, with the appearance
of the lady (Beatrice) in all of her plenitude and grace. It extends through the remainder of the poem in a perfect lyric
circulation that captures not only some essential quality of
the *donna* but also and especially the perfection of desire
that she effects as she passes.[21] In fact, the poem stages a
double epiphany: the encounter with the miracle that is
Beatrice as she is made manifest, as well as the interioriz-
ation of the experience, which changes the beholder. His
heart ('cor'), like the heart of anyone who looks at her, is
pervaded by sweetness ('dolcezza'), and his soul assents to
the 'spirito soave pien d'amore' that, emanating from her
lips, tells it to sigh.

---

20   The text of Dante's sonnet comes from Dante Alighieri, *Rime giovanili e
      della 'Vita Nuova'*, ed. by Teodolinda Barolini, with notes by Manuele
      Gragnolati (Milan: Rizzoli, 2009).

21   Cf. Harrison, 'Dante's ideal lyric crystallizes, encapsulates, or maxim-
      izes the plenitude of Beatrice's presence, forming [...] a lyric circle of
      incorporation', *The Body of Beatrice*, pp. 94–95.

Most strikingly of all, 'Tanto gentile' conveys an experience of the 'now' in which pleasure and desire coincide and create a sense of fullness that is sustained throughout the poem. Neither is there entropy, nor is the possibility of its production envisioned.[22] Dante's poem of epiphany is properly an experience of ec-stasis and that ec-stasis correlates to an erasure of subjectivity or — better — a movement beyond or outside of it. The effect is expansive and indicates a positive experience of dispossession that contrasts with the more negative passivity of Cavalcanti's poem, in which the capitulation to love is unwilled and produces lack. We can map this difference between the two poets in their use of the verb *sospirare* (to sigh). In Cavalcanti, the subject's passivity refers to the impossibility of controlling the experience of love, and in this sense, the 'sospira' of 'Chi è questa che vèn' can be considered a sign of consternation, foreshadowing the insufficiency of the human mind. Dante's 'sospira', given in the imperative, also indicates a form of passivity, but is a clear invitation to pleasure, and the surrender is positive.[23] It brings about

---

22 The term entropy originates from the field of thermodynamics and is the measure of a system's disorder. The second law of thermodynamics, according to which the entropy of a closed system increases irreversibly, is the basis for the so-called thermodynamic arrow of time. On entropy in relation to language, see Lombardi, *The Syntax of Desire: Language and Love in Augustine, the Modistae, Dante* (Toronto: University of Toronto Press, 2007), p. 71 and p. 182.

23 NB: As a free-standing rima, 'Tanto gentile' includes the variant in line 7, 'Credo che sia una cosa venuta....'. Dante's replacement of 'credo che' with 'par che' in the *Vita Nova* iteration of the sonnet pushes further the movement towards dispossession that is characteristic of the 'stilo de la loda' or praise style, which is not about the subject but about the object of desire. Indeed, in the *Vita Nova*, Dante's praise style is explicitly presented as a way to overcome Cavalcanti's narcissism and insistence on the 'I'. See Manuele Gragnolati, 'Trasformazioni e assenze: la *performance* della *Vita nova* e le figure di Dante e Cavalcanti', *L'Alighieri*, 35 (2010), pp. 5–23.

the ecstatic sweetness that is the poem's purpose and that lies at the heart of the 'stilo de la loda'.[24]

The difference between Dante and Cavalcanti's use of the verb 'mostrare' also consolidates the gap dividing their epiphanic experiences. In Dante's poem it is Beatrice herself who does the 'showing' forth — who participates in the miracle that she brings with her — and who gives herself (*'Mostrasi* sì piacente a chi la mira') to others. She thereby imparts to them directly the experience of sweetness that is the very nature of the epiphany for Dante. In Cavalcanti's sonnet, by contrast, the lady can be seen for what she is but cannot be experienced as such, and certainly not known in her *oltranza* (beyondness).[25] In 'Chi è questa che vèn', her 'excess' (*'che* sembra!'; *'cotanto ...'*; *'non si poria contar...'*) is an obstacle and does not allow the lover to participate in her reality. The fulguration of her presence at the beginning of the poem is spectacular, but it is also exclusory and so contrasts quite dramatically with Dante's experience, which centres on the infusion of grace that Beatrice's presence effects and particularly pervades the tercets. The 'spirito soave pien d'amore' that emanates from Beatrice's lips and speaks to the soul reverses the negative stasis in

---

24   In Harrison's words: 'The entire lyric project of the *Vita nuova* lies in the sigh that ends the poem and brings its subject to rest in aesthetic stasis. Here Beatrice no longer incites desire but placates it. This final sigh seems like a resignation to her intangible otherness but also figures as the inspiration that she dispenses through her proximity. [...] While the poem consummates itself in the sigh, the final expiration also marks the beginning of a lyric retrieval of the plenitude of presence'. Harrison, *The Body of Beatrice*, p. 44. As he later clarifies, this aesthetic stasis is 'not an absence of motion' but a rhythm of giving and holding back to create a paradoxical 'placation' of desire.

25   The notion of *oltranza* or *oltraggio*, and especially of the lady as 'oltra natura', which is a recurrent theme in Cavalcanti's poetry (as, for example, in the ballate, 'Fresca rosa novella', lines 31 and 40; and 'Veggio negli occhi de la donna mia'), also seems implied in 'Chi è questa che vèn'.

which the mind is left in Cavalcanti's poem. It emphasizes instead the receptivity of the soul and Dante's growing awareness of 'how the outside world, other people (particularly Beatrice), and the divine impact his individual corporeality' in a transformative sense.[26]

These intertextual analyses bring us to a more fundamental perception of the disparity between Dante and Cavalcanti's poems. While Cavalcanti's sonnet aims at 'canoscenza' (knowledge), a state of 'felicità mentale' (the joy of intellection, knowledge, abstraction), but never arrives there — indeed can barely start to access to it — Dante's poem aims at '*provare* dolcezza' (*experiencing sweetness*), which carries a distinctly mystical charge and indicates a move away from intellection and towards experience. [27] The latter is something that the temporality of Dante's sonnet enacts by making the space and time of the epiphany the space and time of the 'prova' — the experience itself, which does not require anything further to come after it. In a way, it is an equivalent state to the mystical experience of Paradise that Caroline Walker Bynum refers to as 'desire is *now*'.[28] In this sense, the double negation that appears in line 11, 'che 'ntender *no*·lla può chi *no*·lla prova' stresses a possibility of knowledge. However, that "'ntender', insofar as it designates the receipt of sweetness and the experience of it in the heart, is something that can only be perceived or felt, not theorized. In other words, the understanding of sweetness is not rational, but if you experience it you

26   Webb, *The Medieval Heart*, p. 79.

27   See Maria Corti, *Felicità mentale: nuove prospettive per Cavalcanti e Dante* (Turin: Einaudi, 2003), pp. 3–71.

28   See Caroline Walker Bynum, *The Resurrection of the Body in Western Christianity* (New York: Columbia University Press, 1996), p. 339 (italics in the original).

know what it is. Unlike the 'canoscenza' of Cavalcanti's poem, Dante's poetics of *provare* is not about trying to transport the mind somewhere else but about receiving and experiencing the thing that is offered as a loving gift. It is a (temporary) leap into the instantaneity of glory, which the poem does not so much describe as actively perform each time that it is read.[29]

Consequently, even as Dante reprises some very Cavalcantian terms — 'tremando', 'sospira' — for describing the physiology of love and the phenomenal effects of the lady's passing, his sonnet resignifies them. The 'tremando', for example, like the other verbs of movement — especially the 'si mova' (a privileged Dantean cipher for desire) — indicate not the presence of disturbance, affective variation, or flux, but the fact that desire itself is happening and that the experience is one of pleasure.[30] Moreover, through the insistent use of the present tense and the gerund (including the *presente progressivo* (present progressive) construction, 'va dicendo'), the poem extends the pleasure of the 'now' indefinitely.

---

29   In so many lyric poems, 'the sense of *now* is palpable', Jonathan Culler has argued; we might even call it a '"floating now" that is repeated each time the poem is read'. See his *Theory of the Lyric*, pp. 293–94 and also Francesco Giusti's reading of Dante's 'Tanto gentile' in dialogue with Culler's book, 'Rispondere solo a Beatrice. "Tanto gentile e tanto onesta pare" e il rischio della ripetizione lirica', *Revue des études dantesques*, 2 (2018), pp. 87–109 (esp. pp. 97–102).

30   In *Purgatorio* xviii, 32, Dante defines desire as 'moto spiritale'. On desire as motion in Dante see, for example, Elena Lombardi's reading in *The Wings of the Doves: Love and Desire in Dante and Medieval Culture* (Montréal: McGill-Queen's University Press, 2012), esp. pp. 81–84.

PERSEVERING

While Cavalcanti's poem stages a failure and Dante's incarnates an achieved experience, Petrarch's depicts a memory (or fantasy in the guise of remembrance) that destabilizes the epiphany from the outset:[31]

> Erano i capei d'oro a l'aura sparsi
> che 'n mille dolci nodi gli avolgea,
> e 'l vago lume oltra misura ardea
> di quei begli occhi, ch'or ne son sì scarsi;
>
> e 'l viso di pietosi color' farsi,
> non so se vero o falso, mi parea:
> i' che l'ésca amorosa al petto avea,
> qual meraviglia se di súbito arsi?
>
> Non era l'andar suo cosa mortale,
> ma d'angelica forma; et le parole
> sonavan altro che pur voce humana:
>
> uno spirito celeste, un vivo sole
> fu quel ch'i' vidi: et se non fosse or tale,
> piagha per allentar d'arco non sana.

> (Her golden hair fluttered in the breeze, | twisting into a thousand sweet knots, | and those beautiful eyes which once shone beyond measure | are now deprived of their enchanting light. || Her face seemed to colour with compassion | (whether real or imagined I do not know): | and should I, Love's captive, | wonder if I suddenly caught fire? || She walked not like a mortal woman, | but like an angelic creature, and when she spoke, | the loveliness of her words did not resemble any human voice. || A celestial spirit, a living sun, | this is what I saw; and even if she were no longer so, | the wound doesn't heal, though the bow be slack.) (*Rvf* 90)

---

31 On the crucial role of remembrance in Petrarch's epiphanies, through which Petrarch undertakes a 'deconstruction of Dante', see Warning, 'Seeing and Hearing', p. 113.

Whereas Cavalcanti's poem hints at something that doesn't properly begin, and the poetic subject is excluded from participation in the miracle of the epiphany, Petrarch's poem begins from a post-eventual perspective, already after the fact. His epiphany is in the past: in the sonnet the lyric 'I' remembers Laura's previous beauty and how, upon seeing her, he immediately fell in love. The passing of time may have made her less beautiful, and he may even have been mistaken in his original perception of her ('non so se vero o falso mi parea'), but he loves her still.

At the start of the poem, the epiphany is drastically qualified and that qualification is temporal — the imperfect tenses of the first quatrain leave no doubt as to the lady's distancing in the present and her subjection to time and decay.[32] Even the 'gold' (oro) of her hair, loosed to the breeze (a play on Laura's name), hints at the insidious presence of time ('or' (now); 'ora' (hour)).[33] According to Adelia Noferi, the effect of this first line is vertiginous, as it catapults the reader back in time.[34] Petrarch's paradoxical epiphany comes as part of a recollection, and its instantaneity ('subito') is mediated through memory, 'qual meraviglia se di sùbito arsi?'. In that moment, there was no time for thinking; thinking came afterwards, as did the awareness of time, although both are ultimately sub-

---

32 Santagata has noted in his commentary to Petrarch's poem that the dimmed light of Laura's eyes could be an 'allusione "realistica" a una malattia', in Petrarca, *Canzoniere*, p. 445. Georges Güntert has underscored, in turn, how 'Erano i capei d'oro' is followed by two sonnets that have funerary themes (*Rvf* 91 on the death of a friend's lady and *Rvf* 92, composed in honour of Cino da Pistoia), 'Sonetti occasionali e capolavori (*RVF* 90–99)', in *Il Canzoniere: Lettura micro e macrotestuale*, ed. by Michelangelo Picone (Ravenna: Longo, 2007), pp. 243–60.

33 This is a point Güntert has made in 'Sonetti occasionali', p. 251.

34 Adelia Noferi, *L'esperienza poetica del Petrarca* (Florence: Le Monnier, 1962), p. 9.

sumed to the uninterrupted and all-encompassing time of desire and its power.[35] Indeed the poem begins with something like pure entropy but makes of that entropy its means of going somewhere else — taking the lover-poet, and his reader, into a different time and space. This is a time for capturing something that perhaps cannot exist outside of poetry — the 'or' of Petrarch's poem, which both measures and collapses the distance between that 'now' and what came before. The poet's careful configuration of the temporal frame means that the lyric 'I' 'captures and caresses the past as he conjures it and holds it in memory'.[36] As such, Petrarch's poem begins 'post-loss' but it also manages to move beyond loss by the end, subsuming all of time to the continuous present of the aphoristic last line, 'piagha per allentar d'arco *non sana*'.

In other words, in his sonnet as a whole, Petrarch gives us a kind of 'history', which is also a history of temporal loss, in order at once to retrieve the prior event of presence *and* reconfigure it in the 'now' of the poem. As a result, 'Erano i capei d'oro' incorporates an even more complex kind of temporality than either Dante's or Cavalcanti's poems since it encompasses priority (in Petrarch's use of the imperfect tense and *passato remoto*), presentness (in his use of the present tense), and a third time — the time of poetry — which through the vehicle of memory and/or fantasy succeeds in absorbing all these other times within it. Through accepting, manipulating, and even own-

---

35 On the poem's transfiguration of Laura's past beauty into its own particular temporal and spatial mode, see Noferi, *L'esperienza poetica del Petrarca*, pp. 9–10 where she speaks of 'una mitica, delirante memoria che restituisce le cose in una sostanza incorrutibile ed assoluta'; and Giuseppe Mazzotta, *The Worlds of Petrarch* (Durham, NC: Duke University Press, 1993), pp. 60–61.

36 See Barolini, 'Petrarch as the Metaphysical Poet', p. 206.

ing time, Petrarch manages to reformulate it to a degree through poetry. He is able to intervene in his experience in a way that Cavalcanti cannot do, stuck as Cavalcanti's subject is in the inexorable frame of his natural philosophy from which there is no exit or consolation, not even in the beauty of poetry.

Thus, while Petrarch poses a question at line 4, as Cavalcanti does, it is purely rhetorical and not the interrogative of Cavalcanti's poem, which really seeks an answer and finds it tragically lacking. In fact, for Petrarch there is *no* question, or the question is unimportant. Although the 'I' declares that he does not know ('non so') if the vision of Laura was 'real or imagined' (vero o falso), there is no anxiety in that doubt, and knowledge is not at issue. If, with Cavalcanti, we are at the level of pre-cognition and in Dante, with the time of experience, with Petrarch we are within the paradoxically pleasurable effects of memory in the 'now'. As Barolini has argued, 'Erano i capei d'oro' is the 'paradigmatic sonnet' for exploring the 'temporality of eros' in Petrarch; moreover, for this poet, 'desire is more important as a modality through which to experience the passing of time than it is as an experience in itself'.[37]

Within the context of the *Rerum vulgarium fragmenta* as a whole, which explores a constant tension between the poet's love for Laura and his desire for God, given that Laura has aged and become less beautiful, the dissipation of the beloved object in time could finally allow Petrarch to relinquish his desire, but he holds onto it.[38] As Rainer

---

37 See Barolini, 'The Making of a Lyric Sequence', p. 15 n. 30; and her, 'Petrarch Who is the Metaphysical Poet', p. 206.

38 The question of Laura's beauty and her status as a 'mortal thing', the desire for which prevents the Petrarchan 'I' from reaching heaven, is a core topic of Book III of Petrarch's *Secretum*. On these tensions in Petrarch, see Marco Santagata, *I frammenti dell'anima: Storia e rac-*

Warning has argued, memory for Petrarch is an agent of *vo-luptas*, which 'coincides in part with sensual desire, nostal-gia for the beloved in her worldly corporeality [...] which the poetic imagination cannot forego'.[39] This tenacity explains the irreducibility of Petrarchan desire and, in 'Erano i capei d'oro', gives us the image of a rather 'heroic' if masochistic Petrarch who refuses to give up on love and instead embraces desire, for all its contradictions, as an experience of intensity.[40] His poem stages a spectral kind of presence — he no longer possesses everything that initiated the desire in the first place (and that too might have been a mirage — *parere* suggests mere 'seeming' as opposed to the mystical, even visionary, sense it carried in Dante or its phenomenal valence in Cavalcanti), but desire is not diminished for all that. If anything, desire is energized by its refusal to give in to time. In fact, the poet turns the inexorability of time and ageing into an opportunity to state the fidelity and enduring quality of his desire for Laura despite everything. In other terms, in Petrarch's poem there is a kind of suspension — a lingering in pleasure — that allows the initial moment of desire to continue indefinitely.

It is revealing in this respect that the recollection of the epiphany in lines 12–13 ('uno spirito celeste, un vivo sole | fu quel ch'i' vidi') syntactically mirrors the first two lines of Dante's sonnet insofar as, like Dante, Petrarch also de-

---

conto nel 'Canzoniere' di Petrarca (Bologna: Il Mulino, 2004), especially 'Dall'amore-passione alla *caritas*', pp. 209–42; Barolini, 'The Making of a Lyric Sequence'; Moevs, 'Subjectivity and Conversion'; and Mazzotta, *The Worlds of Petrarch*, pp. 33–79.

39   See Warning, 'Seeing and Hearing', p. 113.

40   On Petrarch and masochism see Chapters 1 and 2 of this book; and Georges Barthouil, 'Toujours aimer, toujours souffrir, toujours mourir ou fatalité et volontarisme chez Pétrarque', in *Francesco Petrarca: Père des renaissances, Serviteur de l'amour et de la paix* (Avignon: Aubanel, 1974), pp. 183–208.

ploys a strong enjambement to create a feeling of presence. Yet by putting the verb ('fu') in *rejet* in the enjambement, Petrarch underscores both the absolute fracture between past and present *and* the (poetic) collapse of the past into the present and the elision of the distance between them. The poet *saw* 'a celestial spirit, a living sun', but in line 12 these entities are, for a moment, purely nominal and thus timeless. As qualified as Petrarch's epiphany seems at the outset, what keeps it going is not the experience of beauty per se but the unyielding quality of desire and the perseverance that poetry allows. The result is a paradoxical epiphany that draws its energy from the past — the epiphany took place *in the* past — but by the end of the poem the past is also in the present, since the temporal line that runs from the 'sùbito' to the present has not been broken and in fact has been forged by the poem. To this extent, the 'now' of poetry contrasts entropy and even overcomes it.

***

Our concluding observations address how temporality relates, on the one hand, to desire and subjectivity and, on the other, to pleasure.

Cavalcanti inserts knowledge into the discourse of desire, and we can regard desire in his poetry as an extension towards knowledge. Yet in 'Chi è questa che vèn', the subject of the poem falls short from even beginning the process of cognition and never reaches pleasure. The phrase in line 12 of the poem, 'Non *fu* sì alta *già* la mente nostra', with its striking use of the negative 'non', past historic 'fu' and temporal marker, 'già', indicates that the time of desire is that of a preemptive negation, in the past, of a possibility that consequently will never come: the mind never was powerful enough to grasp the nature of the lady and never will be. Cavalcanti's closing statement comes as one of fact and opens up a space of resignation in the present that acknowledges an impossibility and blocks desire. The final tercet of the poem consequently marks the moment when the 'not yet' truly becomes a 'never there' and not only negates the possibility of knowledge but even makes the desire for it pointless.

By contrast, desire in Dante's sonnet is a fully positive experience of pleasure and hence programmatically different from Cavalcanti's.[41] What sets Dante's experience apart in 'Tanto gentile' is the mystical moment of 'now': felicity and pleasure lie in ecstatic dispossession and an expansion of the 'I' beyond itself. That expansion happens through the dilation of the final sigh, which is itself a confirmation of the experience of presence. In Dante's case, poetry activates this presence, and while the reader of Cavalcanti's 'Chi è questa che vèn' is, by the end of the poem, faced with the bleakness of an inevitable lack, the reader of 'Tanto gentile' experiences a perfect and unassailable sweetness.

With Petrarch, too, things change. His poem begins emphatically in the past, which conveys the epiphany's imperfection and would theoretically impair the presence of its effects. In practice, though, the potential to experience sweetness endures, albeit with a paradoxical slant. Like Cavalcanti, the subject knows that the object of desire (knowledge for Cavalcanti, Laura for Petrarch) is flawed and that desire is doomed; and yet, as in Dante's 'Tanto gentile', 'Erano i capei d'oro' is about creating an enduring pleasure. What is striking in Petrarch's poem is that the awareness of loss does not preclude presence and indeed

---

41   While the failure of 'canoscenza' is the general mode, there are some poems by Cavalcanti where 'canoscenza' does take place. See especially Cavalcanti, *Rime*, XXIII–XXVI.

makes poetry's capacity to recuperate its trace ever more vital. Ultimately, in *Rvf* 90, poetry becomes the space where
memory has the power to suspend time and allows desire
to persist while recognizing the defectiveness of the object
but embracing it still in a fascinating gesture of masochistic
perseverance.

5. Extension
Reaching the Beloved in Cavalcanti, Dante, and Petrarch

As in Chapter 4, we read here three poems by Cavalcanti, Dante, and Petrarch that have to do with the encounter with the beloved and its effects on the lover: the *ballata* 'Perch'i' no spero di tornar giammai' and the sonnets 'Oltra la spera che più larga gira' and 'Levòmmi il mio penser in parte ov'era' (*Rvf* 302). In these poems, the modality of the encounter is not so much epiphany and the lady's manifestation to the poet-lover, as much as the poet-lover moving towards her and thereby bridging an initial separation or filling an absence. Notably, Cavalcanti's 'Perch'i' no spero' belongs to the traditional genre of the *ballata* of separation, common in the Romance tradition, and the distance that separates the poet-lover from the beloved is geographical. In contrast, the distance in Dante's 'Oltra la spera' and Petrarch's 'Levòmmi il mio penser' is metaphysical insofar as the beloved has died, and the poet continues to love her on earth. Nevertheless, in all three cases there is a strong sense of movement towards the beloved, of bridging the

gap and reaching her in a post-mortem encounter modelled upon the beatific vision. In different ways, all three
cases also endow poetry with a particular role in extending
desire into pleasure.[1]

POSTHUMOUS ENCOUNTER

Our starting point is the 'ballata di lontananza' 'Perch'i' no
spero di tornar giammai', one of Cavalcanti's most celebrated poems, in which the poet-lover laments being kept
apart from Tuscany, where his lady resides. As Michelangelo Picone has shown, the motif of the separation from
the beloved has its origin in Ovid's lament of the aban-
doned heroine in the *Heroides*. It enters Troubadour verse
through a reversal involving both gender (since it is now
the male poet that suffers) and the very value of separation (which now becomes a means for affirming fidelity to
the beloved and a desire to return to her). The motif then
became quite common in Duecento Italian lyric poetry,
where it often blended historical and political themes, such
as the poet's exile from his own city.[2] What is distinctively
Cavalcantian about our poem is the very tragic tone established from the opening line through a double negation
('no [...] giammai'), which states the impossibility of the
poet returning to Tuscany ever again:

> Perch'i' no spero di tornar giammai,
> ballatetta, in Toscana,
> va' tu, leggera e piana,

---

1   On this form of extension, see Elena Lombardi, 'Desire', in *The Wings
     of the Doves*, pp. 86–131 (esp. pp. 113–31).

2   Michelangelo Picone, 'Addii e assenza amorosa', in his *Percorsi della lir-
     ica duecentesca. Dai Siciliani alla 'Vita Nova'* (Florence: Cadmo, 2003),
     pp. 125–43; Raffaella Zanni, 'Dalla lontananza all'esilio nella lirica itali-
     ana del XIII secolo', *Arzanà*, 16–17 (2013), pp. 325–63.

dritt' a la donna mia,
che per sua cortesia
ti farà molto onore.

Because I do not ever hope to return, | little ballata,
to Tuscany, | go forth, light and nimble, | straight
to my lady, | who, courteous as she is, | will do
you much honour. ('Perch'i' no spero di tornar
giammai', 1–6)

The hopelessness of the poet's condition affects the form
of the poem, which is given the task of carrying his parting
words to the lady and, as critics have acknowledged, is conceived of as an extended *envoi*.[3] As Marco Berisso has noticed, already the refrain contains many characteristics that
are typical of the *congedo* that usually concludes the text —
directly addressing the poem, sending it to the lady, and the
expectation that she will receive it.[4] If the desperate nature
of the situation is established from the beginning and distinguishes the poem as Cavalcantian, equally Cavalcantian
is that this desperation is conveyed through a limpid and el-
egant style that contributes to creating a composed tone of
resignation: the *ballata* is indeed 'leggera e piana' and, not
surprisingly, has often been considered as a fine example of
that exquisite 'leggerezza' indicated by Italo Calvino as one
of the ciphers of Cavalcanti's poetry.[5]

The first stanza continues the mode of *congedo* by
delineating its audience — in this case, as is typical for

3   See for instance De Robertis and Rea in their editions of Cavalcanti's
     Rime, respectively p. 135 and p. 194.

4   *Poesie dello Stilnovo*, ed. by Marco Berisso (Milan: Rizzoli, 2006), p. 183.

5   See Italo Calvino, *Lezioni Americane. Sei proposte per il prossimo mil-
     lennio* (Milan: Mondadori, 1993), pp. 7–35. On the 'rassegnata dis-
     perazione' of the poem, see Rea's commentary, p. 194, and on the
     expression of motif of 'sweetness' of language and style through the
     gendering of the text in the poetry contemporary with Cavalcanti, see
     Elena Lombardi, *Imagining the Woman Reader in the Age of Dante* (Ox-
     ford: Oxford University Press, 2018), pp. 132–35.

Cavalcanti, a selective one composed only of those people 'di gentil natura' — and explains that all hope is gone because the poet's death is imminent. Death is then lingered on in the following stanzas:

> Tu porterai novelle di sospiri
> piene di dogli' e di molta paura;
> ma guarda che persona non ti miri
> che sia nemica di gentil natura:
> chè certo per la mia disaventura
> tu saresti contesa,
> tanto da lei ripresa
> che mi sarebbe angoscia,
> dopo la morte, poscia
> pianto e novel dolore.
>
> Tu senti, ballatetta, che la morte
> mi stringe, sì che vita m'abbandona;
> e senti come 'l cor si sbatte forte
> per quel che ciascun spirito ragiona.
> Tanto è distrutta già la mia persona,
> ch' io non posso soffrire:
> se tu mi voi servire
> mena l' anima teco,
> (molto di ciò ti preco)
> quando uscirà del core.

(You will bring news of sighs | full of pain and fear; | but be sure that nobody looks upon you | who appreciates not a noble nature: | for surely, learning of my ill fortune | they would stop you in your tracks | and rebuke you, so much | that, in the end, death | would give me anguish, | after tears and after new pain. || Little ballata, you perceive that death's | grip is so tight that life forsakes me; | and you know how hard my heart beats | at what my vital spirits are saying. | My entire person is already so destroyed | that I cannot bear it: | if you want to serve me, | lead my soul away with you | when it takes leave of my heart, | this I beg of you.) ('Perch'i' no spero di tornar giammai', 7–26)

Love is not mentioned explicitly, but the poet's unbearable suffering is here described in terms familiar to readers of Cavalcanti's poems and along all the lines of what Tonelli has termed the 'physiology of passion': an experience of love connected to the senses that debilitates the body, impairs its functioning, and impedes the rational capacity of the lover, even leading him to death. Indeed, whether understood epistemologically as the interruption of reasoning or physically as the cessation of the vital faculties, death is the veritable cipher of Cavalcanti's poetry.[6]

The tragic spectacle presented in the *ballata* is strikingly similar to that staged in the sonnet 'L'anima mia vilment' è sbigotita', where the destruction and fragmentation of the self is explicitly induced by Love:

> L'anima mia vilment' è sbigotita
> de la battaglia ch'e[l]l'ave dal core:
> che s'ella sente pur un poco Amore
> più presso a lui che non sole, ella more.
>
> Sta come quella che non ha valore,
> ch'è per temenza da lo cor partita;
> e chi vedesse com' ell'è fuggita
> diria per certo: 'Questi non ha vita'.
>
> Per li occhi venne la battaglia in pria,
> Che ruppe ogni valore immantenente,
> sì che del colpo fu strutta la mente.
>
> (My soul is wretchedly bewildered | by the battle fought with my heart: | so much so that, when the soul feels Love advance, | even just a little closer to it, it perishes. || It's like one that's lost all power, | and has left the heart for fear; | anyone seeing how it fled | would surely say: 'This man is lifeless'. || The assault came first through the eyes | and shattered all my strength at once, | so that my mind was fractured by the blow.) (1–11)

---

6   See Chapter 4, n. 16.

In 'Perch'i' no spero di tornar giammai', one finds all the usual elements of Cavalcanti's dysphoric concept of love, but the combination of the motif of impending death with that of the definitive separation from the lady has resulted in the *ballata* being considered Cavalcanti's last poem, apparently written in exile in Sarzana, where, fallen sick with malaria, he would give 'a last farewell to his beloved'.[7] This late date of composition is supposedly confirmed by its position in Guido Favati's edition, based on an ideal chronology, but it is now discredited by contemporary editors, who deny its autobiographical character.

Recently Claudio Giunta, while reminding us of the highest degree of formalization of medieval lyric, which follows strict rhetorical conventions and does not necessarily imply any real or biographical reference, has maintained that Cavalcanti's poem is unusual for the detailed precision with which it indicates that the distant beloved is not generically absent but specifically in Tuscany. Giunta has also maintained that the *ballatetta* is unique within the Cavalcantian *corpus* for not presenting the poet's impending death as a consequence of love but as death *tout court*. He has thereby concluded that 'Perch'i' no spero di tornar giammai' is not a love poem but a 'ballata-testamento', a testament-poem originating from a specific, 'real' situation of Cavalcanti's life, which for Giunta is not be to be identified with the exile in Sarzana but most likely with Cavalcanti's journey to Santiago de Compostela.[8] As Giunta has convincingly shown, and as was already men-

---

7   Natalino Sapegno speaks of 'ultimo saluto alla donna amata dall'esilio', echoing similar judgments by Ugo Foscolo and Francesco De Sanctis, *Disegno storico della letteratura italiana*, 2nd edn (Florence: La Nuova Italia, 1973), p. 24. See Giunta, 'Guido Cavalcanti', pp. 47–48.

8   Rea, in his note to 'Perch'i' no spero di tornar giammai', has commented that in this poem 'la distanza dalla donna da psicologica si fa geografica', in Cavalcanti, *Rime*, p. 194.

tioned in Chapter 2, the poem deploys some significant features of contemporary testaments, especially the motifs of the *commendatio anime*, the testator's recommendation of his soul to Christ, and of the wish to enjoy the eternal contemplation of God that usually follows on from that recommendation.[9]

In our view it does not seem necessary to deny, as Giunta has, that the poet's death is caused by love, given that, as was mentioned above, for Cavalcanti, passion can lead even to physical death. Moreover, as has been widely observed, the term 'disaventura' (11) connects 'Perch'i' no spero di tornar giammai' with 'Io temo che la mia disaventura' and 'La forte e nova mia disaventura', two poems that open by stressing the condition of 'disgrazia amorosa' (ill fortune in love),[10] and that in Favati's ordering are placed just before our *ballatetta*. Nonetheless Giunta's point is well taken: the poem's testamentary character is of prime importance. If, as we have seen, the whole poem is conceived of and constructed as an adieu to the beloved, the final two stanzas offer an equally original combination of courtly and eschatological motifs.

Whereas traditionally it is the poet's heart that is sent to the lady as a means of spiritual union between them while separated from one another,[11] in Cavalcanti's *ballata* the poet commends his 'anima', i.e., the sensitive soul and site of sensations that normally resides in the heart, to her, allowing for communion with her after *he* will have died, since there is no hope of them being reunited in this life. Of particular significance to our argument is that while in the traditional envoy of the heart the hope remains alive

9   Giunta, 'Guido Cavalcanti', pp. 45–61.
10   See the note by Rea in the commentary to 'Io temo della mia disaventura' in Cavalcanti, *Rime*, p. 186.
11   Zanni, 'Dalla lontananza all'esilio'.

of return and physical reunion with the beloved, in Cavalcanti's text, as we have seen, the initial 'giammai' negates that possibility from the outset. And yet it is precisely and paradoxically the testamentary, posthumous mode of the poem that allows it to open a space for an encounter. The end of the second stanza implies this possibility by suggesting that the *ballatetta*, which we know from the refrain is meant to travel to the lady, take the 'anima' with it when it leaves the heart (24–26). It is in the third stanza that, within the usual Cavalcantian arena of physiological components and affects, this recommendation is first picked up ('menala teco' in line 29 recalls 'mena l'anima teco' in line 24) and then developed in all its potential and force:

> Deh, ballatetta mia, a la tu' amistate
> quest'anima che trema raccomando:
> menala teco, nella sua pietate,
> a quella bella donna a cu' ti mando.
> Deh, ballatetta, dille sospirando,
> quando le sè presente:
> 'Questa vostra servente
> vien pe·ristar con voi,
> partita da colui
> che fu servo d'Amore'.

(Ah, little ballata, to your friendship | I commend this trembling soul: | take it with you, in its suffering, | to the beautiful lady to whom I send you. | Ah, little ballata, when you are in her presence, | say to her, sighing: | 'This servant of yours | comes to reside with you; | she leaves behind a man | who was once a servant of Love'.) ('Perch'i' no spero di tornar giammai', 27–36)

A veritable turn is staged here, and it becomes evident that as also happens in other poems by Cavalcanti,[12] the

---

12   See Lombardi, *Imagining the Woman Reader*, pp. 95–96.

departing 'anima' is not lost or left alone; in being carried by the *ballata* towards the lady, it is enabled to reach her and to continue the service of love when the poet will have died ('colui | che *fu* servo d'Amore').

There is no cessation of desire but rather an intensification of it, which culminates in the final stanza. The *fronte* extends the physiology of passion that has been present since the beginning of the poem and also introduces the voice as a third *dramatis persona*, which emerges weeping from the poet's grieving heart ('ch'esci piangendo de lo cor dolente').[13] The voice is not lost either and is invited to join the 'anima' and the poem in conversing with the lady about the lover's complete collapse, in particular the disintegration of his 'mente', the faculty predisposed to understanding:

> Tu, voce sbigottita e deboletta
> ch'esci piangendo de lo cor dolente,
> coll'anima e con questa ballatetta
> va' ragionando della strutta mente.

> (Bewildered and frail voice, | you who weeping leave my grieving heart, | with my soul and this little ballata | tell her of my fractured mind.) ('Perch'i' no spero di tornar giammai', 38–40)

---

13 On the relationship of the heart to poetic voice in the Duecento poets and Cavalcanti specifically, see Agamben, *Stanzas*, pp. 124–31; and Federica Anichini, *Voices of the Body: Liminal Grammar in Guido Cavalcanti's Rime / Voci del corpo: grammatica liminale nelle Rime di Guido Cavalcanti* (Munich: Meidenbauer, 2009). The voice that remains of the poet, and which combines with the 'anima' and the 'ballata', is similar to the one that is presented in 'Voi che per li occhi passaste 'l core' as the only element to survive Love's decimation of the poet and the emptying of his spirits to become 'figura sol en segnoria [d'Amore]' (7) and 'voce alquanta, che parla in dolore' (8). On the relationship of this posthumous 'voce' to Echo, see Francesco Giusti's reading of the motif in Cavalcanti in his *Il desiderio della lirica. Poesia, creazione, conoscenza* (Rome: Carocci, 2017), pp. 146–48.

In the *volta* the motif of reaching the lady culminates with
the wish for eternal happiness, offering quite an unexpec-
ted outcome in relation to the initial separation from the
beloved. The poem concludes by boldly imagining a form
of beatific vision in which eternal contemplation of God is
replaced by that of the lady:

> Voi troverete una donna piacente,
> di sì dolce intelletto
> che vi sarà diletto
> starle davanti ognora.
> Anim', e tu l'adora
> sempre, nel su' valore.

> (You will find a dazzling lady, | with such sweet
> intellection | that it will delight you | to remain
> eternally in her presence. | Then, my soul, adore
> her | always, in all her valour.) ('Perch'i' no spero
> di tornar giammai', 41–46)

Line 41, 'Voi troverete una donna piacente', reaffirms the
encounter with the beloved in her desirability and opens
the way to a form of knowledge and subsequent pleasure, to
which poetry — through the triad of 'voce'-'anima'-'ballata'
— opens up. While line 42 'di sì dolce intelletto' is often
read as referring to the lady, in her ability 'to listen and
understand lovingly', we find suggestive Marti's interpretation of that line as meaning 'così dolce a chi ne intenda
appieno il valore' (so sweet for the one who fully grasps her
worth), where 'intelletto' would refer not to rational understanding (which is indeed denied by the phrase 'strutta
mente' in the previous line) but rather to an experiential
form of knowledge that brings sweetness.[14] This experience of sweetness has mystical overtones along the lines

---

14   On the first interpretation see Rea's note in Cavalcanti, *Rime*, p. 138;
      and the recent discussion in Lombardi, *Imagining the Woman Reader*,

of 'che fier per gli occhi una dolcezza al cuore | che 'in-
tender no·lla può chi no·lla prova' in Dante's 'Tanto gentile
e tanto onesta pare', as discussed in Chapter 4. In Cavalcanti's poem, we find particularly significant that this form
of 'intelletto' rhymes with 'diletto', tying it to pleasure and
introducing a different modality, one less tragic yet also
different from that of the 'positive' poems envisioning the
possibility of intellecting the lady (as for instance 'Posso
degli occhi miei novella dire' or 'Veggio negli occhi della
donna mia').[15] In 'Perch'i' no spero' the 'diletto' is a form of
ecstatic surrender and dispossession that turns the promised vision of God into an adoration of the beloved.

As suggested by the adverbs 'ognora' and 'sempre',
which emphatically contrast the initial 'giammai', this experience of pleasure also coincides with abandoning temporality and entering a form of eternity. We find here
a quite peculiar, courtly version of 'earthly eschatology',
maybe the only one conceivable for a poet who focused
on immanence and did not seem to conceive of life after
death. In 'Perch'i' no spero' we are indeed in a posthumous
dimension where survival can only be poetic and moves
on a horizontal plane, but it is no less powerful for all that:
the departed 'anima' is carried by the *ballata* and, through
the exhortatory mode that defines the poem's rhetoric, is
given the task, and the pleasure, of perpetual adoration as
a promise of prospective fulfilment.[16]

---

pp. 89–100. On the second, see Mario Marti, *Storia del Dolce Stilnovo*
(Lecce: Milella, 1973), cited in De Robertis's note to the line in Cavalcanti, *Rime*, p. 138.

15 We would like to thank Franco Costantini for pointing out the rhyme
between 'intelletto' and 'diletto'.

16 See Raffaella Zanni, 'Prendre congé de sa propre poésie: *Perch'i' no
spero di tornar giammai* de Guido Cavalcanti', in *Les Deux Guidi:
Guinizzelli et Cavalcanti. Mourir d'aimer et autres ruptures*, ed. by Mar-

LUMINOUS PRESENCE

If Cavalcanti's 'Perch'i' no spero' culminates with a fantasy of posthumous contemplation, Dante's 'Oltra la spera che più larga gira' is eschatological and is set after the beloved's death. In this sonnet, the poet imagines that a sigh which emanates from his 'grieving heart' journeys to the other world and gets to the Empyrean (the furthest heaven where God and the blessed reside). There it contemplates the lady, before returning to earth and relating the vision. 'Oltra la spera' famously concludes the *Vita Nova* but was written before and, according to the 'libello' (*VN* XLI/30), was composed as a 'cosa nova' (new, or wondrous, thing) to accompany the gift of some other poems to two noble ladies. We quote the sonnet in its pre-*Vita Nova* version:[17]

> Oltra la spera che più larga gira
> passa il sospiro ch'esce del mio core;
> intelligenza nova che l'Amore
> piangendo mette in lui poi sù lo tira.
>
> E quando è giunto là dove disira,
> vede una donna che riceve onore
> e luce sì che per lo suo splendore
> lo pellegrino spirito la mira.
>
> Vedela tal, che quando il mi ridice
> io no·llo 'ntendo, sì parla sottile
> al cor dolente che lo fa parlare.
>
> So io che parla di quella gentile,
> perché sovente ricorda Beatrice,
> sì che lo 'ntendo ben, donne mie care.
>
> (The sigh that leaves my heart | passes beyond the outermost heaven; | Love, weeping, instils it with

---

ina Gagliano, Philippe Guérin, and Raffaella Zanni (Paris: Presses Sorbonne Nouvelle, 2016), pp. 141–56.

17   The text is quoted from Dante, *Rime giovanili e della 'Vita Nuova'*.

a new intelligence | that draws it ever upwards. ||
And having reached the source of its desire, | it sees
a woman who receives such honour | and shines
so luminously, that, for her splendour, | the pilgrim
spirit gazes in wonder. || It sees her such, that, when
it tells me, | my comprehension fails, so subtly does
it address | the grieving heart which makes it speak.
|| But one thing I know: it speaks of that graceful
woman, | for it often mentions the name of Beatrice,
| and this much, dear ladies, I understand.)

The beloved's absence is caused by her death, and as such,
the sonnet might have suggested an even more insur-
mountable separation than the geographical distance of
Cavalcanti's *ballata*. The motif of weeping, whether it refers
to Love or the sigh, indicates the sorrow of that separation,
yet the real cipher of the poem is not a sense of loss but one
of reaching, vertiginously instilled from the very beginning
of the text by the combination of the opening adverb, 'Oltra', the reference to the *Primum mobile* (the most distant
physical heaven from earth, beyond which lies the Empyrean), and the enjambement between lines 1 and 2. The verb
'passa', which is to be united with 'Oltra' to form a single
word, conveys the sigh's extraordinary ability to reach and
a sense of ease and flow. The adverb 'su' in line 4 highlights
the verticality of the sigh's journey towards a transcendental dimension and contrasts quite dramatically with the
horizontal movement of Cavalcanti's poem, which remains
firmly on earth. In 'Oltra la spera', something exceptional
is taking place when the sigh is empowered by Love with
a new, wonderous faculty ('intelligenza nova') that pulls
it upwards to the Empyrean. This infusion seems to ap-
propriate, in a courtly context, the theological concept of
lumen gloriae, the 'light of glory' given to the separated soul
in heaven, which enables it to overcome a rational form

of understanding and enjoy instead an intuitive vision of God.[18]

The effects of that extraordinary infusion are presented in the second quatrain, which follows closely from the first (also causally). Line 5, 'E quando è giunto *là dove disira*', is striking in its emphasis on the attainment and fulfillment of desire. The same fullness imbues the following three lines, which open and close by describing the vision of the lady ('Vede una donna') and the contemplation of her in glory ('la mira') by the sigh, now become a 'spirit' (8). The exceptional character of the journey, which was anticipated by the adjective 'nova', is reinforced by the adjective 'pellegrino' (8), which as Picone has explained, signifies at once that the spirit has left earth behind and reached heaven, and that in heaven it is a 'foreigner' insofar as it is there only temporarily.[19] While it is there, time is suspended, and eternity is accessed. The dazzling nature of its experience is indicated by the intensity with which the lady shines ('luce sì') and by the radiating light in which the spirit contemplates her ('per lo suo splendore [...] la mira').

As seen in Chapter 4, the phrase 'la mira' is the same one that Dante used in the sonnet 'Tanto gentile e tanto onesta pare' to express the miracle of gazing on Beatrice on earth. In the *Paradiso*, 'mirare' refers to the contempla-

---

18   On the concept of *lumen gloriae*, see Simon Gilson, *Medieval Optics and Theories of Light in the Works of Dante* (New York: Edwin Mellen Press, 2000), pp. 252–56.

19   Michelangelo Picone, 'Esilio e *peregrinatio*: Dalla *Vita Nova* alla "Canzone montanina"', *Italianistica: Rivista di letteratura italiana*, 36.3 (Sept–Dec 2007), pp. 1–14 (p. 15 n. 3). Note that the 'sospiro' of line 2 has become a 'spirito' and that this is slippage is corrected by the prose of the *VN*, which first explains that 'sospiro' is to be understood as 'pensero', thereby dematerializing it, and then that that 'pensero' is called 'spirito' because it goes to heaven 'spiritualmente' (XLI, 5/30.5).

tion of God, and one only need think of *Paradiso* XXXIII, 97–99 ('Così la mente mia, tutta sospesa, | mirava fissa, immobile e attenta, | e sempre di mirar faceasi accesa') or 109–11 ('Non perché più ch'un' semplice sembiante | fosse nel vivo lume ch'io mirava, | che tal è sempre qual s'era davante') to appreciate its ecstatic character. In 'Oltra la spera', the phrase 'la mira' conveys an almost mystical sense of perfection and fullness that nonetheless remains courtly, and the sonnet can be considered as transposing into the other world the epiphany that 'Tanto gentile' stages on earth. However, in 'Oltra la spera' there is a strong emphasis on the individual experience of love in contrast to the collective, participatory mode of 'Tanto gentile', in which Beatrice affects all onlookers equally ('Mostrasi sì piacente *a chi* la mira | che fier per gli occhi una dolcezza al core | che 'ntender no·lla può *chi* no·lla prova', 9–11).[20] Notwithstanding the shift in emphasis from the lady as a miracle descended to earth to the beloved as a beatified soul joined in heaven, the verb 'mira' conveys in both instances a sense of ecstatic bedazzlement and encapsulates a unique balance between the erotic and the divine. In this respect, the two sonnets perfectly represent that exclusively Dantean matrix that Teodolinda Barolini has called a 'theologized courtly love'.[21]

The contemplative experience flows into the sestet and is even intensified by the opening phrase 'Vedela tal' in line 9. It recalls both 'vede' of line 6 and 'la mira' of line 8, creating a sort of 'conceptual' *cobla capfinida* — a rhetorical feature also present, in the same place, in 'Tanto gentile'.[22]

---

20   On the latter, see Giusti, 'Rispondere solo a Beatrice', p. 98.

21   Barolini, 'Dante and the Lyric Past', p. 30.

22   In 'Tanto gentile', the structure of *coblas capfinidas* is created through the words 'mostrare', which concludes line 8, and 'Mostrasi', which opens line 9.

In its indefiniteness, the capacious qualifier 'tal' represents
the zenith of the poem and the maximum vision that is
intuitively attained through the 'intelligenza nova' and ec-
statically enjoyed beyond all earthly possibility. A caesura
follows 'tal', and the return of the temporal conjunction
'quando' (9 and 5) marks a transition out of timelessness
as the temporally suspended experience of vision cedes to
the time of retelling ('quand il mi *ri*dice') that is already
a looking back. This temporal shift also coincides with a
movement downward: the spirit returns to earth and tries
to relate the essence of its vision, but the 'I' cannot grasp
it: 'io no·llo 'ntendo sì parla sottile | al cor dolente che lo
fa parlare' (10–11). These lines seem to imply that a gap
has opened up, which could hinder the sense of perfection
staged so far: the heart is still grieving — where the phrase
'cor dolente' is typically Cavalcantian and, as we have seen,
also present in line 38 of 'Perch'i' no spero' — and the
spirit's words are too hermetic to understand insofar as
the vision was attained beyond earthly means and, like all
ecstatic experiences, cannot be fully retained or expressed.
'[I]o no·llo 'ntendo' could even be a 'translation' of the
Pauline 'nescio' following his *raptus* to heaven ('Et scio
huiusmodi hominem (sive in corpore sive extra corpus nescio, Deus scit) quoniam raptus est in paradisum, et audivit
arcana verba quae non licet homini loqui'; *Corinthians* II
xii 2–4). As has been noticed, the motif of ineffability will
return in the *Paradiso* and there refer to the impossibility
of relating in full the heavenly experience.[23] However, it
is important to note that whether the sonnet is read independently from the *Vita Nova* or as its final text, in 'Oltra
la spera' no vision of God is contemplated or expressly

---

23   See Barolini's commentary in *Rime giovanili*, p. 515.

desired, and the vision of Beatrice is described with a comparable intensity and remains the ultimate goal.

'Oltra la spera' does not finish with this declaration of ineffability. Once we move into the final tercet, we appreciate that the mention of the 'I''s epistemological lack ('no·llo 'ntendo') is in fact a strategy designed to reaffirm certainty. Line 12 opens with the affirmative 'So io', which, like the 'So' found in line 3 of 'Io sono stato con Amore insieme' and discussed in Chapter 4, points back to a degree of knowledge that despite the excess of the vision just experienced, the 'I' nonetheless continues to possess. As Barolini has indicated, the mention of Beatrice's name in the following line as that which is remembered functions as a mark of epistemological and intellectual possession that culminates with the phrase 'lo 'ntendo ben' in the final line of the sonnet.[24] While the *giocoso* poet Cecco Angiolieri famously detected an incongruence between 'lo 'ntendo ben' and 'io no·llo 'ntendo' of line 11, several critics have shown that there is no contradiction, and in fact, the play between the two phrases has the effect of emphasizing that some understanding persists even after the journey to the Empyrean is concluded.[25] Moreover, a trace of the ecstatic excess is seemingly not only preserved but also conveyed. If one remembers that in the *Vita Nova* (which must be almost contemporary with the composition of our sonnet) 'nomina sunt consequentia rerum' (names are a consequence of things; XIII, 4/6.4), one can

---

24   Ibid., p. 519.

25   Cecco Angiolieri accused Dante of this incongruence in the sonnet, 'Dante Alleghier, Cecco tu' servo amico', whose sestet is dedicated to the contradiction he perceived in Dante's: 'Ch'al mio parer, ne l'una muta dice | che non intendi su' sottil parlare, | a que' che vide la tua Beatrice; || e poi hai detto a le tue donne care | che ben lo intendi; e dunque contradice | a se medesmo questo tu' trovare' (9–14). Cited ibid.

also see that, as Suzanne Akbari has pointed out, by regis-
tering Beatrice's name, 'the poet comes as close as he can
to conveying her essence'.[26] By inscribing in its textuality
the beloved's name, which signifies 'the one who beatifies',
the sonnet has her continue to be present and also suggests
that from the Empyrean she continues to bestow bliss and
pleasure. It is as though the 'diletto' of contemplation that
at the end of Cavalcanti's 'Perch'i' no spero' was deferred
to a posthumous situation, is realized in 'Oltra la spera' and
even extended indefinitely in the sonnet itself.

DUBIOUS FANTASY

Like Dante's and Cavalcanti's poems, Petrarch's 'Levòmmi
il mio penser in parte ov'era' (*Rvf* 302) is also a poem of
separation that through a post-mortem encounter with the
beloved overcomes lack and allows for the articulation of
a particular kind of pleasure. As in Dante, the separation
comes in the wake of the beloved's death, and the poem
describes a journey to reach her in the other world. But the
poem does not realize the fullness of Dante's sonnet, and
as in Cavalcanti's *ballata*, the eschatology is earthly and the
encounter more tenuous.

As Rosanna Bettarini has noted in her commentary
of the text, together with *Rvf* 297, 298, 300, and 301,
Petrarch's sonnet forms part of a sub-sequence of poems
within the *rime in morte* that is especially concerned with
the absence of Laura's body and stages a tension between

---

26   Suzanne Conklin Akbari, *Seeing Through the Veil: Optical Theory and
     Medieval Allegory* (Toronto: Toronto University Press, 2004), p. 125.
     On the significance of names with the *Vita Nova*'s linguistic theory, see
     Elena Lombardi, 'Il pensiero linguistico nella *Vita nova*', in *Vita nova,
     Fiore, Epistola XIII*, ed. by Manuele Gragnolati and others (Tavarnuzze
     [Florence]: SISMEL · Edizioni del Galluzzo, 2018), pp. 115–34.

heaven and earth.[27] What is particular about *Rvf* 302 (and a feature it shares only with *Rvf* 362) is that, in this sonnet, rather than imagining Laura descending from heaven to comfort him (as in *Rvf* 359), or reappearing in the *locus amoenus* of Vaucluse (as in, for instance, *Rvf* 281), the poet moves towards her:

> Levòmmi il mio penser in parte ov'era
> quella ch'io cerco, et non ritrovo, in terra:
> ivi, fra lor che 'l terzo cerchio serra,
> la rividi piú bella et meno altera.
>
> Per man mi prese, et disse: — In questa spera
> sarai anchor meco, se 'l desir non erra:
> i' so' colei che ti die' tanta guerra,
> et compie' mia giornata inanzi sera.
>
> Mio ben non cape in intelletto humano:
> te solo aspetto, et quel che tanto amasti
> e là giuso è rimaso, il mio bel velo. —
>
> Deh perché tacque et allargò la mano?
> Ch'al suon de' detti sí pietosi et casti
> poco mancò ch'io non rimasi in cielo.

(My thought lifted me to the place where she dwelt, | the one I search for on earth but do not find: | there, among the souls of the third heaven, | I beheld her once more, lovelier and less proud. || She took me by the hand and said: 'in this sphere | you will join me again, if desire doesn't err: | I am she who caused you such strife, | and I ended my day before dusk. || Human intellect cannot comprehend my goodness: | I wait only for you, and for that which you so loved, | which remains down below, my lovely veil'. || Ah, why did she fall silent and

27   See Bettarini's note in Petrarca, *Canzoniere*, p. 1329: she writes that Petrarch copies this sonnet as the last of a series on page 3r of his notebook together with 297, 298 and 301, to which on 3v we find also 300, which shares with 302 the same rhymes in 'terra', 'serra', and 'guerra'.

release my hand? | For at the sound of such merciful
and chaste words | I almost remained in heaven.)
(*Rvf* 302)

Several critics have set the sonnet in dialogue with 'Oltra
la spera', and it is in particular the first quatrain that invites a parallel between the two sonnets.[28] The initial verb,
'Levòmmi', immediately recreates the vertical movement
of 'Oltra la spera', and the verbs 'cerco' and 'non ritrovo'
in line 2 indicate the lack and desire that have also initiated this movement. The 'I' reaches heaven and, as in the
Dantean antecedent, has a vision of the beloved.

Yet as Paul Olson has suggested, if the surface of the
sonnet appears very Dantesque, maybe more so than in
any other poem by Petrarch, the differences are equally
significant.[29] The 'thought' in line 1 points back to Dante's
sonnet insofar as the prose of the *Vita Nova* had glossed the
more physiological 'sospiro'/ 'spirito' of 'Oltra la spera' as
'pensero' (xLI, 3/30.3), but there is no extraordinary faculty ('intelligenza nova') allowing for an ecstatic encounter
beyond human limits. Instead it is the 'I' that is elevated,
and this happens merely by the power of its 'pensero',
which 'everything indicates [...] is almost pure memory
— mixed, of course, with constantly renewed desire'.[30]
Petrarch's vision has a 'retrospective character', and while
Dante's spirit sees ('vede') and contemplates the beloved
in a transfigured state ('per lo suo splendore [...] la mira'),
the Petrarchan 'I' sees her again ('la rividi'), and her transformation appears a more perfect version of her earthly self

---

28   See in particular, Paul Olson, 'Two Sonnets of Heavenly Vision', *Italica*,
     35 (1958), pp. 156–61; Bettarini's note to 'Levòmmi' in Petrarca, *Can-
     zoniere*, II, pp. 1329–30; and Lombardi, '"I Desire Therefore I Am"', pp.
     2–30.

29   See Olson, p. 156.

30   Ibid., p. 157.

('più bella e meno altera'). The extension of the two journeys is significantly different too: whereas Dante's 'sospiro'
journeys through the nine physical heavens and reaches the
Empyrean, Petrarch's journey stops in the third heaven. As
Bettarini has noticed, Petrarch's 'terzo cerchio' combines
Dante's *Paradiso*, where the third heaven is that of Venus,
with Paul's *raptus* in II *Corinthians* xii 2 ('Scio hominem
in Christo… raptum huiusmodi usque *ad tertium caelum*'),
which is also recalled in Dante's sonnet in terms of ineffability. However, in the rest of Petrarch's poem the Pauline
reference fades away, and the sense remains that the third
heaven is merely that of Venus as the abode of the amatory
spirits and love poets (also mentioned in *Rvf* 287).[31]

Ineffability is not what is at stake in Petrarch's poem,
which apparently succeeds in relating what the poet experienced in paradise. It presents heaven not as a space for
excess but primarily as a fantasy that displaces into the afterlife an improved version of earthly desire. In 'Levòmmi il
mio penser' there is not the abandon to the adoration of the
beloved that follows Cavalcanti's posthumous encounter,
nor is there an equivalent experience to Dante's dazzling
vision of Beatrice in glory. The phrase 'la rividi' does not
carry any sense of ecstatic contemplation and is not the
endpoint of the encounter. Instead, it opens a space for
interaction in a heaven where everything points back to
earth but just seems to work better (for the poet). The
beloved is more amenable and even becomes approach-
able and active. She takes the poet by the hand, and the
phrase 'Per man mi prese' is striking for recalling the reciprocation of desire expressed in Cavalcanti's *ballata* 'In
un boschetto trova' pasturella', his most sensual text, that

---

31   'Ma ben ti prego che 'n la terza spera | Guitton saluti, et messer Cino,
     et Dante, | Franceschin nostro, et tutta quella schiere' (9–11).

even culminates with erotic consummation: 'Per man mi prese, d'amorosa voglia, | e disse che donato m'avea 'l core' (She took me by the hand, with amorous intent, | and said that she had given me her heart; 21–22). The reference to Laura's hand also recalls the *Triumphus Mortis* II, in which the beloved appears in a dream the morning after her death and offers the poet her hand before fulfilling his fantasy of ultimate reciprocation: 'e *quella man*, già tanto desiata, | a me, parlando e sospirando *porse*, | onde eterna dolcezza al cor m'è nata' (and, speaking and sighing, | *she stretched out to me that hand* already so long desired, | whence eternal sweetness is born in my heart; 10–12).

In sonnet 302, Laura also speaks, and her speech runs through lines 5–11. Oscillating between past and present, she fulfils all of Petrarch's wishes, compensating for the sufferings that she caused him while alive and for her untimely death, both recalled in lines 7–8 ('i' so' colei che ti die' tanta guerra, | et compie' mia giornata inanzi sera'). Yet this fantasy does not reach the intensity of 'Oltra la spera', and although in the second quatrain Laura states emphatically that Petrarch *will* be with her in the third heaven ('In questa spera | *sarai* anchor meco'), the hypothetical — and ambivalent — clause 'se 'l desir non erra' (6) makes that promise unstable.[32] As Peter Hainsworth has underscored, Laura's words add a 'disturbing qualifier that both stresses the strength of her feelings and leaves some room for uncertainty'.[33]

---

32   The most common reading given to the clause 'se 'l desir non erra' refers to Laura's desire, but the text also allows a reading that would refer to the poet's desire, or even to both his and Laura's. In any case, the coupling of desire and errancy is a recurrent feature of Petrarch's lyric sequence.

33   Hainsworth, *Petrarch the Poet*, p. 167.

A similar dynamic is also visible in the first tercet. It opens with Laura's assertion that heavenly bliss is incommensurable for the human intellect: 'Mio ben non cape in intelletto umano' (9), a statement that is theologically accurate and not only recalls lines 9–11 of 'Oltra la spera' but also would not be out of place in Dante's *Paradiso*. Also theologically correct is the desire that Laura, as a separated soul, expresses for her resurrection body. However, the remainder of lines 10–11 convey an earthly fantasy so outrageous that they undermine that correctness and lead us back into the poet's wishful thinking: Laura refers to her body as the 'bel velo' which the poet loved so much ('quel che tanto amasti'),[34] and she even states that the only other thing she lacks is the poet himself ('te solo aspetto').

The instability that has by now entered the poem feeds into the question that opens the final tercet. It is introduced by the interjection, 'Deh', which is another mark of that uncertainty recalled by Hainsworth: 'Deh perché tacque et allargò la mano?'. Laura's silence and holding back of her hand have an almost Orphic character,[35] causing the vision to dissipate and the beloved to be lost again. Whereas Cavalcanti's *ballatetta* ends by imagining a form

---

34   The term 'velo' is used to refer to Laura's body on several occasions in the *Rerum vulgarium fragmenta*. The adjective 'bel' reminds us of the way in which Beatrice refers to her beautiful limbs now scattered in earth in earthly paradise ('le belle membra in ch'io | rinchiusa fui, e che so' 'n terra sparte', *Purg.* XXXI, 50–51). Nancy Vickers has given an intertextual reading of these associations in her 'Re-membering Dante: Petrarch's "Chiare, fresche et dolci acque"', *MLN*, 96.1, Italian Issue (January 1981), pp. 1–11.

35   Cf. Virgil, *Georgics* IV. 499–502: 'dixit et ex oculis subito, ceu fumus in auras | commixtus tenuis, fugit diversa, neque illum | prensantem nequiquam umbras et multa volentem | dicere praeterea vidit', cited from Virgil, *Eclogues, Georgics, Aeneid Books 1–6*, trans. by H. R. Fairclough, revised by G. P. Goold (Cambridge, MA: Harvard University Press, 1916).

of posthumous union that is set to continue eternally, and Dante's 'Oltra la spera' concludes with the presencing power of Beatrice's name that from heaven continues on earth, 'Levòmmi il mio penser' ends abruptly without answering the question in line 12 and by collapsing downwards and away from the beloved. 'Non rimasi in cielo' emphatically contrasts with the initial '[l]evòmmi', and reading back to the beginning of the sonnet one sees that the present tenses 'cerco, et non ritrovo' already indicate that the journey of the poet towards his lady in heaven has not lasted. Nonetheless, not everything is lost in Petrarch's sonnet either. Bettarini may be going too far when she proposes that at the end of the poem the 'I''s 'ecstatic' ascent to heaven is not suspended but reaffirmed ('è rilanciata in chiusura'); but the last two lines are indeed delightfully Petrarchan in the ambivalent way they suggest some presence or at least a trace of it. In an 'almost' fashion beautifully conveyed by the confusing construction 'poco mancò [...] non', the fantasy of fullness is gone, and yet it lingers on poetically and in memory (which, as we have seen in Chapter 4 and will also consider in Chapter 6, are often hard to extricate in Petrarch). We agree with Hainsworth when he writes that 'It may or may not be that heaven will provide such an impossible reconciliation of opposites: all that is certain is that it can be imagined in a poem, that there the pleasure and power of the imagined or imaginary world in all their uncertainties can be represented'.[36]

What is striking is that pleasure comes not *despite* the ambivalence and instability that are the hallmark of Petrarchan desire but *because* of them. In 'Levòmmi il mio penser', we find neither the lightness of Cavalcanti's 'Perch'i' no spero' nor the epistemological robustness of

---

36   Hainsworth, *Petrarch the Poet*, p. 167.

'Oltra la spera'. Neither do we find the mystical excess that, in different ways, both of these poems imagine as the ultimate mode of encounter and subsequent bliss. Instead, as we have seen, for Petrarch the journey to heaven is mainly a pretext for imagining a version of earth 'in cielo', where his fantasies can be realized. Whether it is neurotic fixation or heroic fidelity, earthly desires are carried across to the heavenly sphere. In Petrarch's fantasy of heaven, the 'I' is very much present and, with it, all its uncertainties, instabilities, and disorientation. Roland Barthes can be of help in understanding this condition when, in a 'Supplément' to *Le plaisir du texte*, he discussed the concept of drift ('dérive') as a practice of in-consistency ('une pratique d'in-consistance') that resists the strictures of cohesion and solidity, as the active search for a dissociation ('la recherche active d'une dissociation') that challenges the oppression of wholeness.[37] As in the other Petrarchan poems we have analysed, this 'pratique d'in-consistance' also seems to be the mode of 'Levòmmi il mio penser': not only of the equivocal encounter it stages and the pleasure it induces in the poetic subject, but also of the experience of reading the poem. If we want to let ourselves be inspired by the conclusive line of the sonnet itself — 'poco mancò ch'io non rimasi in cielo' — we could call this mode — of pleasure and of poetry — an 'almost-mode', one that suggests wholeness and perfection but not quite, one that is even ready to accept failure in order not to yield to the constrictions of totality and closure.[38] It is a mode that

---

37 Roland Barthes, 'Texte supplément to *Le plaisir du texte*', *Art Press*, 4 (1973).

38 For a positive understanding of failing to conform to the heteronormative model of subjectivity not as a limit but as a space for new possibilities, see Judith Halberstam, *The Queer Art of Failure* (Durham, NC: Duke University Press, 2011). On the issues of totality and closure,

embraces errancy and drift and invites the reader to get lost in the bewildering labyrinth of the lines that express them.

---

see *De/Constituing Wholes: Towards Partiality Without Parts*, ed. by Manuele Gragnolati and Christoph F. E. Holzhey (Vienna: Turia + Kant, 2017).

6. Body
Dante's and Petrarch's Lyric Eschatologies

This chapter continues to investigate the intersection between lyric and eschatology that we have explored in the previous chapter, but while Chapter 5 focused on lyric poems incorporating eschatological motifs, this chapter considers how a lyric fervour continues to enrich two inherently eschatological texts that one would expect to stage a 'conversion' from erotic passion to Christian values. We bring Dante's *Paradiso* and Petrarch's *Triumphus Eternitatis* (henceforth *TE*) into dialogue in order to highlight some crucial tensions around the continuing presence of a fundamentally erotic component within the imagination of Christian paradise. In our analysis, 'lyric' stands for an aspect of subjectivity bound up with the relation to the beloved and to a desire contained in the body and expressed in the longing for it. In particular, we aim to examine the different ways in which Dante and Petrarch reimagine the doctrine of the resurrection of the body as conveying a relational sense of identity bound up with the individual's memory, desires, and history that both complicates and opens up their understanding of poetry and ultimate happiness.

'DISIO D'I CORPI MORTI'

Our point of departure is the shores of Dante's Purgatory,
where the pilgrim encounters a shade who has also just
arrived at the realm of purgation: the shade of Casella, an
old friend from the times of youth when Dante had not
yet been exiled from Florence.[1] This episode rewrites the
Virgilian motif of the impossible embrace between a living
person and a shade: the pilgrim and his old friend try to
embrace each other, but they cannot because, as Statius
explains in *Purgatorio* xxv, shades in Dante's afterlife have
an aerial body that gives them an appearance — 'aspetto'
— but no substantiality.[2] As the poet laments, shades in
the otherworld are 'vane', empty:

> Ohi ombre vane, fuor che ne l'aspetto!
> tre volte dietro a lei le mani avvinsi,
> e tante mi tornai con esse al petto.
>
> (Oh empty shades, except in seeming! | Three times
> I clasped my hands behind him | only to find them
> clasped to my own chest.) (*Purg.*, ii, 79–81)

What is important to note is that both friends, who have
just arrived in Purgatory, are still entrapped by their earthly

---

1   On this episode, see Gragnolati, *Amor che move*, pp. 91–103, and
     'Ombre e abbracci. Riflessioni sull'inconsistenza in Dante', in *Passages,
     seuils, sauts: du dernier cercle de l'Enfer à la première terrasse du Pur-
     gatoire (Enf. xxxii – Purg. xii)*, ed. by Manuele Gragnolati and Philippe
     Guérin (= *Chroniques italiennes web*, 35 (2020)), pp. 68–81.

2   See in particular Statius's description of the formation of the aerial
     body in *Purg.* xxv, 85–108, and Manuele Gragnolati's discussion of it in
     Experiencing the Afterlife: Body and Soul in Dante and Medieval Culture
     (Notre Dame, IN: University of Notre Dame Press, 2005), pp. 67–77.
     Quotations from the *Commedia* are from Petrocchi's edition. English
     translations come from: Dante Alighieri, *The Divine Comedy*, trans. by
     Robert Hollander and Jean Hollander. 3 vols (New York: Doubleday
     2000–2007).

desires. Casella tells Dante that although he is now a soul deprived of his mortal body, he continues to love his friend in the same way that he did on earth: 'Così com'io t'amai | nel *mortal corpo*, così t'amo sciolta' (Even as I loved you in *my mortal flesh,*' he said, | 'so do I love you freed from it'; *Purg.* ii, 89–90). Dante also shows nostalgia for the past and asks his friend to sing in the same way he used to sing in their youth. Casella performs Dante's *canzone* 'Amor che nella mente mi ragiona' in such a way that everybody in Ante-Purgatory remains enchanted by its sweetness:

> 'Amor che ne la mente mi ragiona'
> cominciò elli allor sì dolcemente,
> che la dolcezza ancor dentro mi suona.
>
> ('Love that converses with me in my mind', | he then began, so sweetly | that the sweetness sounds within me still.) (*Purg.* ii, 112–14)[3]

The rest of the episode, with Cato's harsh reprimand of the souls' indulging in song and emotion ('Che è ciò, spiriti lenti?'; 120), shows that the mutual affection which the two friends still feel for each other is wrong and that in Purgatory the attachment to the mortal body, the affection for friends and beloved, and the nostalgia for the past must change.[4] Indeed, the moral structure of Dante's Purgatory

---

3   'Amor che nella mente mi ragiona' is one of Dante's *Rime*, included in Book iii of *Convivio*, where it heralds the transfer of Dante's affection from Beatrice to Lady Philosophy. On the importance of this auto-citation in the *Commedia*, see Teodolinda Barolini, *Dante's Poets: Textuality and Truth in the 'Comedy'* (Princeton, NJ: Princeton University Press, 1984), pp. 31–40.

4   For readings of this episode, see for example, John Freccero, 'Casella's Song: *Purgatorio* ii, 112', in his *Dante: The Poetics of Conversion*, ed. by Rachel Jacoff (Cambridge, MA: Harvard University Press, 1986), pp. 186–94; and Robert Hollander, '*Purgatorio* ii: Cato's Rebuke and Dante's *Scoglio*', *Italica*, 52.3 (Autumn 1975), pp. 348–63.

prescribes that the souls learn to detach themselves from anything transient and instead redirect all their desires towards God: according to Dante's Augustinian 'paradigm' of desire, attachments to one's earthly body and nostalgia for the earthly affections symbolized by it are considered as distractions that the purging soul must abandon if it wants to attain the complete love for God that is necessary to reach heaven.[5] Purgatory is precisely the place that provides the experience, at once painful and productive, that allows the soul to transform personal and individual love into *caritas*, that is, the absolute and unconditional love for God which is also gratuitous love for one's neighbour and implies the possibility to free oneself from self-obsession and sin's monomonia and to open oneself to others.[6]

This Augustinian paradigm of desire is made clear by Beatrice in her scolding of the pilgrim in the garden of Eden, when, pointing to her beautiful limbs now scattered on earth and reduced to ashes — her 'belle membra [...] | che so' 'n terra sparte' (*Purg.* XXXI, 50–51) — she explains that it is precisely when her body died that the pilgrim should have loved her most because this would have meant

---

5   See Chapter 5 of Teodolinda Barolini, *The Undivine 'Comedy': Detheologizing Dante* (Princeton, NJ: Princeton University Press, 1992), pp. 99–121 (especially pp. 103–08).

6   On the notion of productive pain in the *Purgatorio*, see Manuele Gragnolati, 'Gluttony and the Anthropology of Pain in Dante's *Inferno* and *Purgatorio*', in *History in the Comic Mode: Medieval Communities and the Matter of Person*, ed. by Rachel Fulton and Bruce W. Holsinger (New York: Columbia University Press, 2007), pp. 238–50; and Gragnolati: *Experiencing the Afterlife*, pp. 89–137. On sin in hell as 'obsessive monomania', see Peter Hawkins, *Dante: A Brief History* (London: Blackwell, 2006), p. 40. On the political significance of the experience of Purgatory, which also teaches the souls to reconstruct societal bonds and rebuild a sense of community, see Joan Ferrante, *The Political Vision of Dante's 'Comedy'* (Princeton, NJ: Princeton University Press, 1984), pp. 198–252.

loving her soul, the immortal part of her that will never
fail him. Actually, he should love her more now that she
is a shade than when she was in her fleshly body on earth:
albeit beautiful, the earthly body is mortal, and one should
neither love it as though it were not doomed to die nor, as
the pilgrim did after Beatrice's death, replace it with some
other mortal good that distracts from fully directing one's
love to God:

> Mai non t'appresentò natura o arte
> piacere, quanto le bella membra in ch'io
> rinchiusa fui, e che so' 'n terra sparte,
> e se 'l sommo piacer sì ti fallio
> per la mia morte, qual cosa mortale
> dovea poi trarre te nel suo disio?
> Ben ti dovevi, per lo primo strale
> de le cose fallaci, levar suso
> di retro a me che non era più tale.

(Never did art or nature set before you beauty |
as great as in *the lovely members* that enclosed me,
| now scattered and reduced to dust. | And if the
highest beauty failed you | in my death, what *mortal
thing* | should then have drawn you to desire it? |
Indeed, at the very first arrow of deceitful things,
you should have risen up | and followed me who
was no longer of them.) (*Purg.* XXXI, 49–57)

Beatrice's words confirm that one should not love earthly
goods too much and also suggest that there is something
problematic in the mortal, fleshly body that is related to
an intimate desire for others that must be overcome. Flesh
would not seem to be required in the eschatological pan-
orama of the *Commedia*, where by releasing a body of air,
the souls are able to acquire the corporeality that is necessary for the full experience of the afterlife and the full
expression of the self. In this respect, Dante's poem is in line

with contemporary eschatological assumptions, which had shifted emphasis from the idea of a collective judgment at the end of time and the subsequent reward or punishment of resurrected humankind in either hell or heaven. They were interested instead in the full experience of the soul in the afterlife right after its separation from the body. As the *Inferno* and *Purgatorio* place emphasis on the intensity of the souls' pain, so the *Paradiso* indicates that in heaven the fleshless souls have access to the beatific vision, which satisfies all their desires and grants them perfect bliss ('pace'):

> Lume è là sù che visibile face
> lo creatore a quella creatura
> che solo in lui vedere ha la sua pace.

> (There is a light above that makes the Creator |
> visible to every creature | that finds its only peace
> in seeing Him.) (*Par.* xxx, 100–02)[7]

Several studies have argued that the condition of bliss achieved and manifested by the souls in heaven corresponds to a state of merging with God that opens up the self and radically changes it. Thus, for instance, Lino Pertile and Steven Botterill have indicated that Beatrice, insofar as she represents attachment to the past as well as erotic and lyric desire, must also eventually leave and be replaced by St Bernard before the pilgrim can reach the ultimate union with God and the Universe.[8] Robin Kirkpatrick has

---

7   On the fullness of the separated souls' experience in Dante's hell and
     heaven, see Gragnolati: *Experiencing the Afterlife*, pp. 77–87, and his
     Amor che move, pp. 69–90.

8   Lino Pertile, *La punta del disio: Semantica del desiderio nella 'Com-
     media'* (Fiesole: Cadmo, 2005), especially pp. 235–46, 'Dimenticare
     Beatrice'; Steven Botterill, *Dante and the Mystical Tradition: Bernard of
     Clairvaux in the 'Commedia'* (Cambridge: Cambridge University Press,
     1994)), pp. 64–86, where he speaks of Dante's 'process of […] detach-
     ment from Beatrice' as realized through Bernard's replacement of her
     as guide (p. 85).

spoken of a 'spirit of dispossession' that characterizes the condition of being in heaven, while Christian Moevs has indicated that the redirection of desire from mortal to immortal goods can be understood as a 'spontaneous crucifixion of the self' and that 'love is selflessness, and self is lovelessness'.[9]

There is something fascinating about the loss of self that uniting with God implies in Dante's concept of heaven and in the kind of subjectivity that this loss entails.[10] However, if an important component of the heavenly state that Dante imagines is constituted by this transformation and shattering of the self, nonetheless there is something about their past that the souls in heaven continue to be attached to and that cannot be tamed, disciplined, or fully relinquished — an identity, that is, that goes in the opposite direction of transformation. Central to this dimension is the celebration of the resurrection of the flesh that takes place in *Paradiso* xiv, a moment in the *Commedia* in which Dante conveys with sublime intensity the nostalgia for one's own mortal body and the intimate affections that it represents. In replying to the pilgrim's doubt about what will happen to heavenly bliss at the end of time, Solomon explains that the final resurrection of the body will allow for an increase of the souls' beatific vision and subsequent happiness:

---

9   See Robin Kirkpatrick, 'Polemics of Praise: Theology as Text, Narrative and Rhetoric in Dante's *Commedia*', in *Dante's 'Commedia': Theology as Poetry*, ed. by Vittorio Montemaggi and Matthew Treherne (Notre Dame, IN: University of Notre Dame Press, 2010), pp. 14–35 (p. 23); and Christian Moevs, *The Metaphysics of Dante's 'Comedy'* (New York: Oxford University Press, 2005), pp. 89–90.

10   See Heather Webb, *Dante's Persons: An Ethics of the Transhuman* (Oxford: Oxford University Press, 2016), and Nicolò Crisafi and Manuele Gragnolati, 'Weathering the Afterlife: The Meterological Psychology of Dante's *Commedia*', in *Weathering: Ecologies of Exposure*, ed. by Christoph F. E. Holzhey and Arnd Wedemeyer (Berlin: ICI Berlin Press, 2020), pp. 63–91.

Come la carne glorïosa e santa
fia rivestita, la nostra persona
più grata fia *per esser tutta quanta*:
    per che *s'accrescerà ciò che ne dona*
di gratüito lume il sommo bene
lume ch'a lui veder ne condiziona;
    onde la visïon *crescer* convene,
crescer l'ardor che di quella s'accende,
crescer lo raggio che da esso vene.

(When we put on again our flesh, | glorified and
holy, then our persons | will be more pleasing *for
being all complete*, | so that *the light, granted to us
freely* | *by the Highest Good, shall increase*, | the light
that makes us fit to see Him. | From that light, vision
must *increase* | and love *increase* what vision kindles,
| and radiance *increase*, which comes from love.)
(*Par.* xiv, 43–51)

The souls react joyfully to Solomon's idea that they will be
reunited with their fleshly body — that mortal body which
has remained on Earth and is now a corpse:

Tanto mi parver sùbiti e accorti
e l'uno e l'altro coro a dicer 'Amme!',
che ben mostrar *disio d'i corpi morti*:
    forse non pur per lor, *ma per le mamme,*
per li padri e per li altri che fuor cari
anzi che fosser sempiterne fiamme.

(So quick and eager seemed to me both choirs | to
say their *Amen* that they clearly showed | *their desire
for their dead bodies*, | not perhaps for themselves
alone, *but for their mothers*, | *for their fathers, and
for others whom they loved* | before they all became
eternal flames. (*Par.* xiv, 61–66)

The eagerness with which the souls ratify Solomon's promise reveals the intensity of their nostalgia for their bodies

('disio d'i corpi morti').[11] Unlike many other passages of the *Paradiso* that stress the souls' current happiness, here Dante's poem emphasizes that they are still longing to reunite with their bodies and that, when they do so, they will be happier. In particular, the rhyme words 'amme' | 'mamme' | 'fiamme' express that after the recovery of what are now dead bodies, the separated souls — which in heaven have become splendid lights, enflamed by their beatitude and love for God — will become again veritable individuals with their own singularity, made of relations and memory.

The souls' joyful reaction at the idea of recovering their dead bodies is connected not only with the increase of their vision of God but also with their personal attachments and can be considered as the passionate 'expression of their desire to love fully in heaven what they loved on earth'.[12] In this way, the souls' 'disio d'i corpi morti' seems to contradict the Augustinian paradigm of detachment, which, as we have seen, depicts the process of Purgatory as a transformation towards selflessness and dispossession. Moreover, the relational sense expressed by the souls' desire for their resurrected bodies was somewhat of a novelty with respect to contemporary theologians, who focused mainly on the

11   On the motif of the resurrection of the body in the *Commedia*, see Gragnolati, *Experiencing the Afterlife*, pp. 139–78, and his *Amor che move*, pp. 104–10 and pp. 149–61, both with ample bibliography. See also Anna Maria Chiavacci Leonardi, '"Le bianche stole": il tema della resurrezione nel *Paradiso*', in *Dante e la Bibbia. Atti del Convegno Internazionale promosso da 'Biblia': Firenze, 26–27–28 settembre 1986*, ed. by Giovanni Barblan (Florence: Olschki, 1988), pp. 249–71; and Caroline Walker Bynum, 'Faith Imagining the Self: Somatomorphic Soul and Resurrection Body in Dante's *Divine Comedy*', in *Faithful Imagining: Essays in Honor of Richard R. Neibuhr*, ed. by Sang Huyn Lee, Wayne Proudfoot, and Albert Blackwell (Atlanta, GA: Scholars Press, 1995), pp. 81–104.

12   Barolini, *The Undivine 'Comedy'*, p. 138.

exclusive relation of the individual to God and were less
interested in the idea that personal and individual attachments continue in heaven among the blessed.[13] The connection Dante makes in *Paradiso* xiv between the body's
materiality and fleshliness, memory, and individuality, is
striking for its personal character. It reveals a tension run-
ning through the *Paradiso* between the understanding of
heaven as a state of transformation of the self as dissolution into God and the blessed souls' 'disio d'i corpi morti',
which for Dante arguably includes not only the desire to
embrace Casella at the end of time but also to recuperate
Beatrice in all her erotic and lyric depth. Indeed, as Regina
Psaki, Lombardi, and Barolini have convincingly shown by
analysing the ubiquitous presence of the amatory language
of lyric poetry in *Paradiso*, the figure of Beatrice does not
lose her lyric character in heaven, nor does the pilgrim ever
tame his erotic desire for her, even when it would seem
logically incompatible with the love for God.[14]

---

13   See Colleen McDannell and Bernhard Lang, *Heaven: A History* (New
     Haven: Yale University Press, 1998), pp. 90–94. For example, Bernard
     of Clairvaux does not permit any notion of interaction between the
     saints in his concept of heaven, notwithstanding his praise of friendship
     on earth. On Bernard in particular, see Anna Harrison, 'Community
     among the Saints in Heaven in Bernard of Clairvaux's *Sermons for the
     Feast of All Saints*', in *Last Things: Death and Apocalypse in the Middle
     Ages*, ed, by Caroline Walker Bynum and Paul Freedman (Philadelphia:
     University of Pennsylvania Press, 2000), pp. 191–204.

14   See F. Regina Psaki, 'Dante's Redeemed Eroticism', *Lectura Dantis*,
     18–19 (1996), pp. 12–19, her 'The Sexual Body in Dante's Celestial
     Paradise', in *Imagining Heaven in the Middle Ages: A Book of Essays*, ed.
     by Jan Swango Emerson and Hugh Feiss (New York: Garland, 2000),
     pp. 47–61, and her 'Love for Beatrice: Transcending Contradiction
     in the *Paradiso*', in *Dante for the New Millennium*, ed. by Teodolinda
     Barolini and H. Wayne Storey (New York: Fordham University Press,
     2003), pp. 115–30; Elena Lombardi, 'Identità lirica e piacere linguist-
     ico: una lettura di *Paradiso* xxvi', *Studi danteschi*, 82 (2017), pp. 51–80
     and her *Imagining the Woman Reader*, pp. 117–53; Teodolinda Barolini,
     'La poesia della teologia e la teologia della poesia dalle *Rime* di Dante

Our final point regards the last cantos of *Paradiso* and the representation of the Empyrean, a heaven of pure intellectual light (xxx, 39), a dimensionless point ('punto') equal to the mind of God, where everything is simultaneously co-present ('il punto | a cui tutti li tempi son presenti', xvii, 17–18) — a state that theologians called *totum simul*.[15] In the Empyrean, something significant takes place that has to do with the resurrection. On a thematic level, the resurrection of the body is anticipated and imagined before the end of time when the pilgrim Dante enters the Empyrean: not only is he granted the privilege of seeing the blessed with the resurrected bodies that they will receive only at the Last Judgment, but his own 'living' body has acquired the characteristics of a resurrected body.[16]

In linguistic and formal terms, as Gary Cestaro has noticed, in the last ten cantos of *Paradiso* dedicated to the pilgrim's experience in the Empyrean, one finds the resurgence of the image of the child suckling at the mother's breast, which is central to Dante's meditation on the vernacular as a corporeal, affective, and fluid language acquired by imitating the wet nurse (*De vulgari eloquentia* I, i, 2).[17] For instance, it is present when the pilgrim enters the Empyrean and observes a river of light turning into a circle:

al *Paradiso*', in *'Il mondo errante'. Dante fra letteratura, eresia e storia; atti del convegno internazionale di studio: Bertinoro, 13–16 settembre 2010*, ed. by Marco Veglia, Lorenzo Paolini, and Riccardo Parmeggiani (Spoleto: Centro di studi italiani sull'alto medioevo, 2013), pp. 537–45.

15 On the concept of *totum simul*, originally in Boethius, see Barolini, *The Undivine 'Comedy'*, pp. 168–69.

16 See Gragnolati, *Experiencing the Afterlife*, pp. 161–78.

17 Gary Cestaro, *Dante and the Grammar of the Nursing Body* (Notre Dame, IN: University of Notre Dame Press, 2003), pp. 154–56.

Non è fantin che sì subito rua
col volto verso il latte, se si svegli
molto tardato da l'usanza sua,

   come fec' io, per far migliori spegli
ancora de li occhi, chinandomi a l'onda
che si deriva perché vi s'immegli;

   e sì come di lei bevve la gronda
da le palpebre mie, così mi parve
di sua lunghezza divenuta tonda.

(No infant, waking up too late | for his accustomed
feeding, will thrust his face | up to his milk with
greater urgency, | than I, to make still better mirrors
of my eyes, | inclined my head down toward the
water | that flows there for our betterment, | and no
sooner had the eaves of my eyelids | drunk deep of
that water than to me it seemed | it had made its
length into a circle.) (*Par.* xxx, 82–90)

The image of the child craving his mother's milk expresses
here the intensity of the pilgrim's desire to see God and
is deployed at the crucial moment in which the pilgrim,
now close to attaining the ultimate vision, is about to abandon a linear dimension of temporality (like that on Earth
or in Purgatory) and enter instead the circular and extra-
temporal dimension of Eternity.

Our hypothesis, which draws on Cestaro's reading but
pushes it further through Bersani's concept of 'aesthetics'
with which we have often engaged in this book, is that
the complex and multivalent desire informing the eschatological imagination of the *Commedia* is also replicated in
the movement of its textuality. It is indeed quite significant
that the image of suckling at the mother's breast appears
in precisely the three cantos of the *Paradiso* (xxiii, xxx
and xxxiii) in which, as Barolini has shown, the *Commedia*
deploys a different kind of textuality — a textuality that is
no longer rational, logical, or linear but 'jumping': a tex-

tuality that transgresses the common mode, which is dis-
cursive, logical, linear, 'chronologized', and intellective, by
being instead 'lyric', by which Barolini means 'nondiscurs-
ive, nonlinear or circular, dechronologized and affective'.[18]
This jumping mode is inaugurated with the attempt to capture the ineffable experience of Beatrice's smile in canto
XXIII, 55–60, so overwhelming that the sacred poem is
forced to jump ('qui convien saltare lo sacrato poema', 60).
This form of textuality is 'resistant to subdivision and hence
to logical exposition, and is characterized by apostrophes,
exclamations, heavily metaphoric language, and intensely
affective similes', subverting linearity and conveying the
circular and extra-temporal dimension of Eternity, where
everything is simultaneously co-present.[19]

Ultimately, our point is that the final cantos of the
poem not only represent the resurrection of the body (for
both the blessed and the pilgrim) before the end of time
but also perform it. As we have seen, the heavenly state can
be interpreted as the paradoxical condition of combining
the dissolution of too rigid an identity into the movement
of God's cosmic order and his love ('l'amor che move il
sole e l'altre stelle', Par. XXXIII, 145) with a strong sense
of individuality which is accepted in its singularity and
relationality and persists in the body and in the desire

18   See Barolini, The Undivine 'Comedy', pp. 218–56 (p. 221). Her notion
      of a 'jumping' textuality as fundamentally lyric rather than narrative in
      nature derives from her analysis of the terzina from Paradiso XXIII, 61–
      63, in which Dante acknowledges that he must leap over the moment
      of ecstatic, lyric, mystical vision he cannot describe and rejoin his path
      further up: 'e così, figurando il paradiso, | convien saltar lo sacrato
      poema | come chi trova suo cammin reciso'. On the poetic language of
      the high Paradiso as incorporating a Kristevan dimension of semiotic
      affect which recuperates the fluid and maternal component of the ver-
      nacular, see Cestaro, Dante and the Grammar, especially pp. 135–66;
      and Gragnolati, Amor che move, pp. 149–61.

19   Again see Barolini, The Undivine 'Comedy', p. 221.

for it ('disio d'i' corpi morti', *Par.* XIV, 63). One could
say that the subject which is not a subject anymore, re-
found and replicated in the poem's textuality and rhythm,
not only opens itself up to a state of cosmic dissolution
but also maintains a corporeal depth that is connected
with its affective history, including, in the case of Dante,
Beatrice and the lyric past associated with her. One could
therefore say that, together with the sense of progression
typical of Dante's poem and its epic form, the pyrotechnic,
ardent, 'resurrected' character of the lyric textuality of the
Paradiso's last cantos replicates the paradoxical pleasure
not only of losing but also of continuing to find oneself
again.

DESIRING LAURA'S BODY

Bearing in mind Dante's enactment and embrace of paradox as the essence of desire in the *Paradiso*, we can turn
to Petrarch's *Triumphi* and consider the eschatology and
textuality they embody, particularly the final *TE*. The *Triumphi*, likely composed between 1352 and 1374, are written in the form of a vision and in *terza rima* — the meter
Dante invented for his *Commedia*, and as such, they explicitly invite a comparison with Dante's magnum opus.
They narrate a triumphal procession of six allegorical figures, each of which is defeated in turn by a greater victor —
Love, Chastity (represented by Laura, Petrarch's beloved),
Death, Fame, and Time — until Eternity triumphs over
them all. As in the *Commedia* with respect to the *Vita Nova*,
in the *Triumphi* the lyric poetry composing Petrarch's *Rvf*
gives way to a more universal, didactic, and narrative dimension that culminates with a vision of paradise and
supposedly supplants eros. In turn, the epic framework of
the *Triumphi* (modelled on the classical epic as much as on

Dante's vernacular one) and the forward movement gener-
ated by the *terza rima* itself instigate a 'vertical' drive largely
absent from the *rime sparse*.[20]

In particular, we would like to focus on the notion
of desire that the *Triumphi*'s finale conveys. As we shall
see, it offers a depiction of heaven that goes against the
development of some key theological assumptions about
the afterlife in the late Middle Ages, specifically regard-
ing the beatific vision and Dante's own eschatology in the
Commedia. As hinted earlier, the eschatological focus had
shifted during this period from a concern with the event of
the Last Judgment and the resurrection of the body at the
end of time towards the experience of the separated soul
in the time between death and the resurrection. This development concluded with the 1336 promulgation of the
papal bull *Benedictus Deus*, which officially declared that
in heaven a separated soul enjoys ultimate beatitude and
does not need its body in order to have access to full vision
of God. This edict was passed in Avignon, the place where
Petrarch lived and worked in and around the papal curia,
and it is not surprising that, as Maria Cecilia Bertolani has
shown, he knew well contemporary theological debates on
the beatific vision.[21] In c.1336, Petrarch even wrote a letter

---

20 On the poetics of the *Triumphi* and the nature of Petrarch's vernacular
    project in that work, see at least, Zygmunt G. Barański: 'The *Triumphi*',
    in *The Cambridge Companion to Petrarch*, ed. by Albert R. Ascoli and
    Unn Falkeid (Cambridge: Cambridge University Press, 2015), pp.
    74–84; Fabio Finotti, 'The Poem of Memory: Petrarch's *Triumphi*',
    in *Petrarch: A Critical Guide to the Complete Works*, ed. by Victoria
    Kirkham and Armando Maggi (Chicago: University of Chicago Press,
    2009), pp. 63–83; Marco Ariani, 'I *Triumphi*', in his *Petrarca* (Rome:
    Salerno, 1999), pp. 286–310; and Marguerite Waller, 'Negative Stylist-
    ics: A Reading of Petrarch's *Trionfi*', in her *Petrarch's Poetics and Literary
    History* (Amherst: University of Massachusetts Press, 1980), pp. 107–
    32. On the notion of a 'vertical' drive in the *Triumphi*, see Finotti, 'The
    Poem of Memory', p. 63.

21 For example, see those those put forward by Robert of Anjou, Benedict
    XII, and Durand of St Pourçain. See the first two chapters of Maria

to Benedict XII in which he acknowledged the Pontiff's view that the resurrection of the body is not necessary for the blessed souls' glory and that they are granted the beatific vision straight after physical death.[22]

Yet the *TE* imagines quite a different eschatology, not only focussing on the resurrection of the body but imbuing this theological doctrine with a courtly tenor. Instead of redirecting desire from a mortal lady to an immortal God, the vision of eternity in the last Triumph seems to justify the poet-lover's desire for his lady by imagining that the resurrection of her body will cure it of the imperfections that had made it so problematic. As such, the beatific experience of the *TE* is not located in the gratuitous giving of the self to God or to others (or vice versa) but in a carefully choreographed vision of the triumph of the beloved, which eschews any known eschatological parameters in the strictest sense.

The *TE* opens by staging a poetic subject still shaken and dispersed by the vicissitudes of desire, time, and history depicted in the earlier Triumphs, particularly in the *Triumphus Temporis*. Acknowledging the instability and volubility of the world and recognizing his own responsibility in his predicament, the Petrarchan subject is presented as being on the point of conversion, preparing to move into the infallible God:

> Da poi che sotto 'l ciel cosa non vidi
> stabile e ferma, tutto sbigottito
> mi volsi a me, e dissi: 'In che ti fidi?'

Cecilia Bertolani, *Petrarca e la visione dell'eterno* (Bologna: Il Mulino 2005), pp. 1–126; and Bynum's discussion of the controversy over the beatific vision in *The Resurrection of the Body*, pp. 283–91.

22   The letter in question is *Epistola* I, 5, analysed by Bertolani, *Petrarca e la visione*, pp. 99–126.

Risposi: 'Nel Signor, che mai fallito
non à promessa a chi si fida in lui.
ma ben veggio che 'l mondo m'ha schernito,
    e sento quel ch'i' sono e quel ch'i' fui,
e veggio andar, anzi volare il tempo,
e doler mi vorrei, né so di cui;
    ché la colpa è pur mia, che più per tempo
deve' aprir gli occhi, e non tardar al fine,
ch'a dir il vero omai troppo m'attempo.
    Ma tarde non fur mai gratie divine;
in quelle spero che 'n me anchor faranno
alte operatïoni e pellegrine'.

(Since I saw nothing beneath heaven that was stable
or firm, all dismayed, I turned to myself and said
'What do you trust in?'. || I replied 'In the Lord, who
has never broken a promise made to one who trusts
in him. But I see well that the world has mocked me,
|| and I perceive that which I am and what I was, and
I see Time moving on, indeed flying, and I would
like to complain but I don't know about whom; ||
because the fault is entirely my own: for I should
have opened my eyes sooner, not waiting until the
end, since to tell the truth I've already let too much
time pass by. || But divine grace has never come too
late and I put my hope in it that it will still produce
high and wondrous things in me'.) (*TE*, 1–15)

While absorbed in these meditations, which recall the typically Petrarchan situation that we analysed in Chapter 1
in relation to *Rvf* 70 (and that is most emblematically expressed in *Rvf* 264 and in the *Secretum*), the 'I''s thoughts
take an explicitly eschatological turn, shifting towards a
question about the end of time: 'Or, se non stanno | queste
cose che 'l ciel volge e governa, | dopo molto voltar, che
fine avranno?' (And now, if these things that the heavens
move and govern never stand still, after so much turning,
what will become of them?; 13–15). There is no interest
for the eschatological period between physical death and

the Last Judgment; instead the 'I' has a sudden vision that transports him directly to the final transfiguration of the world and to the stopping of time and variation:

> Questo pensava; e mentre più s'interna
> la mente mia, veder mi parve un mondo
> novo, in etate immobile ed eterna,
>   e 'l sole e tutto 'l ciel disfar a tondo
> con le sue stelle, anchor la terra e 'l mare,
> e rifarne un più bello e più giocondo.
>   Qual meraviglia ebb'io, quando ristare
> vidi in un punto quel che mai non stette,
> ma discorrendo suol tutto cangiare!
>   E le tre parti sue vidi ristrecte
> ad una sola, e quella una esser ferma
> sì che, come solea, più non s'affrette;
>   e quasi in terra d'erbe ignuda ed herma,
> né 'fia', né 'fu', né 'mai', né 'inanzi' o ''indietro',
> ch'umana vita fanno varia e 'nferma!
>   Passa il penser sì come sole in vetro,
> anzi più assai, però che nulla il tene.
> O, qual gratia mi fia, se mai l'impetro,
>   ch'i'veggia ivi presente il sommo bene,
> non alcun mal, che solo il tempo mesce
> e con lui si diparte e con lui vène.

(I was thinking this, and while my mind was turning ever further in on itself, I seemed to see a new world appear, in an immobile and eternal time, || and the sun and all of heaven and its stars around disappear, and the earth and the sea too, and to see another world remade more beautiful and more pleasing. || What wonder I felt when I saw motionless in one point that which has never stopped moving, but racing on changes everything! || And I saw its three parts contained in one alone, and that one staying still, not hurrying on as it used to do; || and, like in a grassless and remote stretch of land, neither 'will be', nor 'was', nor 'ever', neither 'before' nor 'after', that make human life so unstable and infirm. || Thought passes on like sun through glass, indeed

even more so, since nothing holds it back. O what
grace it will be, if I should obtain it, || that I should
see there present the supreme good, and no evil that
time alone furnishes, and that with it comes and
goes.) (*TE*, 19–39)

We have now moved from the personal reflection on God
as the infallible endpoint of every promise to an Apo-
calyptic perspective of the 'new heaven and new earth'
(Apoc. 21). The focus is almost exclusively on vision and
the visionary ('veder mi parve'; 'vidi'; 'vidi'; 'veggia'), yet
Petrarch's reading and appropriation of Apocalypse turns
out to be partial and restrictive: while he emphasizes the
importance of revelation and the unprecedented power of
the vision of the 'new world' (mondo novo) to subsume
the old, he underplays the theocentric, sustaining, and ti-
tanic presence of God as 'Alpha and Omega' (Apoc. 1, 8)
as well as the final victory of the Lamb (Apoc. 5, 6), which
one might otherwise expect from engaging with the Book
of Revelation.

Petrarch's appropriation of Dante is arguably even
more radical. The phrase 'mentre più s'interna | la mente
mia' (19–20) recalls *Par.* XXXIII, 85, where the verb
's'interna' refers to Dante's vision of the mystery of how
the universe, in all its multiplicity, is actually unified in the
Godhead — a mystical meaning that Petrarch picks up
in *Rvf* 327, 10–11: 'fra li spiriti electi, | ove nel suo factor
l'alma s'interna' (among the blessed spirits, where the
soul immerses itself in contemplation of its maker). The
TE thereby creates the expectation that the Petrarchan
subject will have a transcendent vision of God. However,
as Moevs has shown, the verb 's'interna', together with the
recasting of the equally Dantean 'punto' mentioned in our
analysis of the *Paradiso*, indicates Petrarch's resistance to
metaphysics, as well as his doubt about the ontological

foundations of the soul and its relationship to its maker. Able to join with God only through a superhuman effort of the will that would quell all other desires, the Petrarchan subject does not possess that innate desire propelling it to reunite with its source and the ground of all being. Rather, it has to strive even just to seek God among the things of the world.[23]

As a consequence, in the *TE*, Petrarch's eternity results in:

> a strange affair: it is not a transcendence of time and flux, but rather it is time and flux frozen, fixed, stopped. It is not a beatific vision of the divine light, of pure being or consciousness as the ontological foundation of the world; it is rather a dream that the fleeting world itself could be made a 'cosa... stabile e ferma' [...]: in short, a spatiotemporal world that is non-contingent, stable, unchanging, permanently new, whole, dependable and gathered together.[24]

In other words, for both Dante and Petrarch, eternity is without end and, insofar as time is suspended, timeless too. But whereas for Dante the 'punto' has a metaphysical valence and coincides with the 'transcendent God' that gives meaning to creation and is the source and end of all desire (see for example its manifold presence in *Par.* XXVIII), Petrarch's 'punto' merely corresponds to a perfected version of earth, cured of its instability and subjection to time.[25] It is definitively not the *totum simul* of Dante's *Paradiso*, where, as we have seen above, the poet actually aims to recreate textually the experience of 'ontological

---

23   See Moevs, 'Subjectivity and Conversion', p. 242 and p. 246.

24   Ibid, p. 234.

25   Ibid, p. 237.

simultaneity': eternity not as mere duration but as God's 'plenitude of presence in a never-fading instant'.[26]

As Moevs also has suggested, the insistence on thinking (*TE*, 19; 34) indicates that the Petrarchan subject remains bound to a finite mode of understanding and ultimately never transcends himself or his earthly desires. Unlike the progression that informs the *Commedia*, where in a paradoxical way the self keeps its memory and affective identity but also changes and opens up to fusing with God, in the *TE*, we find at most a pseudo-progression: a simulated movement toward what we think might be the beatific vision of God but which is merely a prelude of (or even a pretext for) Laura's final return in all her perfection.

Instead of reflecting on the beatific vision that the blessed enjoy as soon as they get to heaven and that will increase at the resurrection, the remainder of the *TE* insists on eternity as the freezing of time, first as a way to imagine that a never-ending fame will be possible and then as a possibility for the body — especially Laura's glorified body — to resurrect in a changeless manner. In this conception, having a taste of beatitude is not about opening up or turning oneself inside out to merge with God but instead involves focusing exclusively on one individual in all her (lyric and erotic) specificity. In the passage quoted above, the 'sommo bene' (37) is usually read as referring to God. Indeed, as Vinicio Pacca has pointed out in his commentary, it is a common phrase for God in both Dante's and Petrarch's other works (see e.g. *Rvf* 13, 10; 99, 3). At the same time, given how the *TE* evolves, it could equally be a symbol of Laura in her fully corporeal glory and per-

---

26   Barolini, *The Undivine 'Comedy'*, p. 168.

fection at the resurrection, her body no longer fragmented
or scattered as it is represented in the *Rvf*.[27]

Indeed, Petrarch's eschatology fully unfolds in the moment when Laura herself appears in the text of the *TE*:

> O felici quelle anime che 'n via
> sono o seranno di venire al fine
> di ch'io ragiono, quandunque e' si sia.
>
> E tra l'altre leggiadre e pellegrine
> beatissima lei, che morte occise
> assai di qua dal natural confine!
>
> Parranno allor l'angeliche divise
> e l'oneste parole e i penser casti
> che nel cor giovenil natura mise.
>
> Tanti volti, che Morte e 'l Tempo à guasti,
> torneranno al suo più fiorito stato;
> e vedrassi ove, Amor, tu mi legasti,
>
> ond'io a dito ne sarò mostrato:
> 'Ecco chi pianse sempre, e nel suo pianto
> sovra 'l riso d'ogni altro fu beato!'
>
> E quella di ch'anchor piangendo canto
> avrà gran meraviglia di se stessa,
> vedendosi fra tutte dar il vanto.

(O happy those souls who are, or will be, on their
way to reaching the end of which I speak, whenever
it may be! || And among the other graceful and
peregrine souls, most blessed she whom Death ex-
tinguished much before the natural time! || Then
will appear the angelic looks and honest words and
chaste thoughts that Nature placed in her young
heart. || So many faces, which Death and Time have
ravaged, will return in fullest flower and it will be
seen where you, Love, bound me, || so that I will

---

27   On the synecdochic representation of Laura in the *Rvf*, see for example,
      Mazzotta, *The Worlds of Petrarch*, pp. 9–10 and pp. 78–79; Cesare Segre,
      'Les Isotopies de Laure', in *Exigences et perspectives de la sémiotique:
      recueil d'hommages pour Algirdas Julien Greimas*, ed. by Herman Perret
      and Hans-George Ruprecht, 2 vols (Amsterdam: J Benjamins, 1985),
      II, pp. 811–26; and Freccero, 'The Fig Tree and the Laurel', pp. 34–40.

be singled out: 'Here's one who wept always and,
in his tears, was more blessed than anyone in their
laughter!'. || And she for whom I still weep and
sing will marvel greatly at herself seeing how she is
praised above all the others.) (*TE*, 82–99)

Once more, Petrarch's text takes on a clear eschatological
perspective, emphatically looking forward to the end of
time ('fine'). There is no doubt that the resurrection of
the body will take place ('sono o seranno', 'paranno allor',
'torneranno', 'vedrassi'), and the beginning of this passage
looks like it might be a celebration of that ultimate happiness or *gaudium*, which, theologically, should coincide
with a perfect enjoyment of the *visio Dei*. Instead, Petrarch
takes this as an opportunity to recapitulate his entire erotic
history and its inextricable links to poetry. As the poet
interpolates the god of Love (here *Amor* is the lyric figure
representing eros and not the Christian God) and even
himself into that vision as a kind of celebrity (*TE*, 93–96),
Petrarch's eschatological vision takes a decisive turn back
towards earthly desires. There is a resurgence of the lyric
past in all its specificity and — in Petrarch's case — exclusivity as the poet imagines that when the resurrection of the
body takes place, it will be Laura who will be most beautiful
and blessed, her face standing out among all the rest, the
same face to which Amor first bound him and continues to
do so.

   There is no sense of dispossession or transformation of
the self in Petrarch's vision of eternity here. Instead, what
keeps it together is the persistence and indissolubility of
identity, which is a fundamentally lyric entity that carries
an unwavering and erotic attachment to the corporeal dimension of an individual and their personal history. To
speak of 'lyric' in relation to the *Paradiso* and the *TE* is
precisely to emphasize the corporeal, intersubjective, and

relational aspect of their poetic eschatologies. In Dante's case, we have called 'lyric' that undisciplinable, affective component bound up with the body as the site of desire, memory, and relationality, and ultimately with Beatrice.[28] In Dante, as we have seen, this lyric dimension resists being fully subsumed into the more mystical, self-dissolving union with God that propels the narrative of the *Commedia*, remaining instead in paradoxical tension right to the end of the poem. In Petrarch's *TE* by contrast, the lyric and erotic dimension is the one that takes over, becoming the only element that matters, to the exclusion of everything else, including God. We find neither the experience of *caritas*, nor the radical openness of the self to the Other that is implied by ecstatic union and the *visio Dei*, nor is there any other interest beyond that for Laura herself, with whom the poem exclusively concludes:

> Ne l'età più fiorita e verde avranno
> con immortal bellezza eterna fama.
> Ma innanzi a tutte ch'a rifarsi vanno
> è quella che piangendo il mondo chiama
> con la mia lingua e con la stancha penna:
> ma 'l ciel pur di vederla intera brama.
> A riva un fiume che nasce in Gebenna,
> Amor mi die' per lei sì lunga guerra,
> che la memoria ancora il cor accenna.
> Felice sasso che 'l bel viso serra!
> Che, poi che avrà preso il suo bel velo,
> se fu beato chi la vide in terra,
> or che fia dunque a rivederla in cielo?

---

28   For this understanding of lyric in Dante, see Manuele Gragnolati and Elena Lombardi, 'Volgarizzazione lirica e piacere linguistico in Dante', in *Toscana bilingue (1260–1430). Per una storia sociale del tradurre medievale*, ed. by Sara Bischetti and others (Berlin: de Gruyter, forthcoming); and Francesca Southerden, 'The Lyric Mode', in *The Oxford Handbook of Dante*, ed. by Manuele Gragnolati, Elena Lombardi, and Francesca Southerden (Oxford: Oxford University Press, forthcoming).

(In the most blossoming and greenest age they will have immortal beauty and eternal fame. But supreme among all those who will be remade || is she for whom the world cries out, weeping, with my tongue and my weary pen, while heaven's only desire is to see her whole again. || Along a riverbank that rises in Gebenna, Love gave me so long a war for her, that my heart still preserves the memory. || Happy the gravestone that encloses that face! For when she will have put on again her mortal veil, if it was bliss to see her on earth, || what will it be to see her again in heaven?) (*TE*, 133–45)

While we do remain within the Christian framework of heavenly eternity, there is no reference to Christ, the Trinity, or God, but only to the never-ending fame and beauty that the blessed will enjoy, Laura above all. It is in equal parts an eschatological and lyric fantasy, which culminates with intense yearning for a vision of Laura's body alone. The poet even states without irony that all of heaven desires, with almost cupidinous force (the word Petrarch uses is 'brama'), to look upon Laura's body in its restored corporeal wholeness and to celebrate her exceptional and enduring beauty and fame ('dar il vanto'). In other words, the experience of heaven has a place only to validate the supremacy of Laura's image in relation to Petrarch's gaze and to the resurrected landscape of his heart. As the memory of the lyric past floods back, the prospect of entering a celestial Jerusalem (if it ever existed) is completely supplanted by the vision of a new and timeless Vaucluse transposed into this paradise at the end of time (139–41). The reader is led back all the way to the 'loco chiuso' (enclosed place) with which the *Triumphi* began (*Triumphus Cupidinis* I, 8), i.e., to the scene of both the writing subject's dream and his subjection to Love, here both redeemed and valourized in light of the final, imagined vision of Laura's resurrected body.[29] In this vision of eternity, God cannot but be absent: within the confines of Petrarch's redeemed lyric universe of the *Triumphi*, when Laura will be restored to presence, if she takes God's place, He will be relegated below, in a stunning reversal of the substitution of the beloved by the Virgin Mary in *Rvf* 366.[30]

Being 'beato' (144) in this fantasy does not mean fusing with God but re-experiencing in heaven, in an even more wondrous manner, the pleasure of gazing on Laura on earth. Yet notwithstanding its vertical drive and final burst of lyric energy, the *TE* ends not with a sense of fullness but rather with a kind of suspension, conveyed both in the still-unrealized status of wish and in the hypothetical and interrogative mode of the closing lines. We are reminded of the 'almost mode' that marked the poet's vision of heaven in *Rvf* 302, which, as analysed in Chapter 5, similarly resisted certainty, closure, and perfection. In the sonnet, the lyric fantasy is one of interaction with the beloved, which brings pleasure but appears tenuous from the start and doesn't last; in the *TE*, the ultimate pleasure is projected towards the timeless future and therefore envisaged as lasting, but it hasn't happened yet and also lacks intimacy and reciprocation. Laura remains an object of beauty to be contemplated at a distance, rather than the subject of an interaction that would truly allow for an intersubjective experience of affective union.

---

29 Cf. *Triumphus Cupidinis* I, 8, and Marco Ariani's intertextual reading of the two moments of the work in Francesco Petrarca, *Triumphi*, ed. by Marco Ariani (Milan: Mursia, 1988): 'è dunque il corpo glorioso di Madonna che fa rifiorire la landa desolata del tempo annientato: il topos del plazer primaverile, corroso all'inizio del poema, ritorna, alla fine, in un cerchio perfettamente concluso, radicalmente riavvalorato' (p. 384).

30 See Southerden, *Dante and Petrarch in the Garden of Language.*

As outlined above in the final cantos of Dante's *Paradiso*, with the collapse of eschatology into poetry there is a resurrection of lyric textuality, whereby the pilgrim actually experiences the resurrection, and the poem replicates its fullness in the text. Everything is simultaneously present in a form of openness that paradoxically preserves and extends desire and memory into the eschatological present of the resurrection itself. By contrast, Petrarch's language is less dazzling, and what seems to be missing is precisely the fullness that feels so present in the *Paradiso*'s 'jumping' textuality. One could say that the *TE* is therefore lyric in a different way. For Petrarch, the moment of ultimate reunion with Laura can be imagined, and the subject can gain satisfaction from the fantasy, but it cannot be experienced or expressed except between the lines and, as the final — open — question testifies, at the very margins of the text. In other words, with the textual 'fireworks' Dante stages at the end of the *Paradiso*, the pilgrim's own desire and will ('disio' and '*velle*') are brought into a perfect cosmological circulation with 'l'amor che move il sole e l'altre stelle' (*Par.* XXXIII, 142–45); but at the end of the *TE*, the fulfilment of desire is deferred with a quintessentially Petrarchan sense of non-closure.[31] Dante's *Paradiso* is sustained by presence, to the extent that even when, as in *Paradiso* XIV, the body is felt as absent, the lack of it can still be celebrated as joyous. In Petrarch, by contrast, a sense of virtuality, even spectrality, remains, and what is absent really *isn't* there: in the *Rerum vulgarium fragmenta* Laura dissolves even when she comes back (see, for example, *Rvf* 359), and in the *TE*, the lack of her *mortal corpo* remains irreducible even in the face of its promised return at the end of time as indicated by the reference to the 'happy gravestone' (felice

---

31   Cf. Heyworth, *Desiring Bodies*, pp. 179–227 (p. 218).

sasso, 143) that the poet still covets.[32] As Jennifer Rush-worth has noted, the poet and the world continue to mourn for Laura ('quella che *piangendo* il mondo chiama | con la mia lingua', 136–37), and 'in the rhyme of "chiama" and "brama", Laura emerges as an unlocatable absence, a denizen of neither heaven nor earth'.[33]

Rather than encounter the extraordinary fullness and realization of the *Paradiso*, we find here another, equally extraordinary, form of intensity, this time based on distance, incompletion, and deferral: the delay in desire's ultimate fulfilment and the quite radical gesture of supplanting God with Laura while still contemplating her from a distance are still forms of pleasure for Petrarch. As we have seen throughout this book, in this paradoxical form of desire, fore-pleasure counts as much as end-pleasure, and the subject seeks to remain in that state as long as possible since it too can be — paradoxically — satisfying.[34]

---

32   A similar fantasy of the resurrection of Laura's body is found in poems such as *Rvf* 302, 313, 319, and 362.

33   Rushworth, *Discourses of Mourning*, p. 84.

34   See especially the discussion of Bersani's concept of masochistic pleasure in Chapters 1 and 2 of this book.

Radure / Clearings
ANTONELLA ANEDDA ANGIOY

a Pia Pera

Translation by Jamie McKendrick

Tra il dicembre 1933 e il gennaio 1934 Osip Mandel'štam traduce per la 'Vsemirniaia literatura' quattro sonetti da Francesco Petrarca. Sono gli stessi anni del saggio della 'Conversazione su Dante'. Lo aspettano le poesie dei 'Quaderni di Voronež', le 'Ottave', il confino, il carcere e infine la morte, nel 1937 in un campo di transito. Secondo il racconto di un racconto fatto a Ilja Eremburg e sempre negato dalla moglie Nadežda, Mandel'štam avrebbe letto Petrarca ai compagni di detenzione.

Cosa aggiungono le traduzioni di Mandel'štam agli studi su Petrarca? E cosa aggiunge la lettura di Petrarca a una ulteriore comprensione dell'opera di Mandel'štam? Probabilmente la possibilità di continuare il lavoro assegnato dallo stesso Mandel'štam ai suoi interlocutori: ripercorrere i testi, interrogarli di nuovo rendendoli vicini, azzerare il tempo per farlo rivivere nello spazio del linguaggio.

Gli studi su Mandel'štam traduttore di Petrarca concordano, anche se con diversi punti di vista, sul fatto che non si tratta di traduzioni ma di riscritture, versioni, variazioni. Forse un altro modo per definirle è 'virate', virate del respiro petrarchesco. *Virata di respiro* infatti è una delle possibili traduzioni di *Atemwende*, il titolo di una raccolta di versi di Paul Celan. Celan è il primo a tradurre Mandel'štam traghettandolo in tedesco, il primo a vedere nella sua opera quello stratificarsi minerale, quella capacità di conciliare distanza e prossimità in un nodo di luce-suono-senso che ne farà l'interlocutore di altri grandi poeti come Philippe Jaccottet.

'Virata' è anche un termine nautico. Ancora di Paul Celan i versi finali della lirica 'Lösspuppen' (Crisalidi di Löss), che allude all'esilio di Mandel'štam: 'Petrarca | ist wieder | in Sicht' (Petrarca è di nuovo in vista). Cosa significa?

Between December 1933 and January 1934 Osip Mandel-
stam translated four of Petrarch's sonnets for 'Vsemirniaia lit-
eratura'. It was during these years that he wrote 'Conversation
about Dante'. Ahead of him lay the poems of the 'Voronezh
Notebooks' and the 'Octaves', his internal exile, prison, and
then his death in a transit camp in 1937. According to a
story recounted to Ilya Erenburg and always denied by his
wife Nadezhda, Mandelstam read out Petrarch to his fellow
prisoners.

What do Mandelstam's translations add to Petrarch studies? And what does a reading of Petrarch add to a further
understanding of Mandelstam's work? My belief is that
they act as a spur to continue that work which Mandelstam
himself assigns to his 'addressees': to reread the texts, to
bring them closer by further questioning, to annul time so
as to make it live again in the space of language.

Studies on Mandelstam as a translator of Petrarch
agree, even if from differing perspectives, on the fact that
these are not translations but rewritings, versions, variations. Perhaps another way to define them would be *virate*
(turns, veerings, or tackings), veerings from the Petrarchan
breath. *Breathturn*, in fact, is one of the possible translations of *Atemwende*, the title of one of Paul Celan's poetry
books. Celan was the first translator to ferry Mandelstam
into German, the first to see in his work that mineral strat-
ification, that ability to reconcile distance and closeness in
a knot of light-sound-sense that will make him the ideal
addressee of other great poets such as Philippe Jaccottet.

'Tacking' is primarily a nautical term. Staying with
Paul Celan, the final lines of his poem 'Lösspuppen' (Loess
Dolls) which alludes to Mandelstam's exile: 'Petrarca | ist
wieder | in Sicht' (Petrarch's | in sight | again). What does

Petrarca è vicino, avvistabile, ancora una volta possibile per l'Occidente. Con l'istinto rabdomantico che lo contrad-distingue Celan stabilisce il legame Petrarca-Mandel'štam. Probabilmente, come nota Andrea Cortellessa nel saggio 'Petrarca è di nuovo in vista', Celan non conosceva, perché non ancora pubblicate, le traduzioni di Mandel'štam da Petrarca. Eppure potremmo dire in un precipitare che Celan 'sa' che Mandel'štam 'sapeva già' quello che Petrarca sapeva e teneva in serbo per noi. In 'Es ist alles anders' (È tutto diverso), una delle due poesie di *Die Niemandsrose* dedicate a Mandel'štam, si legge:

> der Name Ossip kommt auf dich zu, du erzählst ihm,
> was er schon weiß [...]
> — was abriß, wächst wieder zusammen —
> da hast du sie, da nimm sie dir, da hast du alle beide,
> den Namen, den Namen, die Hand, die Hand,
> da nimm sie dir zum Unterpfand,
> er nimmt auch das, und du hast,
> wieder, was dein ist, was sein war
>
> (Il nome Ossip ti viene incontro, tu gli racconti
> quel che sa già [...]
> — quanto divelto si salda di nuovo —
> eccoli, prendili, eccoli entrambi,
> il nome, il nome, la mano, la mano,
> ecco prenditeli in pegno,
> lui prende anche questo, e tu hai
> di nuovo ciò che è tuo, ciò che era suo)

Tu gli racconti quel che sa già. Avere di nuovo ciò che è tuo, che è nostro, significa ritrovarlo all'indietro. Ciò che è tuo, nostro, ritorna attraverso ciò che è stato nelle parole di un morto. I corpi che abbiamo conosciuto e amato: mani e nomi sono stati dati in pegno perché, appunto, 'quanto divelto si saldi di nuovo'.

this mean? Petrarch is nearby, discernible, still possible for the West. With that rhabdomantic instinct which distinguishes Celan, he establishes, without placing them in direct contact, the Petrarch-Mandelstam link. Probably, as Cortellessa notes, Celan did not know Mandelstam's Petrarch translations as they had yet to be published. Still, we might say (in a cascading sequence) that Celan 'knew' what Mandelstam 'already knew' what Petrarch knew and kept safe for us. In 'Es ist alles anders' (Everything's different), one of the two poems in *Die Niemandsrose* dedicated to Mandelstam, we read:

> der Name Ossip kommt auf dich zu, du erzählst ihm,
> was er schon weiß [...]
> — was abriß, wächst wieder zusammen —
> da hast du sie, da nimm sie dir, da hast du alle beide,
> den Namen, den Namen, die Hand, die Hand,
> da nimm sie dir zum Unterpfand,
> er nimmt auch das, und du hast,
> wieder, was dein ist, was sein war

> (The name Osip walks up to you, and you tell him
> what he knows already, [...]
> — what was severed joins up again —
> there you have it, so take it, there you have them both,
> the name, the name, the hand, the hand,
> so take them, keep them as a pledge,
> he takes it too, and you have
> again what is yours, what was his)

You tell him what he already <u>knows</u>. To repossess what is yours, what is ours, means to find again what lies behind us. That which is yours, ours, returns via what lay in the words of a dead man. The bodies we have known and loved: hands and names have been given in pledge because, precisely, 'what was severed joins up again'.

Nelle sue traduzioni Mandel'štam rimodula, adattandolo
alla lingua russa e alla propria voce, tutto di Petrarca, torce
il collo alle traduzioni precedenti, le spoglia di qualsiasi pe-
trarchismo facendo suo quello che ammirava della lingua
dei naturalisti, e di Charles Darwin in particolare, elimi-
nando ogni retorica, spalancando, come scrive in *Viaggio
in Armenia*, in chi legge una 'radura'.

Nella traduzione dal sonetto 164 di Petrarca che ho
scelto di ripercorrere si ritrovano molti elementi della gran-
dezza di Mandel'štam: cortocircuiti vertiginosi tra suono-
senso, fisicità musicale e architettonica, distesa dello spazio
e acuto del tempo. Il linguaggio evade dalle grate, scappa in
avanti in un movimento che cerca lo scorrere dell'acqua, la
libertà. Tra quelli tradotti da Mandel'štam, il sonetto 164 è
l'unico 'in vita di Madonna Laura' eppure 'Laura non c'è',
anzi 'è andata via' — per usare le parole di Andrea Zanzotto
(grande lettore di Petrarca e di Celan), che cita a sua volta
una nota canzone del Festival di san Remo. In questo caso
Laura s'identifica in Olga Vaskel, morta suicida a Stoccol-
ma. L'amore è andato via dissolto dal destino, incalzato
dalla storia.

Così, se è vero che, come nota Irina Semenko, la 'catastrofe spirituale di Petrarca diventa in Mandel'štam una
catastrofe geologica', è altrettanto vero che in questa di-
scesa, come in altre liriche, Mandel'štam trova non solo
fossili ma radici: 'Mi piego alle umili radici', scriveva in uno
dei versi più belli dei *Quaderni di Voronež*. Petrarca *è* una
radice. Mandel'štam si china continuamente sulla lingua
italiana, legge Petrarca lasciandosi attraversare da ricordi
di voci passate, 'risponde' facendo 'risonare contemporaneamente le voci di Orazio, Puškin, l'epos russo, Belyj'
(Bonola) per guardare meglio in faccia ogni perdita, per
rendere il linguaggio, duttile, vivo, coraggioso.

In his translations Mandelstam reshapes, adapting to the Russian language and his own voice, all of Petrarch, twists the neck of the previous translations, strips them of whatever Petrarchan mannerism, and makes his own what he admired in the language of the naturalists and of Charles Darwin in particular: eliminating all rhetoric, opening wide, as he writes in *Journey to Armenia*, a 'clearing' in whoever reads.

In his translation of sonnet 164 (that I've chosen to dwell on) many of the elements that reveal Mandelstam's genius can be found: vertiginous short-circuits of sound and sense, a musical and architectonic physicality, an extension of space and a compression of time. Language throws off its chains, and escapes in a movement like the flow of water, like freedom. Among the sonnets that Mandelstam translates, this is the only one in which 'Madonna Laura' is still alive, although 'Laura is not present' or rather 'has gone off somewhere' to use the expression of Andrea Zanzotto (excellent reader both of Petrarch and of Celan), who in turn quotes a well-known song from the San Remo Festival. In this case Laura assumes the identity of Olga Vaskel, who died by suicide in Stockholm. Love has gone off, undone by destiny, pursued by history.

So, if it's true, as Irina Semenko claims, that 'Petrarch's spiritual catastrophe becomes in Mandelstam a geological catastrophe', it's equally true that in this descent, Mandelstam finds not only fossils but also roots: 'To these humble roots obedient' he wrote in one of the most beautiful lines from the *Voronezh Notebooks*. Petrarch *is* a root. Mandelstam continually leans down over the Italian language: he reads Petrarch letting him be traversed by memories of earlier voices, 'he replies' by making 'the voices of Horace, Pushkin, the Russian epos, Bely resonate at the same time' (Bonola) but so as better to confront every loss, to render the language ductile, alive, courageous.

Tutto torna: Petrarca è Petra e Arca (Corrado Bologna). Come non pensare che Pietra (*Kamien*) è la traduzione del primo libro di Mandel'štam, il cui riferimento spaziale è Pietroburgo, città di Pietro, pietra su cui edificare altre pietre?

In un saggio del 1921 intitolato 'La parola e la cultura' Mandel'štam aveva scritto 'tutto questo è già esistito'. E aveva aggiunto che il poeta non teme la ripetizione. Non teme infatti di intitolare *Tristia* la sua seconda raccolta ritrovando i *Tristia* di Ovidio. Allo stesso modo le traduzioni da Petrarca si ri-frammentano e si rifrangono per schegge nelle poesie dal 1933 al 1937, quando la dialettica poesia–potere diventa inseguimento della poesia da parte del potere incarnato nel secolo–lupo. Non a caso, nella variazione dal sonetto 164 c'è il fiutare, che appare anche nell'attacco della poesia contro Stalin, recitata — sembra — davanti a un funzionario di polizia, nel 1933: 'Viviamo senza fiutare più sotto di noi il paese'. Fiutare significa percepire fisicamente la terra, sentirla concretamente sotto di sé e dover fiutare per non mettere i piedi nel vuoto.

(È sempre Zanzotto a correggere l'immagine di un Petrarca cortigiano sostituendola con quella di un poeta moderno, tanto in anticipo sui tempi da essere consapevole del prezzo da pagare per avere uno spazio dove scrivere, pensare).

Senza alcuna pretesa di tradurre dal russo, cercando a tentoni ogni parola, sviscerandola e interrogandola sono ritornata attraverso Mandel'štam a Petrarca e attraverso Petrarca di nuovo a Mandel'štam. Qui di seguito compaiono quattro testi: il sonetto 164 di Petrarca, la versione di Mandel'štam, la traduzione di Irina Semenko e infine una mia lettura offerta come una possibilità, un possibile spalancamento di linguaggio, una sua radura.

Everything returns: Petrarch is Petrus and Arc (as Bologna notes). How can one not think that 'pietra' (stone) is the Italian translation of Mandelstam's first book *Kamien*, whose geographic reference is St. Petersburg, Peter the Great's city, to build which stone has been placed on stone.

In a 1921 essay titled 'The Word and Culture' Mandelstam wrote 'all this has happened before'. And he added that the poet does not fear repetition. He had no fear in titling his second collection *Tristia* with its re-evocation of Ovid. Likewise the translations from Petrarch fragment again and reform from splinters in the poems from 1933–37 when the dialectic poetry-power becomes the persecution of poetry by power incarnated in the wolf-century. It's not incidental that, in the variations of sonnet 164, the same Russian word for 'sniff' or 'sense' appears in his Stalin epigram which says, as though before a commissar: 'We live without feeling the country beneath us'. To sniff here means to physically perceive the earth, to sense it concretely beneath one's feet so as not to step into the void.

(It's once again Zanzotto who corrects the image of a courtly Petrarch, substituting that with the figure of a modern poet, so far in advance of his time as to be aware of the price he had to pay for a space in which to write and think.)

Without any claim to have translated from the Russian, groping for every word, turning it inside out, and questioning its interstices, I have returned via Mandelstam to Petrarch, and once more via Petrarch to Mandelstam. Here follow four texts: Petrarch's sonnet 164, Mandelstam's version, the translation of Irina Semenko, and finally my own reading offered as a possibility, a possible opening up of language, a clearing.

Or che 'l ciel et la terra e 'l vento tace
et le fere e gli augelli il sonno affrena,
Notte il carro stellato in giro mena
et nel suo letto il mar senz'onda giace,

vegghio, penso, ardo, piango; et chi mi sface
sempre m'è inanzi per mia dolce pena:
guerra è 'l mio stato, d'ira et di duol piena,
et sol di lei pensando ò qualche pace.

Così sol d'una chiara fonte viva
move 'l dolce et l'amaro ond'io mi pasco;
una man sola mi risana et punge;

e perché 'l mio martir non giunga a riva,
mille volte il dì moro et mille nasco,
tanto da la salute mia son lunge.
(Petrarca, *Rvf* 164)

Когда уснет земля и жар отпышет,
А на душе зверей покой лебяжий,
Ходит по кругу ночь с горящей пряжей,
И мощь воды морской зефир колышет, —

Чую, горю, рвусь, плачу - и не слышит,
В неудержимой близости все та же:
Целую ночь, целую ночь на страже
И вся как есть далеким счастьем дышит.

Хоть ключ один - вода разноречива,
Полужестка, полусладка.
Ужели Одна и та же милая двулична…

Тысячу раз на дню, себе на диво,
Я должен умереть на самом деле
И воскресаю так же сверхобычно.
(Osip Mandel'štam, *Polnoe sobranie sochinenii*, I, p. 190)

Now heaven and earth are hushed and the wind doesn't stir,
the beasts of the field and the fowls of the air
succumb to sleep, and night's starry chariot wheels above
and the sea lies abed without the heave of a wave,

I stay awake and brood and yearn and weep:
always before me stands that sweet destructive grief.
At war within, wracked with anger and pain —
only the thought of her gives some faint relief.

So from a single clear and living fountain
flow the sweet and the bitter waters I take;
a single hand both wounds and heals me,

and since my torment is a shoreless sea
a thousand times a day I die and am reborn,
and ever further off's the cure I crave.
(Petrarch translated by JM)

Когда уснет земля и жар отпышет,
А на душе зверей покой лебяжий,
Ходит по кругу ночь с горящей пряжей,
И мощь воды морской зефир колышет, —

Чую, горю, рвусь, плачу - и не слышит,
В неудержимой близости все та же:
Целую ночь, целую ночь на страже
И вся как есть далеким счастьем дышит.

Хоть ключ один - вода разноречива,
Полужестка, полусладка.
Ужели Одна и та же милая двулична...

Тысячу раз на дню, себе на диво,
Я должен умереть на самом деле
И воскресаю так же сверхобычно.
(Osip Mandelstam, *Polnoe sobranie sochinenii*, I, p. 190)

Quando la terra s'assopisce e la calura s'estingue
e nell'anima delle fiere c'è una calma da cigno,
la notte gira attorno con una filatura ardente
e la possanza dell'acqua lo zefiro marino dondola.

Fiuto, ardo, bramo, piango — e non ascolta
nell'irrefrenabile vicinanza sempre lei;
l'intera notte, l'intera notte di guardia
e tutta com'è spira di lontana felicità.

Benché la fonte sia una sola, l'acqua è discorde,
per metà crudele, per metà dolce. Davvero
è la stessa, una sola amata bifronte?

Mille volte al giorno, a me stesso meraviglia,
io devo morire proprio per davvero
e risorgo altrettanto miracolosamente.
(Mandel'štam, tradotto da Irina Semenko)

Quando la terra si addormenta e la canicola si spegne
e nell'animo delle bestie c'è la pace del Cigno
la notte gira in tondo con la sua filatura ardente
e la forza del mare muove un'onda-gelatina.

Fiuto, brucio, piango — e lei non sente,
in questa poca distanza inarrestabile sempre lei:
l'intera notte l'intera notte di guardia
e tutto — così com'è — respira una felicità distante.

C'è una sola fonte, eppure l'acqua è discorde
semi–dura, semi-dolce, — è possibile
che la stessa adorata sia bifronte?

Mille volte al giorno, meravigliandomi
devo davvero morire
e resuscitare in modo altrettanto straordinario.
(AAA)

Mandel'štam usa davvero nei confronti di questo sonetto
'una memoria rimpatriante' (Berman). Non solo guarda a
una costellazione di nomi che vanno da Virgilio (forse da
Alcmane?) a Ovidio, a Puškin, ma permette a chi legge di
decifrare ulteriormente la condizione di chi scrive. Siamo

When earth falls asleep and the heat dies down,
And the animals feel a swanlike calm,
Night goes around with her burning yarn,
And a zephyr lulls the seawater's strength, -

I sense, burn, strive, and sob — she doesn't hear,
Unchanging in the elusive nearness:
All night, all night I am vigilant
While she exudes a distant joy.

Though the spring is one, the water is contradictory,
Half-hard, half-sweet. Can it be
That one and the same darling is two-faced …

A thousand times a day, to my amazement,
I must die in point of fact
And rise again just as preternaturally.
(Mandelstam translated by Philippe Leon Redko)

When the earth falls asleep and the dog star is doused
and the Swan's peace possesses the souls of animals
the night circles with its fiery threadwork
and the sea's strength can barely lift a candied wave;

I sniff, I burn, I weep — and she feels nothing,
at that brief relentless distance always her:
the whole night the whole night on guard awake
and everything — as it is — breathes a remote joy.

That has a single source, and yet the water's discordant,
half-hard, half-soft — could it be
the beloved herself is double-featured?

A thousand times a day, I marvel at myself,
as I die and then in an equally
miraculous manner once more revive.
(AAA translated by JM)

Mandelstam does indeed, as Berman claims, employ 'a re-
patriating memory' in his treatment of this sonnet. He not
only looks to a constellation of names from Virgil (perhaps
via Alcman?) to Ovid, and on to Pushkin, but also allows
the reader ultimately to construe the writer's condition. We

nel 1934 al culmine delle purghe staliniste. Mandel'štam
traduce Petrarca incalzato dalla consapevolezza della sua
futura detenzione e morte. Basterà tornare su alcune immagini: la notte ruota in cerchio come ruotano in cerchio
i detenuti e i pazzi (come nel quadro di Van Gogh del
manicomio di Arles?), la notte si intreccia alla veglia della
guardia.

L'uomo che scrive è consapevole del suo stato: febbrile
('жар' nel primo verso è anche il calore della febbre) in
preda alle allucinazioni, tentato dal suicidio in ospedale.

Il ritmo lento e quieto della notte di Petrarca diventa
nelle versione di Mandel'štam asmatico, l'arsura cerca di
estinguersi nelle tregue del testo, nell'acqua marina, nel
vento occidentale: lo zefiro. Nella scelta di questa parola,
Mandel'štam ribadisce come il suo linguaggio, anche il più
legato alla tradizione, si misuri con la realtà. Ripercorriamo
l'ultimo verso della prima quartina nella traduzione di Irina
Semenko: 'la possanza', la forza dell'acqua, muove, 'dondola', lo zefiro. '[Z]ephir' è certamente lo zefiro, il vento
che abita tutta l'opera di Petrarca ma 'zephir' è anche un
dolce di albume leggero e gelatinoso molto diffuso in Russia. Mandel'štam mantiene la sonorità di zefiro, ma forse
non era indifferente alla evocazione, al richiamo concreto
di un cibo popolare. L'onda del mare ondeggia, trema come
una gelatina. Chissà se avrà agito la memoria delle classi
elementari nella cultura ebraica in cui i bambini imparano
l'alfabeto mangiando le lettere di pasta spalmate di mie-
le. Per questo approfittando delle possibilità che sfuggono
dalle grate di questi versi ho sovrapposto alla versione 'la
possanza dell'acqua marina muove lo zefiro' la variazione
dell'onda-gelatina, un'immagine di golosità infantile (ma
Mandel'štam è autore anche di poesie per bambini).

are in 1934 at the height of the Stalinist purges. Mandelstam translates Petrarch pursued by an awareness of his
future detention and death. Several images immediately
suggest this: the night circles much as the prisoners and the
mad wheel in a circle (as in the painting by Van Gogh of the
asylum in Arles?), the night is woven into the sentries on
guard.

The man who writes is aware of his state: feverish
('жар' in the first line also signifies the heat of a fever), prey
to hallucinations, tempted by suicide in the hospital.

The night's slow, calm rhythm in Petrarch becomes
asthmatic and feverish in Mandelstam's version, the
scorching heat tries to douse itself in the poem's pauses, in
the sea water, in the west wind: the Zephyr. In choosing
this word, Mandelstam reveals how his language, even
when most tied to tradition, measures itself against
reality. The word certainly refers to the wind which blows
throughout Petrarch's work, but 'zephyr' is also a sweet
made from a light, jellied egg yolk which was very common
in Russia. Mandelstam retains the classical sonority of the
word, but was perhaps far from indifferent to the chance
of evoking, of making concrete reference to a popular
food. The wave of the sea ripples, and trembles like a
jelly. Who knows if the image awoke in him the memory
of elementary classes in Jewish culture where children
learn the alphabet by eating the pastry letters spread with
honey. So making the most of the possibilities of freedom
that translation provides, I've substituted for the line 'And
a zephyr lulls the seawater's strength' the variant of the
wave that trembles like a jelly, an image of childhood's
greedy appetite — and Mandelstam did, in fact, write
poems for children.

E ancora, nella prima terzina, come in Petrarca (Semenko) anche qui l'amore è contemporaneamente assenza, distanza e presenza, la morte contempla una possibile
rinascita quotidiana. Petrarca distende lo sguardo, rallenta,
dilata, Mandel'štam mette un campo di forze in tensione,
non guarda al cielo ma alla terra. C'è il moto delle ma-
ree, ma anche il dettaglio quotidiano oltre che letterario
(pensiamo a Ovidio) del filare, della stoffa tessuta, della matassa, della filatura — 'пряжа' — che è ardente, in
fiamme: 'горящей'. Mandel'štam parla di un mondo reale,
legato ai commerci, ma anche — è solo un'ipotesi — alla
loro distruzione, a roghi di negozi e case, ai tanti pogrom
del passato, all'intuizione degli orrori futuri.

Leggiamo Petrarca: 'Notte il carro stellato in giro mena',
e poi Mandel'štam: 'la notte gira attorno con una filatura
ardente'. Il respiro di Petrarca, 'le fere e gli augelli il sonno
affrena', si contrae nel confronto tra l'animo delle bestie
e la pace da cigno, che sembra contrapporre la verticalità
dei monti alla orizzontalità calma dello scivolare dei cigni
sull'acqua ma anche forse alludere alla costellazione estiva
del Cigno in possibile dialogo con 'жар' (appunto calore
febbricitante) che nella mia rilettura è diventato canicola.

È vero, Petrarca distingue simmetricamente i
verbi 'veggio e penso' da 'ardo e piango' (Semenko).
Mandel'štam invece inizia la quartina con un'altra
percezione. Non è lo sguardo, ma l'olfatto. Al posto di
vedere, fiuta: 'Чую cuju' è fiutare, fiuta le tracce del suo
desiderio ma fiuta anche la terra, e il dolore per la Russia.

Non c'è malinconia. Mandel'štam trascina Petrarca
nella storia russa del Novecento, mette una scheggia di al-
larme nella trama originale inserendo il termine 'страже',
che evoca la sentinella di guardia. La sentinella controlla
ma anche avvisa, vede.

And we can see that in the first tercet, as in Petrarch, love is at once absence, distance, and presence, and death promises a possible daily rebirth (Semenko). Petrarch distends the gaze, slows it down, and dilates it; Mandelstam puts a force field in place, looking not to the heavens but the earth. There is the force of the tides, but also beyond the literary, the quotidian detail (recalling Ovid) of spinning, of woven material, of hanks of wool, of spun threads — 'пряжа' — which are flaming, on fire: 'горящей'. Mandelstam speaks of an actual world, with the ties of commerce, but also — this is only conjecture — of their destruction, of shops and houses set alight, of the many pogroms in the past, and an intuition of future horrors.

Let's look again at Petrarch: 'night's starry chariot wheels above', and then Mandelstam: 'Night goes around with her burning yarn'. The breath of Petrarch, 'beasts' and 'fowls' that 'succumb to sleep', is contracted into the souls of animals and the swan's peace, which seems to set the verticality of the mountains against the calm horizontal gliding of swans over the water but perhaps also alludes to the summer constellation of the Swan in possible dialogue with 'жар' (feverish heat), which in my rereading becomes the dog star.

As Semenko registers, Petrarch symmetrically distinguishes the verbs 'see and think' and 'burn and weep'. Mandelstam, by contrast, begins the quatrain with another sense perception. It's not the visual, but the olfactory. Instead of seeing, he smells: 'Чую cuju' is to sniff, he sniffs the traces of his desire, but he also sniffs the earth, and sorrow for Russia.

There's no melancholy here. Mandelstam drags Petrarch into Russian twentieth-century history, puts a splinter of alarm into the original weft by inserting the term 'страже', which evokes the figure of the sentry. The sentry guards but also warns and oversees.

Per questo 'Petrarca è di nuovo in vista'. Mandel'štam lo fa ri-vivere, consegnando a noi che leggiamo, pieni di dubbi, confusi dai nostri errori, quello che la sua poesia sapeva già. Questo mi pare sia il senso dell'ultimo verso della versione di Mandel'štam: risorgere, ogni giorno, mille volte, nel modo straordinariamente ('сверхобычн' è straordinario) terreno che è concesso a noi umani.

Grazie agli studi di Antoine Berman, Corrado Bologna, Anna Bonola, Clarence Brown, Manuela Calusio, Piero Cazzola, Andrea Cortellessa, Cesare G. De Michelis, Tom Dolock, Riccardo Donati, Daria Farafonova, Anna Glazova, Peter Hainsworth, Seamus Heaney, Philippe Jaccottet, Ermanno Krumm, Nadežda Mandel'štam, Jamie McKendrick, Camilla Miglio, Igor' A. Pil'ščikov, Renato Poggioli, Philippe Leon Redko, Barbara Ronchetti, Irina Semenko, Natascia Tonelli, Serena Vitale, Andrea Zanzotto.

Grazie a Manuele Gragnolati e a Francesca Southerden che coinvolgendomi in questo lavoro mi hanno fatto riavvistare Petrarca.

In this way, 'Petrarch's in sight again'. Mandelstam makes him live again, consigning to us his readers, full of doubt, confused by our own errors, that which his poetry already knew. It seems to me that this is the sense behind the final line of Mandelstam's version: to rise again, every day, a thousand times, in the extraordinary ('сверхобычн' means extraordinary) earthly manner conceded to us humans.

With thanks to the work of Antoine Berman, Corrado Bologna, Anna Bonola, Clarence Brown, Manuela Calusio, Piero Cazzola, Andrea Cortellessa, Cesare G. De Michelis, Tom Dolock, Riccardo Donati, Daria Farafonova, Anna Glazova, Peter Hainsworth, Seamus Heaney, Philippe Jaccottet, Ermanno Krumm, Nadezhda Mandelstam, Jamie McKendrick, Camilla Miglio, Igor A. Pilshchikov, Renato Poggioli, Philippe Leon Redko, Barbara Ronchetti, Irina Semenko, Natascia Tonelli, Serena Vitale, Andrea Zanzotto.

With thanks to Manuele Gragnolati and Francesca Southerden who by inviting me to participate in this work have made me reread and rethink Petrarch.

WORKS CONSULTED

Berman, Antoine, *L'Épreuve de l'étranger. Culture et traduction dans l'Allemagne romantique: Herder, Goethe, Schlegel, Novalis, Humboldt, Schleiermacher, Hölderlin* (Paris: Gallimard, 1984)

Bologna, Corrado, 'PetrArca petroso', *Critica del testo*, 6.1 (2003), pp. 366–420

Bonola, Anna, 'Traduzione e impulso creativo. Un sonetto di Petrarca nella versione russa di Osip E. Mandel'štam', *L'analisi linguistica e letteraria*, 11.1 (2003), pp. 29–73

Brown, Clarence, *Mandelstam*, rev. edn (Cambridge: Cambridge University Press, 2010)

Cazzola, Piero, 'Osip Mandel'štam, traduttore russo del Petrarca', in *Dynamique d'une expansion culturelle: Pétrarque en Europe, XIVe–XXe siècle; Actes du XXVIe Congrès International du CEFI, Turin et Chambéry, 11–15 décembre 1995: À la Mémoire de Franco Simone* (Paris: Champion, 2001), pp. 401–13

Celan, Paul, 'Everything's different' (Es ist alles anders), in *Selected Poems*, trans. by Michael Hamburger, rev. edn (London: Penguin, 1996)

——'Loess Dolls' (Lösspuppen), in *Snow Part = Schneepart: and other poems (1968-1969)*, trans. by Iain Fairley (Manchester: Carcanet, 2007)

——*Poesie*, ed. by Moshe Kahn and Marcella Bagnasco (Milan: Mondadori, 1976)

Cortellessa, Andrea, 'Petrarca è di nuovo in vista', in *'Un'altra storia. Petrarca nel Novecento italiano'*, atti del Convegno di Roma, 4–6 ottobre 2001, ed. by Andrea Cortellessa (Rome: Bulzoni, 2004), pp. i–xxxi

De Michelis, Cesare G., 'Mandel'štam in URSS', *Rassegna sovietica*, 4 (1970), pp. 5–11

Dolack, Tom, 'Ventriloquio autobiografico: Mandelstam traduttore di Petrarca', *Intersezioni*, 27.3 (2007), pp. 475–86

Glazova, Anna, 'Poetry of Bringing about Presence: Paul Celan translates Osip Mandelstam', *MLN*, Comparative Literature Issue, 123.5 (2008), pp. 1108–26 <https://doi.org/10.1353/mln.0.0073>

Hainsworth, Peter, *Petrarch the Poet: An Introduction to 'Rerum vulgarium fragmenta'* (New York: Routledge, 2014)

Heaney, Seamus, *The Government of the Tongue* (London: Faber and Faber, 1988)

Jaccottet, Philippe, *D'une lyre à cinq cordes* (Paris: Gallimard, 1997)

—— *A partir du mot Russie* (Montpellier: Fata Morgana, 2002)

Mandelstam, Nadezhda Jakovlevna, *Le mie memorie con poesie e altri scritti di Osip Mandel'štam*, trans. by Serena Vitale (Milan: Garzanti, 1972)

Mandelstam, Osip, *Cinquanta poesie*, ed. by Remo Faccani (Turin: Einaudi, 1998)

—— *Polnoe sobranie sochinenii i pisem v trekh tomakh*, ed. by A. G. Mets, 3 vols (Moscow: Progress-Pleiada, 2009–11)

—— *Quaderni di Voronež*, trans. by Manuela Calusio, intro. by Ermanno Krumm (Milan: Mondadori, 1995)

—— *Quasi leggera morte*, ed. by Serena Vitale (Milan: Adelphi, 2017)

—— *Selected Poems*, trans. by David McDuff (New York: Farrar, Strauss and Giroux, 1975)

—— *Simple promesse. Choix de poèmes 1908–1937*, trans. by Philippe Jaccottet, Louis Martinez, and Jean-Claude Schneider (Chêne-Bourg: La Dogana, 1994)

—— *Viaggio in Armenia*, ed. by Serena Vitale (Milan: Adelphi, 1988)

—— *Voronezh Notebooks*, trans. by Andrew Davis (New York: NYRB, 2016)

—— 'The Word and Culture', trans. by Sidney Monas, *Arion: Journal of Humanities and the Classics*, 2.4 (1975), pp. 527–32

McKendrick, Jamie, *The Foreign Connection: Writings on Poetry, Art and Translation* (Oxford: Legenda, 2020)

Miglio, Camilla, *Vita a fronte. Saggio su Paul Celan* (Macerata: Quodlibet, 2005)

Petrarch, Francesco, *Canzoniere*, ed. by Marco Santagata, rev. ed. (Milan: Mondadori, 2010)

Pil'ščikov, Igor' A., 'Petrarca nelle traduzioni dei poeti russi dell'età d'oro e dell'età d'argento', trans. by Bianca Sulpasso, *Russica Romana*, 17 (2010), pp. 89–114

Redko, Philip Leon, *Boundary Issues in Three Twentieth-Century Russian Poets (Mandelstam, Aronzon, Shvarts)* (doctoral thesis, Harvard University, Graduate School of Arts and Sciences, 2019) <https://dash.harvard.edu/handle/1/41121299> [accessed 29 September 2020]

Semenko Irina, 'Mandel'štam traduttore di Petrarca', ed. by Cesare G. De Michelis, *Rassegna sovietica*, 4 (1970), pp. 14–35

Tonelli, Natascia, *Leggere il 'Canzoniere'* (Bologna, Il Mulino, 2017)

Zanzotto, Andrea, 'Petrarca fra il palazzo e la cameretta', in *Scritti sulla letteratura*, ed. by Gianmario Villalta, 2 vols, (Milan: Mondadori, 2001), I, pp. 261–71

References

Agamben, Giorgio, *Stanzas: Word and Phantasm in Western Culture*, trans. by Ronald L. Martinez (Minneapolis: University of Minnesota Press, 1992)

Akbari, Suzanne Conklin, *Seeing Through the Veil: Optical Theory and Medieval Allegory* (Toronto: Toronto University Press, 2004)

Alighieri, Dante, *La Commedia secondo l'antica vulgata*, ed. by Giorgio Petrocchi, 4 vols (Milan: Mondadori, 1966–67)

—— *Dante Alagherii epistolae = The letters of Dante*, trans. by Paget Toynbee, 2nd edn (Oxford: Clarendon Press, 1966)

—— *Dante's Lyric Poetry*, ed. by Kenelm Foster and Patrick Boyde, 2 vols (Oxford: Oxford University Press, 1967)

—— *The Divine Comedy*, trans. by Robert Hollander and Jean Hollander. 3 vols (New York: Doubleday 2000–2007)

—— *Monarchia*, ed. and trans. by Prue Shaw (Cambridge: Cambridge University Press, 1995)

—— *Rime*, ed. by Claudio Giunta (Milan: Mondadori, 2018)

—— *Rime*, ed. by Domenico de Robertis (Tavarnuzze [Florence]: SISMEL · Edizioni del Galluzzo, 2005)

—— *Rime giovanili e della 'Vita Nuova'*, ed. by Teodolinda Barolini, with notes by Manuele Gragnolati (Milan: Rizzoli, 2009)

—— *Vita Nova*, ed. by Guglielmo Gorni (Turin: Einaudi, 1996)

—— *Vita Nuova*, ed. by Domenico De Robertis, (Milan–Naples: Ricciardi, 1980)

—— *Vita Nuova*, ed. by Michele Barbi (Florence: Bemporad, 1932)

Anichini, Federica, *Voices of the Body: Liminal Grammar in Guido Cavalcanti's Rime / Voci del corpo: grammatica liminale nelle Rime di Guido Cavalcanti* (Munich: Meidenbauer, 2009)

Ardizzone, Maria Luisa, *Guido Cavalcanti: The Other Middle Ages* (Toronto: University of Toronto Press, 2002) <https://doi.org/10.3138/9781442675568>

Ariani, Marco, *Petrarca* (Rome: Salerno, 1999)

Auerbach, Erich, 'Passio as Passion', in Time, History, and Literature: Selected Essays of Erich Auerbach, ed. by James I. Porter, trans. by Jane O. Newman (Princeton, NJ: Princeton University Press, 2013), pp. 165–87

Augustine, Opera omnia. PL 32–45 <http://www.augustinus.it> [accessed 15 September 2020]

Barański, Zygmunt G., 'Petrarch, Dante, Cavalcanti', in Petrarch and Dante: Anti–Dantism, Metaphysics, Tradition, ed. by Zygmunt G. Barański and Theodore J. Cachey, Jr (Notre Dame, IN: University of Notre Dame Press, 2009), pp. 50–133 <https://doi.org/10.2307/j.ctvpj78c0.7>

—— 'The Triumphi', in The Cambridge Companion to Petrarch, ed. by Albert R. Ascoli and Unn Falkeid (Cambridge: Cambridge University Press, 2015), pp. 74–84 <https://doi.org/10.1017/CCO9780511795008.009>

Barkan, Leonard, The Gods Made Flesh: Metamorphosis and the Pursuit of Paganism (New Haven, CT: Yale University Press, 1986)

Barnes, John C., and Zygmunt G. Barański, 'Dante's Canzone montanina', The Modern Language Review, 73.2 (April 1978), pp. 297–307 <https://doi.org/10.2307/3727103>

Barolini, Teodolinda, 'Dante and Cavalcanti (On Making Distinctions in Matters of Love): Inferno 5 in its Lyric and Autobiographical Context', in Dante and the Origins of Italian Literary Culture, pp. 70–101 <https://doi.org/10.5422/fordham/9780823227037.003.0004>

—— 'Dante and the Lyric Past', in Dante and the Origins of Italian Literary Culture (New York: Fordham University Press), pp. 23–46 <https://doi.org/10.5422/fordham/9780823227037.003.0002>

—— Dante's Poets: Textuality and Truth in the 'Comedy' (Princeton, NJ: Princeton University Press, 1984) <https://doi.org/10.1515/9781400853212>

—— 'The Making of a Lyric Sequence: Time and Narrative in Petrarch's Rerum vulgarium fragmenta', MLN, 104.1, Italian issue (Jan. 1989), pp. 1–38 <https://doi.org/10.2307/2904989>

—— 'Petrarch as the Metaphysical Poet Who Is Not Dante: Metaphysical Markers at the Beginning of the Rerum vulgarium fragmenta (Rvf 1–21)', in Petrarch and Dante: Anti–Dantism, Metaphysics, Tradition, ed. by Zygmunt

G. Barański and Theodore J. Cachey, Jr (Notre Dame, IN: University of Notre Dame Press, 2009), pp. 195–225 <https://doi.org/10.2307/j.ctvpj78c0.10>

—— 'La poesia della teologia e la teologia della poesia dalle *Rime* di Dante al *Paradiso*', in *'Il mondo errante'. Dante fra letteratura, eresia e storia; atti del convegno internazionale di studio: Bertinoro, 13–16 settembre 2010*, ed. by Marco Veglia, Lorenzo Paolini, and Riccardo Parmeggiani (Spoleto: Centro di studi italiani sull'alto medioevo, 2013), pp. 537–45

—— 'The Self in the Labyrinth of Time: *Rerum vulgarium fragmenta*', in *Petrarch: A Critical Guide to the Complete Works*, ed. by Victoria Kirkham and Armando Maggi (Chicago: Chicago University Press, 2009), pp. 33–62

—— *The Undivine 'Comedy': Detheologizing Dante* (Princeton, NJ: Princeton University Press, 1992) <https://doi.org/10.1515/9781400820764>

Baron, Hans, *Petrarch's 'Secretum': Its Making and its Meaning* (Cambridge, MA: Harvard University Press, 1985)

Barthes, Roland, 'Texte supplément to *Le plaisir du texte*', *Art Press*, 4 (1973)

Barthouil, Georges, 'Toujours aimer, toujours souffrir, toujours mourir ou fatalité et volontarisme chez Pétrarque', in *Francesco Petrarca: Père des renaissances, Serviteur de l'amour et de la paix* (Avignon: Aubanel, 1974), pp. 183–208

Berisso, Marco, ed., *Poesie dello Stilnovo* (Milan: Rizzoli, 2006)

Berman, Antoine, *L'Épreuve de l'étranger. Culture et traduction dans l'Allemagne romantique: Herder, Goethe, Schlegel, Novalis, Humboldt, Schleiermacher, Hölderlin* (Paris: Gallimard, 1984)

Bersani, Leo, *The Freudian Body: Psychoanalysis and Art* (New York: Columbia University Press, 1986)

—— *Homos* (Cambridge, MA: Harvard University Press, 1995)

—— *Is the Rectum a Grave? And Other Essays* (Chicago: University of Chicago Press, 2005)

Bertolani, Maria Cecilia, *Petrarca e la visione dell'eterno* (Bologna: Il Mulino 2005)

Boccignone, Manuela, 'Un albero piantato nel cuore (Petrarca e Iacopone)', *Lettere italiane*, 52.2 (April–June 2000), pp. 225–64

Boggs, Edward L., 'Cino and Petrarch', *MLN*, 94.1, Italian is-
      sue (Jan. 1979), pp. 146–52 <https://doi.org/10.2307/
      2906335>

Boitani, Piero, '*O quike deth*: Love, Melancholy, and the Divided
      Self', in *The Tragic and the Sublime in Medieval Literature*
      (Cambridge: Cambridge University Press, 1989), pp. 56–
      74

Bologna, Corrado, '"Occhi solo occhi" (*Rvf* 70–75)', in *Can-
      zoniere: Lettura micro e macrotestuale*, ed. by Michelangelo
      Picone (Ravenna: Longo, 2007), pp. 183–205

—— 'PetrArca petroso', *Critica del testo*, 6.1 (2003), pp. 366–420

Bolzoni, Lina, *La rete delle immagini: predicazione in volgare dalle
      origini a Bernardino da Siena* (Turin: Einaudi, 2002)

Bonaventure, *Bonaventurae Opera omnia*, ed. by PP. Collegii S.
      Bonaventurae, 11 vols (Quaracchi: Collegium S. Bonaven-
      turae, 1882–1902)

Bonola, Anna, 'Traduzione e impulso creativo. Un sonetto di
      Petrarca nella versione russa di Osip E. Mandel'štam',
      L'analisi linguistica e letteraria, 11.1 (2003), pp. 29–73

Borsa, Paolo, 'L'immagine nel cuore e l'immagine nella mente:
      dal Notaro alla *Vita nuova* attraverso i due Guidi', in *Les
      Deux Guidi: Guinizzelli et Cavalcanti. Mourir d'aimer et
      autres ruptures*, ed. by Marina Gagliano, Philippe Guérin,
      and Raffaella Zanni (Paris: Presses Sorbonne Nouvelle,
      2016), pp. 75–92

—— *La nuova poesia di Guido Guinizzelli* (Fiesole: Cadmo,
      2007)

Botterill, Steven, *Dante and the Mystical Tradition: Bernard of
      Clairvaux in the 'Commedia'* (Cambridge: Cambridge
      University Press, 1994) <https://doi.org/10.1017/
      CBO9780511611735>

Braidotti, Rosi, 'Intensive Genre and the Demise of Gender', *An-
      gelaki*, 13.2 (2008), pp. 45–57 <https://doi.org/10.1080/
      09697250802432112>

—— 'Writing as a Nomadic Subject', *Comparative Critical
      Studies*, 11.2–3 (2014), pp. 163–84 <https://doi.org/
      10.3366/ccs.2014.0122>

Brenkman, John, 'Writing, Desire, Dialectic in Petrarch's *Rime
      23*', *Pacific Coast Philology*, 9 (1974), pp. 12–19 <https:
      //doi.org/10.2307/1316564>

Brown, Clarence, *Mandelstam*, rev. edn (Cambridge: Cambridge University Press, 2010)

Burgwinkle, William, 'Modern Lovers: Evanescence and the Act in Dante, Arnaut, and Sordello', in *Desire in Dante and the Middle Ages*, ed. by Manuele Gragnolati and others (Oxford: Legenda, 2012), pp. 14–28 <https://doi.org/10.4324/9781315094946-2>

Bynum, Caroline Walker, 'Faith Imagining the Self: Somatomorphic Soul and Resurrection Body in Dante's *Divine Comedy*', in *Faithful Imagining: Essays in Honor of Richard R. Neibuhr*, ed. by Sang Huyn Lee, Wayne Proudfoot, and Albert Blackwell (Atlanta, GA: Scholars Press, 1995), pp. 81–104

—— *Metamorphosis and Identity* (New York: Zone Books, 2001)

—— *The Resurrection of the Body in Western Christianity* (New York: Columbia University Press, 1996)

Caiti Russo, Gilda, *Les Troubadours et la Cour des Malaspina* (Montpellier: Presses Universitaires de la Meditérranée, 2005)

—— 'Il marchese Moroello Malaspina testimone ideale di un dibattito tra Dante e Cino sull'eredità trobadorica', *Dante Studies*, 124 (2006), pp. 137–48

Calcaterra, Carlo, *Sant'Agostino nelle opere di Dante e del Petrarca* (Milan: Vita e Pensiero, 1931)

Calvino, Italo *Lezioni Americane. Sei proposte per il prossimo millennio* (Milan: Mondadori, 1993)

Carruthers, Mary, *The Experience of Beauty in the Middle Ages* (Oxford: Oxford University Press, 2013) <https://doi.org/10.1093/acprof:osobl/9780199590322.001.0001>

Carson, Anne, 'Decreation: How Women Like Sappho, Marguerite Porete and Simone Weil Tell God', in *Decreation: Poetry, Essays, Opera* (New York: Knopf, 2005), pp. 155–83

—— *Economy of the Unlost: Reading Simonides of Keos with Paul Celan* (Princeton, NJ: Princeton University Press, 1999)

Cavalcanti, Guido, *Rime. Con le rime di Iacopo Cavalcanti*, ed. by Domenico De Robertis (Turin: Einaudi, 1986)

—— *Rime*, ed. by Roberto Rea and Giorgio Inglese (Rome: Carocci, 2011)

Cazzola, Piero, 'Osip Mandel'štam, traduttore russo del Petrarca', in *Dynamique d'une expansion culturelle: Pétrarque en Europe, xive–xxe siècle; Actes du xxvie Congrès International du CEFI, Turin et Chambéry, 11–15 décembre 1995: À la Mémoire de Franco Simone* (Paris: Champion, 2001), pp. 401–13

Celan, Paul, 'Everything's different' (Es ist alles anders), in *Selected Poems*, trans. by Michael Hamburger, rev. edn (London: Penguin, 1996)

—— 'Loess Dolls' (Lösspuppen), in *Snow Part = Schneepart: and other poems (1968-1969)*, trans. by Iain Fairley (Manchester: Carcanet, 2007)

—— *Poesie*, ed. by Moshe Kahn and Marcella Bagnasco (Milan: Mondadori, 1976)

Cervigni, Dino, 'The Petrarchan Lover's Non-Dialogic and Dialogic Discourse: An Augustinian Semiotic Approach to Petrarch's *Rerum Vulgarium Fragmenta*', *Annali d'Italianistica*, 22 (2004), pp. 105–34

Cestaro, Gary, *Dante and the Grammar of the Nursing Body* (Notre Dame, IN: University of Notre Dame Press, 2003)

Chiavacci Leonardi, Anna Maria, '"Le bianche stole": il tema della resurrezione nel *Paradiso*', in *Dante e la Bibbia. Atti del Convegno Internazionale promosso da 'Biblia': Firenze, 26–27–28 settembre 1986*, ed. by Giovanni Barblan (Florence: Olschki, 1988), pp. 249–71

Cipollone, Annalisa, '"Né per nova figura il primo alloro…": La chiusa di *Rvf* XXIII, il *Canzoniere* e Dante', *Rassegna europea di letteratura italiana*, 11 (1998), pp. 29–46

Cixous, Hélène, *Illa* (Paris: Des Femmes, 1980)

—— *La* (Paris: Gallimard, 1976)

Coccia, Emanuele, *La Vie des plantes* (Paris: Éditions Payot & Rivages, 2016), in English as *The Life of Plants: A Metaphysics of Mixture*, trans. by Dylan J. Montanari (Cambridge: Polity, 2019)

Cortellessa, Andrea, 'Petrarca è di nuovo in vista', in *'Un'altra storia. Petrarca nel Novecento italiano', atti del Convegno di Roma, 4–6 ottobre 2001*, ed. by Andrea Cortellessa (Rome: Bulzoni, 2004), pp. i–xxxi

Corti, Maria, *Felicità mentale: nuove prospettive per Cavalcanti e Dante* (Turin: Einaudi, 2003)

—— 'Il linguaggio poetico di Cino da Pistoia', *Cultura mediolatina*, 12.3 (1952), pp. 185–223

Crevier Goulet, Sarah-Anaïs, 'Du jardin d'essai / *esse* à l'hortus conclusus: Figures de la naissance et du végétal dans l'oeuvre de Hélène Cixous', in *Des jardins autres*, ed. by Paolo Alexandre Néné and Sarah Carmo (Paris: Archives Karéline, 2015), pp. 257–80

Crisafi, Nicolò, and Manuele Gragnolati, 'Weathering the Afterlife: The Meterological Psychology of Dante's *Commedia*', in *Weathering: Ecologies of Exposure*, ed. by Christoph F. E. Holzhey and Arnd Wedemeyer (Berlin: ICI Berlin Press, 2020), pp. 63–91 <https://doi.org/10.37050/ci-17_04>

Culler, Jonathan, *Theory of the Lyric* (Cambridge, MA: Harvard University Press, 2015) <https://doi.org/10.4159/9780674425781>

Deleuze, Gilles, *Expressionism in Philosophy: Spinoza*, trans. by Martin Joughin (New York: Zone Books, 1992)

Deleuze, Gilles, and Félix Guattari, *A Thousand Plateaus: Capitalism and Schizophrenia*, trans. by Brian Massumi (Minneapolis: University of Minnesota Press, 1987)

De Libera, Alain, *Volonté et action: Cours du Collège de France 2014/2015* (Paris: Vrin, 2017)

De Michelis, Cesare G., 'Mandel'štam in URSS', *Rassegna sovietica*, 4 (1970), pp. 5–11

Derrida, Jacques, *The Work of Mourning*, ed. by Pascale-Anne Brault and Michael Naas (Chicago: University of Chicago Press, 2001)

Deuber-Mankowsky, Astrid, 'Diffraktion statt Reflexion. Zu Donna Haraways Konzept des Situierten Wissens', *Zeitschrift für Medienwissenschaft*, 1 (2011), pp. 83–92 <https://doi.org/10.1524/zfmw.2011.0008>

Dinshaw, Carolyn, *Getting Medieval: Sexualities and Communities, Pre- and Post-modern* (Durham, NC: Duke University Press, 1999) <https://doi.org/10.1215/9780822382188>

——, *How Soon is Now: Medieval Texts, Amateur Readers, and the Queerness of Time* (Durham, NC: Duke University Press, 2012) <https://doi.org/10.1215/9780822395911>

Dolack, Tom, 'Ventriloquio autobiografico: Mandelstam traduttore di Petrarca', *Intersezioni*, 27.3 (2007), pp. 475–86

Dronke, Peter, *The Medieval Lyric* (London: Hutchinson, 1968)

Dubrow, Heather, *English Petrarchism and its Counterdiscourses* (Cornell, NY: Cornell University Press, 1995)

Durling, Robert M., 'Introduction', in *Petrarch's Lyric Poems: The Rime Sparse and Other Lyrics*, trans. and ed. by Robert M. Durling (Cambridge, MA: Harvard University Press, 1976), pp. 1–33

—— 'Petrarch's "Giovene donna sotto un verde lauro"', *MLN*, 86.1 (1971), pp. 1–20 <https://doi.org/10.2307/2907460>

Edelman, Lee, *No Future: Queer Theory and the Death Drive* (Durham, NC: Duke University Press, 2004) <https://doi.org/10.1215/9780822385981>

Eisner, Martin, *Boccaccio and the Invention of Italian Literature: Dante, Petrarch, Cavalcanti, and the Authority of the Vernacular* (Cambridge: Cambridge University Press, 2013) <https://doi.org/10.1017/CBO9781107300484>

Enterline, Lynn, 'Embodied Voices: Petrarch Reading Himself Reading Ovid', in *Desire in the Renaissance: Psychoanalysis and Literature*, ed. by Valeria Finucci and Regina Schwartz (Princeton, NJ: Princeton University Press, 1994), pp. 120–45 <https://doi.org/10.1515/9781400821501.120>

—— *The Rhetoric of the Body from Ovid to Shakespeare* (Cambridge: Cambridge University Press, 2000) <https://doi.org/10.1017/CBO9780511483561>

Fenzi, Enrico, 'Ancora sulla *Epistola* a Moroello e sulla "montanina" di Dante (*Rime*, 15)', *Tenzone*, 4 (2003), pp. 43–84

Ferrante, Joan, *The Political Vision of Dante's 'Comedy'* (Princeton, NJ: Princeton University Press, 1984)

Ferrara, Sabrina, 'Io mi credea del tutto esser partito: il distacco di Dante da Cino', in *Cino nella storia della poesia italiana*, ed. by Rossend Arqués Corominas and Silvia Tranfaglia (Florence: Cesati, 2016), pp. 99–111

Finotti, Fabio, 'The Poem of Memory: Petrarch's *Triumphi*', in *Petrarch: A Critical Guide to the Complete Works*, ed. by Victoria Kirkham and Armando Maggi (Chicago: University of Chicago Press, 2009), pp. 63–83

Foucault, Michel, *The Hermeneutics of the Subject: Lectures at the Collège de France, 1981–82*, ed. by Fréderic Gros, trans. by Graham Burchell (New York: Palgrave-Macmillan, 2005)

Fowler, Robert M., *Let the Reader Understand: Reader-Response Criticism and the Gospel of Mark* (Harrisburg: Trinity Press International, 2001)

Freccero, Carla, 'Ovidian Subjectivities in Early Modern Lyric:
    Identification and Desire in Petrarch and Louise Labé', in
    Ovid and the Renaissance Body, ed. by Goran Stanivukovic
    (Toronto: University of Toronto Press, 2001), pp. 21–37
    <https://doi.org/10.3138/9781442678194-003>

—— *Queer/Early/Modern*   (Durham,   NC: Duke   Uni-
    versity   Press,   2006)   <https://doi.org/10.1215/
    9780822387169>

Freccero, John, *Dante: The Poetics of Conversion*, ed. by Rachel
    Jacoff (Cambridge, MA: Harvard University Press, 1986)

—— 'The Fig Tree and the Laurel: Petrarch's Poetics', *Diacritics*,
    5.1 (Spring 1975), pp. 34–40 <https://doi.org/10.2307/
    464720>

Freeman, Elizabeth, ed., *Queer Temporalities* (=*GLQ: A Journal
    of Lesbian and Gay Studies*, 13.2–3 (2007)) <https://doi.
    org/10.1215/10642684-2006-029>

Freud, Sigmund, 'Beyond the Pleasure Principle' (1920), in *The
    Standard Edition to the Complete Psychological Works of
    Sigmund Freud*, ed. and trans. by James Strachey, 24 vols
    (London: Hogarth Press, 1953–74), XVIII (1955), pp. 7–
    64

Friedrich, Paul, 'Lyric Epiphany', *Language in Society*,
    30 (2001), pp. 217–47 <https://doi.org/10.1017/
    S0047404501002032>

Galbiati, Giuseppina Stella, 'Sulla canzone "I' vo pensando" (*Rvf*
    264): L'ascendente agostiniano ed altre suggestioni cultu-
    rali', in *Petrarca volgare e la sua fortuna sino al Cinquecento*,
    ed. by Bruno Porcelli (= *Italianistica*, 33.2 (May–August
    2004)), pp. 109–21

Galvez, Marisa, *Songbook: How Lyrics Became Poetry in Medieval
    Europe* (Chicago: University of Chicago Press, 2012)
    <https://doi.org/10.7208/chicago/9780226280523.
    001.0001>

Gilson, Simon, *Medieval Optics and Theories of Light in the Works
    of Dante* (New York: Edwin Mellen Press, 2000)

Ginsberg, Warren, 'Chaucer and Petrarch: "S'amor non è" and
    the *Canticus Troili*', *Humanist Studies & the Digital Age*, 1.1
    (Winter 2011), pp. 121–27 <https://doi.org/10.5399/
    uo/hsda.1.1.1166>

Giunta, Claudio, 'Guido Cavalcanti, "Perch'i' no spero di tornar giammai"', in *Codici. Saggi sulla poesia del Medioevo* (Bologna: il Mulino, 2005), pp. 45–61

Giusti, Francesco, *Il desiderio della lirica. Poesia, creazione, conoscenza* (Rome: Carocci, 2017)

—— 'Rispondere solo a Beatrice. "Tanto gentile e tanto onesta pare" e il rischio della ripetizione lirica', *Revue des études dantesques*, 2 (2018), pp. 87–109

Glazova, Anna, 'Poetry of Bringing about Presence: Paul Celan translates Osip Mandelstam', *MLN*, Comparative Literature Issue, 123.5 (2008), pp. 1108–26 <https://doi.org/10.1353/mln.0.0073>

Gragnolati, Manuele, *Amor che move. Linguaggio del corpo e forma del desiderio in Dante, Pasolini e Morante* (Milan: il Saggiatore, 2013)

—— *Experiencing the Afterlife: Body and Soul in Dante and Medieval Culture* (Notre Dame, IN: University of Notre Dame Press, 2005)

—— 'Gluttony and the Anthropology of Pain in Dante's *Inferno* and *Purgatorio*', in *History in the Comic Mode: Medieval Communities and the Matter of Person*, ed. by Rachel Fulton and Bruce W. Holsinger (New York: Columbia University Press, 2007), pp. 238–50 <https://doi.org/10.7312/fult13368-022>

—— 'Ombre e abbracci. Riflessioni sull'inconsistenza in Dante', in *Passages, seuils, sauts: du dernier cercle de l'Enfer à la première terrasse du Purgatoire (Enf. XXXII – Purg. XII)*, ed. by Manuele Gragnolati and Philippe Guérin (= *Chroniques italiennes web*, 35 (2020)), pp. 68–81

—— 'Trasformazioni e assenze: la *performance* della *Vita nova* e le figure di Dante e Cavalcanti', *L'Alighieri*, 35 (2010), pp. 5–23

Gragnolati, Manuele, and Elena Lombardi, 'Volgarizzazione lirica e piacere linguistico in Dante', in *Toscana bilingue (1260–1430). Per una storia sociale del tradurre medievale*, ed. by Sara Bischetti and others (Berlin: de Gruyter, forthcoming)

Gragnolati, Manuele, and Christoph F. E. Holzhey, eds, *De/Constituing Wholes: Towards Partiality Without Parts* (Vienna: Turia + Kant, 2017) <https://doi.org/10.37050/ci-11>

Greene, Roland, and Bronwen Tate, 'Lyric Sequence', in *The Princeton Encyclopedia of Poetry and Poetics*, ed. by Roland Greene and others, 4th edn (Princeton, NJ: Princeton University Press, 2012), pp. 834–36

Gregerson, Linda, 'Open Voicing: Wyatt and Shakespeare', in *The Oxford Handbook of Shakespeare's Poetry*, ed. by Jonathan Post (Oxford: Oxford University Press, 2013), pp. 151–66 <https://doi.org/10.1093/oxfordhb/9780199607747.013.0013>

Gregg, Melissa, and Gregory J. Seigworth, eds, *The Affect Theory Reader* (Durham, NC: Duke University Press, 2010) <https://doi.org/10.1215/9780822393047>

Gudder, Stanley, *A Mathematical Journey* (New York: McGraw-Hill, 1994)

Guinizzelli, Guido, *Rime*, ed. by Luciano Rossi (Turin: Einaudi, 2002)

Guérin, Philippe, 'Pétrarque, ou de l'écriture comme odyssée', in *Voyages de papier: Hommage à Brigitte Urbani*, ed. by Perle Abbrugiati and Claudio Milanesi (=*Italies*, 17/18 (2014)), pp. 31–57 <https://doi.org/10.4000/italies.4648>

Güntert, Georges, 'Sonetti occasionali e capolavori (*RVF* 90–99)', in *Il Canzoniere: Lettura micro e macrotestuale*, ed. by Michelangelo Picone (Ravenna: Longo, 2007), pp. 243–60

Hainsworth, Peter, *Petrarch the Poet: An Introduction to 'Rerum vulgarium fragmenta'* (New York: Routledge, 2014)

Halberstam, Judith, *In a Queer Time and Place: Transgender Bodies, Subcultural Lives* (New York: New York University Press, 2005)

—— *The Queer Art of Failure* (Durham, NC: Duke University Press, 2011) <https://doi.org/10.1215/9780822394358>

Haraway, Donna J., *Modest_Witness@Second_Millennium. FemaleMan_Meets_OncoMouse^{TM}: Feminism and Technoscience* (New York: Routledge, 1997)

—— 'The Promises of Monsters: A Regenerative Politics for Inappropriate/d Others', in *Cultural Studies*, ed. by Lawrence Grossberg, Cary Nelson, and Paula A. Treichler (New York, Routledge, 1992), pp. 295–337

Hardie, Philip, 'Ovid into Laura: Absent presences in the *Metamorphoses* and Petrarch's *Rime sparse*', in *Ovidian Transformations: Essays on Ovid's 'Metamorphoses' and its Recep-*

tion, ed. by Philip R. Hardie, Alessandro Barchiesi, and Stephen Hinds (Cambridge: Cambridge University Press, 1999), pp. 254–70

Harrison, Anna, 'Community among the Saints in Heaven in Bernard of Clairvaux's *Sermons for the Feast of All Saints*', in *Last Things: Death and Apocalypse in the Middle Ages*, ed, by Caroline Walker Bynum and Paul Freedman (Philadelphia: University of Pennsylvania Press, 2000), pp. 191–204

Harrison, Robert Pogue, *The Body of Beatrice* (Baltimore, MD: Johns Hopkins University Press, 1988)

Hawkins, Peter, *Dante: A Brief History* (London: Blackwell, 2006)

Heaney, Seamus, *The Government of the Tongue* (London: Faber and Faber, 1988)

Hempfer, Klaus W., 'La canzone CCLXIV, il *Secretum* e il significato del *Canzoniere* di Petrarca', *Studi petrarcheschi*, 14 (1994), pp. 263–87

Heyworth, Gregory, *Desiring Bodies: Ovidian Romance and the Cult of Form* (Notre Dame, IN: University of Notre Dame Press, 2009)

Hollander, Robert, '*Purgatorio* II: Cato's Rebuke and Dante's *Scoglio*', *Italica*, 52.3 (Autumn 1975), pp. 348–63 <https://doi.org/10.2307/478438>

Holmes, Olivia, *Assembling the Lyric Self: Authorship from Troubadour Song to Italian Poetry Book* (Minneapolis: University of Minnesota Press, 2000)

Holzhey, Christoph F. E., 'The Lover of a Hybrid: Memory and Fantasy in *Aracoeli*', in *The Power of Disturbance: Elsa Morante's* Aracoeli, ed. by Manuele Gragnolati and Sara Fortuna (Oxford: Legenda, 2009), pp. 42–58 <https://doi.org/10.4324/9781315085531-5>

—— *Paradoxical Pleasures and Aesthetics: Masophobia, Sexual Difference, and E. T. A. Hoffmann's Kater Murr*, Ph.D. Thesis (Ann Arbor, MI: University of Michigan, 2002).

Iliescu, Nicolae, *Il canzoniere petrarchesco e Sant'Agostino* (Rome: Società accademica romena, 1962)

Inglese, Giorgio, *L'intelletto e l'amore: Studi sulla letteratura italiana del Due e Trecento* (Florence: La Nuova Italia, 2000)

Irigaray, Luce, and Michael Marder, *Through Vegetal Being: Two Philosophical Perspectives* (New York: Columbia University Press, 2016) <https://doi.org/10.7312/irig17386>

Jaccottet, Philippe, *D'une lyre à cinq cordes* (Paris: Gallimard, 1997)

—— *A partir du mot Russie* (Montpellier: Fata Morgana, 2002)

Jackson, Virginia, 'Lyric', in *The Princeton Encyclopedia of Poetry and Poetics*, ed. by Roland Greene and others, 4th edn (Princeton, NJ: Princeton University Press, 2012), pp. 826–34

Jackson, Virginia, and Yopie Prins, eds, *The Lyric Theory Reader: A Critical Anthology* (Baltimore, MD: Johns Hopkins University Press, 2014)

Kaiser, Birgit Mara, and Kathrin Thiele, 'Diffraction: Onto-Epistemology, Quantum Physics and the Critical Humanities', *Parallax*, 20.3 (2014), pp. 165–67 <https://doi.org/10.1080/13534645.2014.927621>

Kay, Sarah, *Parrots and Nightingales: Troubadour Quotations and the Development of European Poetry* (Philadelphia: University of Pennsylvania Press, 2013) <https://doi.org/10.9783/9780812208382>

Keen, Catherine, 'Images of Exile: Distance and Memory in the Poetry of Cino Da Pistoia', *Italian Studies*, 55.1 (2000), pp. 21–36 <https://doi.org/10.1179/its.2000.55.1.21>

Kerrigan, John, 'Between Michelangelo and Petrarch: Shakespeare's Sonnets of Art', in *On Shakespeare and Early Modern Literature: Essays* (Oxford: Oxford University Press, 2011), pp. 23–40 <https://doi.org/10.1093/acprof:oso/9780199248513.003.0002>

Kirkpatrick, Robin, 'Polemics of Praise: Theology as Text, Narrative and Rhetoric in Dante's *Commedia*', in *Dante's 'Commedia': Theology as Poetry*, ed. by Vittorio Montemaggi and Matthew Treherne (Notre Dame, IN: University of Notre Dame Press, 2010), pp. 14–35 <https://doi.org/10.2307/j.ctvpg862d.7>

Knuutila, Simo, *Emotions in Ancient and Medieval Philosophy* (Oxford: Oxford University Press, 2004) <https://doi.org/10.1093/0199266387.001.0001>

Korolec, J. B., 'Free Will and Free Choice', in *The Cambridge History of Later Medieval Philosophy: From the Discovery of Aristotle to the Disintegration of Scholasticism 1100–1600*, ed. by Norman Kretzmann and others (Cambridge: Cambridge University Press, 1982), pp. 629–41 <https://doi.org/10.1017/CHOL9780521226059.035>

Laplanche, Jean, and Jean-Bertrand Pontalis, *The Language of Psycho-Analysis*, trans. by Donald Nicholson-Smith (London: Hogarth Press and Institute of Psycho-Analysis, 1973)

Leupin, Alexandre, 'The *Roman de la Rose* as a Möbius Strip (On Interpretation)', in *The Medieval Author in Medieval French Literature*, ed. by Virginie Greene (New York: Palgrave-Macmillan, 2006), pp. 61–75 <https://doi.org/10.1057/9781403983459_4>

Lombardi, Elena, '"I Desire Therefore I Am": Petrarch's *Canzoniere* between the Medieval and the Modern Notion of Desire', in *Early Modern Medievalisms: The Interplay between Scholarly Reflection and Artistic Production*, ed. by Alicia C. Montoya, Wim van Anrooij, and Sophie van Romburgh (Leiden: Brill, 2010), pp. 19–41 <https://doi.org/10.1163/ej.9789004187665.i-472.14>

—— 'Identità lirica e piacere linguistico: una lettura di *Paradiso* XXVI', *Studi danteschi*, 82 (2017), pp. 51–80

—— *Imagining the Woman Reader in the Age of Dante* (Oxford: Oxford University Press, 2018) <https://doi.org/10.1093/oso/9780198818960.001.0001>

—— 'Il pensiero linguistico nella *Vita nova*', in *Vita nova. Fiore. Epistola XIII*, ed. by Manuele Gragnolati and others (Tavarnuzze [Florence]: SISMEL · Edizioni del Galluzzo, 2018), pp. 115–34

—— *The Syntax of Desire: Language and Love in Augustine, the Modistae, Dante* (Toronto: University of Toronto Press, 2007)

—— *The Wings of the Doves: Love and Desire in Dante and Medieval Culture* (Montréal: McGill-Queen's University Press, 2012)

Love, Heather, *Feeling Backward: Loss and the Politics of Queer History* (Cambridge, MA: Harvard University Press, 2009) <https://doi.org/10.2307/j.ctvjghxr0>

Mandelstam, Nadezhda Jakovlevna, *Le mie memorie con poesie e altri scritti di Osip Mandel'štam*, trans. by Serena Vitale (Milan: Garzanti, 1972)

Mandelstam, Osip, *Cinquanta poesie*, ed. by Remo Faccani (Turin: Einaudi, 1998)

—— *Polnoe sobranie sochinenii i pisem v trekh tomakh*, ed. by A. G. Mets, 3 vols (Moscow: Progress-Pleiada, 2009–11)

—— *Quaderni di Voronež*, trans. by Manuela Calusio, intro. by Ermanno Krumm (Milan: Mondadori, 1995)

—— *Quasi leggera morte*, ed. by Serena Vitale (Milan: Adelphi, 2017)

—— *Selected Poems*, trans. by David McDuff (New York: Farrar, Strauss and Giroux, 1975)

—— *Simple promesse. Choix de poèmes 1908–1937*, trans. by Philippe Jaccottet, Louis Martinez, and Jean-Claude Schneider (Chêne-Bourg: La Dogana, 1994)

—— *Viaggio in Armenia*, ed. by Serena Vitale (Milan: Adelphi, 1988)

—— *Voronezh Notebooks*, trans. by Andrew Davis (New York: NYRB, 2016)

—— 'The Word and Culture', trans. by Sidney Monas, *Arion: Journal of Humanities and the Classics*, 2.4 (1975), pp. 527–32

Mann, Nicholas, 'Petrarca giardiniere (a proposito del sonetto CCXXVIII)', *Letture Petrarce*, 12 (1992), pp. 235–56

Marder, Michael, *The Philosopher's Plant: An Intellectual Herbarium*, with illustrations by Mathilde Roussel (New York: Columbia University Press, 2014)

—— *Plant-thinking: A Philosophy of Vegetal Life* (New York: Columbia University Press, 2013)

Marshall, Cynthia, *The Shattering of the Self: Violence, Subjectivity, and Early Modern Texts* (Baltimore, MD: Johns Hopkins University Press, 2002)

Marti, Mario, *Storia del Dolce Stilnovo* (Lecce: Milella, 1973)

Martinez, Ronald L., 'Francis, Thou Art Translated: Petrarch Metamorphosed in English, 1380–1595', *Humanist Studies & the Digital Age* 1.1 (2011), pp. 80–108 <https://doi.org/10.5399/uo/hsda.1.1.1196>

Massumi, Brian, *Parables for the Virtual: Movement, Affect, Sensation* (Durham, NC: Duke University Press, 2002) <https://doi.org/10.1215/9780822383574>

Mazzotta, Giuseppe, 'Petrarch's Dialogue with Dante', in *Petrarch and Dante: Anti–Dantism, Metaphysics, Tradition*, ed. by Zygmunt G. Barański and Theodore J. Cachey, Jr (Notre Dame, IN: University of Notre Dame Press, 2009), pp. 179–81 <https://doi.org/10.2307/j.ctvpj78c0.9>

—— *The Worlds of Petrarch* (Durham, NC: Duke University Press, 1993) <https://doi.org/10.1215/9780822382614>

McDannell, Colleen, and Bernhard Lang, *Heaven: A History* (New Haven: Yale University Press, 1998)

McKendrick, Jamie, *The Foreign Connection: Writings on Poetry, Art and Translation* (Oxford: Legenda, 2020)

Meeker, Natania, and Antónia Szabari, 'Libertine Botany: Vegetal Sexuality and Vegetal Forms', *Postmedieval: A Journal of Medieval Cultural Studies*, 9.4 (2018), pp. 478–89 <https://doi.org/10.1057/s41280-018-0105-3>

Miglio, Camilla, *Vita a fronte. Saggio su Paul Celan* (Macerata: Quodlibet, 2005)

Moevs, Christian, *The Metaphysics of Dante's 'Comedy'* (New York: Oxford University Press, 2005) <https://doi.org/10.1093/0195174615.001.0001>

—— 'Subjectivity and Conversion in Dante and Petrarch', in *Petrarch and Dante: Anti-Dantism, Metaphysics, Tradition*, ed. by Zygmunt G. Barański and Theodore J. Cachey, Jr (Notre Dame, IN: University of Notre Dame Press, 2009), pp. 226–59 <https://doi.org/10.2307/j.ctvpj78c0.11>

Morton, Timothy, 'Guest Column: Queer Ecology', *PMLA*, 125.2 (2010), pp. 273–82 <https://doi.org/10.1632/pmla.2010.125.2.273>

Nardi, Bruno, 'Filosofia dell'amore nei rimatori italiani del Duecento e in Dante', in *Dante e la cultura medievale. Nuovi saggi di filosofia dantesca*, ed. by Paolo Mazzantini, new edn (Bari: Laterza, 1985), pp. 9–79

Nasti, Paola, 'Nozze e vedovanza: dinamiche dell'appropriazione biblica in Cavalcanti e Dante', *Tenzone*, 7 (2006), pp. 71–110

Noferi, Adelia, *L'esperienza poetica del Petrarca* (Florence: Le Monnier, 1962)

Ochoa, John, 'The Poet Becomes the Poem: The Missing Object and Petrarch's Ends in the *Canzoniere*', *Romance Quarterly*, 65.1 (2018), pp. 38–48 <https://doi.org/10.1080/08831157.2018.1396138>

Olson, Paul, 'Two Sonnets of Heavenly Vision', *Italica*, 35 (1958), pp. 156–61 <https://doi.org/10.2307/477647>

Paterson, Don, *Reading Shakespeare's Sonnets: A New Commentary* (London: Faber and Faber, 2010)

Pertile, Lino, *La punta del disio: Semantica del desiderio nella 'Commedia'* (Fiesole: Cadmo, 2005)

Peterson, Thomas E., '"Amor co la man dextra il lato manco" (*Rvf* 228) as Allegory of Religious Veneration', *MLN*, 135.1 (January 2020), Italian Issue, pp. 17–33 <https://doi.org/10.1353/mln.2020.0013>

Petrarch, Francesco, *Canzoniere*, ed. by Marco Santagata, rev. ed. (Milan: Mondadori, 2010)

—— *Canzoniere*, ed. by Ugo Dotti, with notes by Giacomo Leopardi (Milan: Feltrinelli, 1979)

—— *Canzoniere. Rerum vulgarium fragmenta*, ed. by Rosanna Bettarini, 2 vols (Turin: Einaudi, 2005)

—— *Canzoniere, Trionfi: l'incunabolo veneziano di Vindelino da Spira del 1470 nell'esemplare della Biblioteca civica Queriniana di Brescia con figure dipinte da Antonio Grifo, INC. G V 15*, ed. by Giuseppe Frasso, Giordana Mariani, and Ennio Sandal (Rome: Salerno, 2016)

—— *Opere latine di Francesco Petrarca*, ed. by Antonietta Bufano, 2 vols (Turin: UTET, 1975)

—— 'Petrarch's Coronation Oration', trans. by Ernest Hatch Wilkins, *PMLA*, 68.5 (Dec. 1953), pp. 1241–50 <https://doi.org/10.2307/460017>

—— *Trionfi, Rime estravaganti, Codice degli abbozzi*, ed. by Vinicio Pacca and Laura Paolino (Milan: Mondadori, 1996)

—— *Triumphi*, ed. by Marco Ariani (Milan: Mursia, 1988)

Petrini, Mario, 'La canzone alla Vergine', *Critica letteraria*, 23 (1994), pp. 33–42

Picone, Michelangelo, 'Addii e assenza amorosa', in *Percorsi della lirica duecentesca. Dai Siciliani alla 'Vita Nova'* (Florence: Cadmo, 2003), pp. 125–43

—— 'Esilio e *peregrinatio*: Dalla *Vita Nova* alla "Canzone montanina"', *Italianistica: Rivista di letteratura italiana*, 36.3 (Sept–Dec 2007), pp. 1–14

—— 'I paradossi e i prodigi dell'amore passione (*Rvf* 130–140)', in *Il Canzoniere: Lettura micro e Macrotestuale*, ed. by Michelangelo Picone (Ravenna: Longo, 2007), pp. 313–33

—— 'Petrarca e il libro non finito', in *Petrarca volgare e la sua fortuna sino al Cinquecento*, ed. by Bruno Porcelli (= *Italianistica*, 33.2 (May–August 2004)), pp. 83–94

—— 'La tenzone "de amore" fra Jacopo Mostacci, Pier della Vigna e il Notaro', in *Percorsi della lirica duecentesca* (Florence: Cadmo, 2003), pp. 47–67

Pil'ščikov, Igor' A., 'Petrarca nelle traduzioni dei poeti russi dell'età d'oro e dell'età d'argento', trans. by Bianca Sulpasso, *Russica Romana*, 17 (2010), pp. 89–114

Praloran, Marco, *La canzone di Petrarca: Orchestrazione formale e percorsi argomentativi*, ed. by Arnaldo Soldani (Rome-Padua: Antenore, 2013)

Psaki, F. Regina, 'Dante's Redeemed Eroticism', *Lectura Dantis*, 18–19 (1996), pp. 12–19

—— 'Love for Beatrice: Transcending Contradiction in the *Paradiso*', in *Dante for the New Millennium*, ed. by Teodolinda Barolini and H. Wayne Storey (New York: Fordham University Press, 2003), pp. 115–30

—— 'The Sexual Body in Dante's Celestial Paradise', in *Imagining Heaven in the Middle Ages: A Book of Essays*, ed. by Jan Swango Emerson and Hugh Feiss (New York: Garland, 2000), pp. 47–61

Pézard, André, '*De passione in passionem*', *L'Alighieri*, 1 (1960), pp. 14–26

Quillen, Carol E., *Rereading the Renaissance: Petrarch, Augustine, and the Language of Humanism* (Ann Arbor: University of Michigan Press, 1998) <https://doi.org/10.3998/mpub. 15299>

Rabitti, Giovanna, '"Nel dolce tempo": sintesi o nuovo cominciamento?', in *Petrarca volgare e la sua fortuna sino al Cinquecento*, ed. by Bruno Porcelli (= *Italianistica*, 33.2 (May–August 2004)), pp. 95–108

Redko, Philip Leon, *Boundary Issues in Three Twentieth-Century Russian Poets (Mandelstam, Aronzon, Shvarts)* (doctoral thesis, Harvard University, Graduate School of Arts and Sciences, 2019) <https://dash.harvard.edu/handle/1/41121299> [accessed 29 September 2020]

Roche, Thomas P., Jr, *Petrarch and the English Sonnet Sequences* (New York: AMS Press, 1989)

Rushworth, Jennifer, *Discourses of Mourning in Dante, Petrarch and Proust* (Oxford: Oxford University Press, 2016) <https://doi.org/10.1093/acprof:oso/9780198790877. 001.0001>

Santagata, Marco, *Dal sonetto al canzoniere: Ricerche sulla preisto-ria e la costituzione di un genere* (Padua: Liviana, 1979)

—— *I frammenti dell'anima: Storia e racconto nel 'Canzoniere' di Petrarca* (Bologna: Il Mulino, 2004)

Sapegno, Natalino, *Disegno storico della letteratura italiana*, 2nd edn (Florence: La Nuova Italia, 1973)

Schoenfeldt, Michael, 'Friendship and Love, Darkness and Lust: Desire in the Sonnets', in *The Cambridge Introduction to Shakespeare's Poetry* (Cambridge: Cambridge University Press, 2010), pp. 88–111 <https://doi.org/10.1017/CBO9780511781186.006>

—— 'The Sonnets', in *The Cambridge Companion to Shakespeare's Poetry*, ed. by Patrick Cheney (Cambridge: Cambridge University Press, 2007), pp. 125–43 <https://doi.org/10.1017/CCOL0521846277.008>

Segre, Cesare, 'Les Isotopies de Laure', in *Exigences et perspectives de la sémiotique: recueil d'hommages pour Algirdas Julien Greimas*, ed. by Herman Perret and Hans-George Ruprecht, 2 vols (Amsterdam: J Benjamins, 1985), II, pp. 811–26 <https://doi.org/10.1075/z.23.72seg>

Semenko Irina, 'Mandel'štam traduttore di Petrarca', ed. by Cesare G. De Michelis, *Rassegna sovietica*, 4 (1970), pp. 14–35

Shakespeare, William, *Shakespeare's Sonnets*, ed. by Katherine Duncan-Jones (London: Methuen Drama, 2010)

von Simpson, Otto G., '*Compassio* and *Co-redemptio* in Roger van der Weyden's *Descent from the Cross*', *The Art Bulletin*, 25 (1953), pp. 9–16 <https://doi.org/10.2307/3047456>

Southerden, Francesca, 'The Art of Rambling: Errant Thoughts and Entangled Passions in Petrarch's "Ascent of Mont Ventoux" (*Fam.* IV, 1) and *Rvf* 129', in *Medieval Thought Experiments: Poetry, Hypothesis and Experience in the European Middle Ages*, ed. by Philip Knox, Jonathan Morton, and Daniel Reeve (Turnhout: Brepols, 2018), pp. 197–221 <https://doi.org/10.1484/M.DISPUT-EB.5.114697>

—— *Dante and Petrarch in the Garden of Language* (in progress)

—— 'The Lyric Mode', in *The Oxford Handbook of Dante*, ed. by Manuele Gragnolati, Elena Lombardi, and Francesca Southerden (Oxford: Oxford University Press, forthcoming)

Spiller, Michael R. G., *The Sonnet Sequence: A Study of its Strategies* (New York: Twayne, 1997)

Stabile, Giorgio, 'Volontà', in *Enciclopedia dantesca*, ed. by Umberto Bosco, 6 vols (Roma: Istituto della Enciclopedia Italiana, Fondata da Giovanni Treccani, 1970–78), v, cols 1134–40

Stark, Hannah, 'Deleuze and Critical Plant Studies', in *Deleuze and the Non/Human*, ed. by Jon Roffe and Hannah Stark (London: Palgrave Macmillan, 2015), pp. 180–96 <https://doi.org/10.1057/9781137453693_11>

Stewart, Dana, *The Arrow of Love: Optics, Gender, and Subjectivity in Medieval Love Poetry* (London: Bucknell University Press, 2003)

Sturm-Maddox, Sara, *Petrarch's Metamorphoses: Text and Subtext in the 'Rime Sparse'* (Columbia: University of Missouri Press, 1985)

Suitner, Franco, *Petrarca e la tradizione stilnovistica* (Florence: Olschki, 1977)

Tonelli, Natascia, 'Amor da che convien ch'io mi doglia', in *Dante: Le quindici canzoni. Lette da diversi* (Lecce: Pensa Multimedia, 2012), pp. 255–83

—— *Fisiologia della passione: Poesia d'amore e medicina da Cavalcanti a Boccaccio* (Tavarnuzze [Florence]: SISMEL · Edizioni del Galluzzo, 2015)

—— *Leggere il 'Canzoniere'* (Bologna, Il Mulino, 2017)

—— *Per queste orme: Studi sul 'Canzoniere' di Petrarca* (Pisa: Pacini, 2016)

Tronzo, William, *Petrarch's Two Gardens: Landscape and the Image of Movement* (New York: Italica Press, 2014) <https://doi.org/10.2307/j.ctt1t88w1b>

Tubbs, Robert, *Mathematics in Twentieth-Century Literature and Art: Content, Form, Meaning,* (Baltimore, MD: John Hopkins University Press, 2014)

Vickers, Nancy, 'Re-membering Dante: Petrarch's "Chiare, fresche et dolci acque"', *MLN*, 96.1, Italian Issue (January 1981), pp. 1–11 <https://doi.org/10.2307/2906426>

Virgil, *Eclogues, Georgics, Aeneid Books 1–6*, trans. by H. R. Fairclough, revised by G. P. Goold (Cambridge, MA: Harvard University Press, 1916) <https://doi.org/10.4159/DLCL.virgil-eclogues.1916>

Waller, Marguerite, *Petrarch's Poetics and Literary History* (Amherst: University of Massachusetts Press, 1980)

Warning, Rainer, 'Imitatio und Intertextualität. Zur Geschichte lyrischer Dekonstruktion der Amortheologie: Dante, Petrarca, Baudelaire', in *Lektüren romanischer Lyrik. Von den Trobadors zum Surrealismus* (Freiburg: Rombach, 1997), pp. 104–41

—— 'Seeing and Hearing in Ancient and Medieval Epiphany', in *Rethinking the Medieval Senses: Heritage, Fascinations, Frames*, ed. by Stephen G. Nichols, Andreas Kablitz, and Alison Calho (Baltimore, MD: Johns Hopkins University Press), pp. 102–16

Webb, Heather, *Dante's Persons: An Ethics of the Transhuman* (Oxford: Oxford University Press, 2016) <https://doi.org/10.1093/acprof:oso/9780198733485.001.0001>

—— *The Medieval Heart* (New Haven, CT: Yale University Press, 2010)

Zak, Gur, *Petrarch's Humanism and the Care of the Self* (Cambridge: Cambridge University Press, 2010) <https://doi.org/10.1017/CBO9780511730337>

Zanni, Raffaella, 'Dalla lontananza all'esilio nella lirica italiana del XIII secolo', *Arzanà*, 16–17 (2013), pp. 325–63 <https://doi.org/10.4000/arzana.230>

—— 'Prendre congé de sa propre poésie: *Perch'i' no spero di tornar giammai* de Guido Cavalcanti', in *Les Deux Guidi: Guinizzelli et Cavalcanti. Mourir d'aimer et autres ruptures*, ed. by Marina Gagliano, Philippe Guérin, and Raffaella Zanni (Paris: Presses Sorbonne Nouvelle, 2016), pp. 141–56

Zanzotto, Andrea, 'Petrarca fra il palazzo e la cameretta', in *Scritti sulla letteratura*, ed. by Gianmario Villalta, 2 vols, (Milan: Mondadori, 2001), I, pp. 261–71

Notes on the Authors and Translator

Manuele Gragnolati is Full Professor of Italian Literature at Sorbonne Université and Associate Director of the ICI Berlin, as well as Senior Research Fellow at Somerville College, Oxford. A major part of his research, including his monograph *Experiencing the Afterlife* (2015), focuses on Dante and medieval literature and culture. He has collaborated with Teodolinda Barolini on an edition of Dante's *Rime* (2009) and published essays on medieval and modern authors. His monograph *Amor che move* (2013) offers a 'diffractive' exploration of body, language, and desire in Dante, Pier Paolo Pasolini, and Elsa Morante. At the ICI Berlin and elsewhere, he has run several interdisciplinary projects, which have often resulted in collective volumes, including *The Power of Disturbance* (2010), *Aspects of the Performative in Medieval Culture* (2010), *Dante's Plurilingualism* (2010), *Metamorphosing Dante* (2011), *Desire in Dante and the Middle Ages* (2012), *The Scandal of Self-Contradiction* (2012), *De/Constituting Wholes* (2017), *Vita nova, Fiore, Epistola* XIII (2019), and the forthcoming *Openness in Medieval Culture* and *Oxford Handbook of Dante*.

Francesca Southerden is Associate Professor of Medieval Italian and Tutorial Fellow at Somerville College, Oxford. She has written several articles on Dante and Petrarch and is the author of *Landscapes of Desire in the Poetry of Vittorio Sereni* (Oxford University Press, 2012). She is currently working on a monograph entitled *Dante and Petrarch in the Garden of Language*, and is co-editor, together with Manuele Gragnolati and Elena Lombardi, of *The Oxford Handbook of Dante* (forthcoming with Oxford University Press). These projects, like the present one, are the result of a longstanding interest in exploring the nature and possibilities of lyric and similarly bring medieval texts into dialogue with modern and contemporary theory on desire and affect in particular.

Antonella Anedda Angioy was born in Rome in a Sardinian-Corsican family and is one of Italy's most original and lauded contemporary poets. Since the publication of her first work in 1992, the poetic collection Residenze Invernali (Winter Residences), she has received numerous awards, including the Montale Prize, the Viareggio Prize, and the Pushkin International Prize. Her last collection of poetry is Historiae (2018). She has translated Classical and modern poets,written several essays on literature and art, including *La vita dei dettagli* (The Life of Details, 2009), and *Isolatria* (2013), and collaborated regularly with artists and musicians. Her poetry has been translated in several languages and in 2014 an anthology of her poetry was published in English, translated by Jamie McKendrick. In 2019 she received an honorary doctorate from Sorbonne Université.

Jamie McKendrick was born in Liverpool and is distinguished both as a poet and translator. His seven collections have won the Forward Prize, the Hawthornden Prize and, in 2019, the Cholmondeley Award, and his *Selected Poems* are published by Faber. As a translator he has won the Oxford Weidenfeld Prize and the John Florio Prize (twice), and he is the editor of the *Faber Book of Twentieth-Century Italian Poems* as well as the author of *The Foreign Connection: Writings on Poetry, Art and Translation* (2020).

Index of Works

Index of Names

Cultural Inquiry

EDITED BY CHRISTOPH F. E. HOLZHEY
AND MANUELE GRAGNOLATI